Trade
& Structural
Change

Leslie Stein

CROOM HELM
London & Canberra

ST. MARTIN'S PRESS
New York

To my wife Clara and children, Mark and Karen

© 1984 Leslie Stein
Croom Helm Ltd, Provident House, Burrell Row,
Beckenham, Kent BR3 1AT

British Library Cataloguing in Publication Data

Stein, Leslie
    Trade and structural change.
    1. International economic relations   2. World
    politics – 1975–1985
    I. Title
    337   HF1411
    ISBN 0-7099-0232-8

All rights reserved. For information, write:
St. Martin's Press, Inc., 175 Fifth Avenue, New York, NY 10010
Printed in Great Britain
First published in the United States of America in 1984

Library of Congress Cataloging in Publication Data

Stein, Leslie.
    Trade and structural change.

    Bibliography: p.
    Includes index.
    1. International economic relations. I. Title.
HF1411.S7967   1984   382   83–40181
ISBN 0–312–81205–1

Printed and bound in Great Britain

CONTENTS

Preface

1. **Trade Determination Theories**   1
   Classical Trade Theory   1
   The Heckscher–Ohlin Theorem   3
   Intra-Industry Trade   10
   Linder's Hypothesis   12
   Technology Based Theories   14

2. **Trade Theories Empirically Assessed**   23
   The Ricardian Theory   23
   The Leontief Paradox   25
   The H/O Model and Some of its Rivals   33
   Skills and Technological Factors   37
   The Product Cycle Theory   40
   'Revealed' Comparative Advantage   43
   The Linder Hypothesis   44
   The 'Stages' Approach to Comparative Advantage   46
   Determinants of LDC Trade   48
   Conclusion   49
   Appendix: A Note on the Derivation of Capital Intensities   49

3. **Multinational Corporations in World Trade**   55
   MNC Investments and Exports   56
   MNCs and Current Exports   59
   MNCs and Trade: Some Conceptual Considerations   64
   Intra-firm Trade   65
   MNCs and the Third World   70
   Offshore Processing   71
   Conclusion   74

4. **Protection**   78
   The Theory of Protection   78
   Effective Protection   82
   Non-tariff Barriers   87
   Are Tariffs Economically Justifiable?   88

The Political Economy of Protectionism 92
Tariff Preferences 94
The New Protectionism 99

5. **LDC Imports and Job Displacement** 105
Recent Export Trends 105
Employment and Trade 108
The Relative Job Impact of LDC Exports 111
Trade Benefits and Adjustments 113
Conclusion 115

6. **Trade Adjustment Policies** 118
Trade Adjustment Assistance in the US 120
Trade Adjustment Assistance in Canada 123
Trade Adjustment Assistance in Australia 125
An Evaluation of the US, Canadian and Australian Schemes 127
General Measures Assisting Adjustments 129
Adjustment Under the Canadian-American Automobile Pact 130
Negative Adjustments and the Clothing and Textile Industries 131
Adjustment Assistance to the Canadian Clothing and Textile
Industries 132
Protection of the Australian, Clothing, Footwear and Textile
Industries 133
Issues in Easing the Adjustment Process 135
Conclusion 138

Appendix: Emmanuel's Unequal Exchange Thesis: A Critique 143
The Meaning of Unequal Exchange 144
Emmanuel on Comparative Costs 153
The Independent Wage Assumption 159
Conclusion 160

Bibliography 163
Index 182

PREFACE

During the 1960s the world economy grew at an unprecedented rate. Expanded trade volumes were accommodated with a minimum of friction as the advantages emanating from trade and specialisation were widely realised and perceived. Similarly, tariffs and other trade barriers were steadily dismantled in the general expectation that within a relatively free trade regime, the world economy would become increasingly integrated and prosperous. Unfortunately, with the advent of recessionary forces which manifested themselves with menacing vigour in the wake of OPEC price rises, and of the near univeral imperative to contain inflation, hopes for immediate and continued economic progress withered. Industrial nations have begun to doubt the value of unfettered free trade and disaffected elements within them have been seeking to bolster flagging incomes and employment prospects through the curtailment of imports. This trend has been particularly ominous for the newly emerged industrial less developed countries (LDCs) which, despite the world recession, have made dramatic headway in gaining comparative advantages in fields which have hitherto been the exclusive prerogative of the wealthy. As matters now stand, if the OECD countries are yet again to derive maximum trade gains and if their economic recoveries are to be founded on sustainable and healthy foundations, sooner or later they have to respond to the changing international environment by undertaking various structural adjustments. With this issue in mind, this book attempts to enhance the reader's understanding of the implications of living in a period of imminent trade induced adaptations. Hopefully, this greater understanding will be achieved through the provision of a concise review of the forces that generate trade and those that retard it, and of the difficulties entailed in coming to terms with the decline of traditional industrial activities.

This book can readily be followed by anyone with a basic knowledge of first year university/college or even high school economics. It is partly based on material presented in an undergraduate international economics course at Macquarie University but it would also be of value to postgraduate students wishing to obtain a bird's eye view of salient trade issues. I have attempted to economise on verbiage and, accordingly, I sincerely hope that any prospective reader fearing that on account of the book's apparent brevity, major considerations are not comprehensively reviewed, would soon have such fears allayed. In short, I have tried to provide a comprehensive yet compact rendition of our current understanding of some trade and structural transformation problems.

I would like to acknowledge with thanks, the editor of the *Malayan Economic Review* for permitting me to include (in Chapter 3) contents which first appeared in the April 1983 edition of his journal; the editor of *Kyklos* for allowing me to reproduce material (in Chapters 4 and 5) that originated in *Kyklos*, vol. 34, fasc. 1, 1981; and to the editor of the *American Journal of Economics and Sociology* for permission to include (in Chapter 6) material that was first published in his journal, vol. 41, no. 3, July 1982.

Various colleagues in Canada, the UK, Israel and Australia have either read sections of the manuscript or have attended my deliveries at staff seminars. Without singling out anyone in particular, I would like to express my thanks for their useful comments and advice. An especially warm note of thanks and gratitude is accorded to my wife Clara for not only encouraging me in the pursuit of my writings but for bearing with good grace and patience the many hours that I have separated myself from her. Finally, I would like to thank Daphne Gordon for her prompt assistance in completing the typing of the manuscript.

Leslie Stein,
Macquarie University

1 TRADE DETERMINATION THEORIES

Classical Trade Theory

From the late eighteenth century, with the advent of Adam Smith's pioneering tract *The Wealth of Nations*, the probable causes and consequences of international trade have preoccupied the minds of renowned economists. Until fairly recently, Ricardo's comparative advantage doctrine held sway. In its most rudimentary form, the Ricardian or classical theory assumes a two country world in which each country produces the same two commodities with one homogeneous production factor; labour. Fixed input-output ratios, which may differ across industries within a country or within an industry between countries, exist. Labour is assumed to be fully employed and internally mobile. Perfect competition prevails so that internal pre-trade prices are equal to marginal costs which are determined by labour-product coefficients. Within this general setting, the potential for profitable international exchange lies in differences in each country's relative price structure. This is so, even if one country is absolutely more efficient in the production of both goods. If for instance, in one country, say the USA, a unit of each product, say cloth and wheat, is produced by 4 and 2 labour units respectively, and in the other country, say the UK, 8 labour units yield a unit of either commodity, mutually advantageous trade could still occur. Despite the USA's overall technological superiority, its comparative advantage lies only in wheat, while the UK has a competitive forte in cloth. From the USA's viewpoint, the internal opportunity cost of acquiring a unit of cloth involves the sacrifice of two units of wheat. In the UK by contrast, the cost of a unit of cloth is equivalent to only one foregone wheat unit. Suppose that in the international arena, cloth and wheat are exchanged at a price ratio lying somewhere between each country's individual autarchic one, say at the rate of 1 cloth for 1.3 wheat.[1] Should the USA wish to acquire 1 cloth from its own industry, it would have to expend 4 labour units but if it availed itself of the opportunity of acquiring 1 cloth indirectly, by exporting 1.3 wheat, it need only deploy 2.6 labour units for that purpose. Likewise, in the UK, the option to obtain 1.3 wheat from its own farmers necessitates the use of 10.4 labour units whereas if that quantity of wheat were imported,

1

Figure 1.1

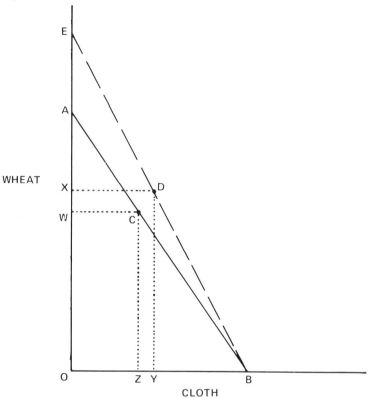

only 8 labour units need be employed in producing the 1 cloth required to finance wheat imports. Trade, by permitting both countries to economise on their resources, facilitates simultaneous living standard improvements.

The nature of the aforementioned trade gains can be highlighted iconographically with the use of simple co-ordinate geometry. In Figure 1.1, AB represents the production possibility curve of a certain country. Reflecting the constant cost assumption, it is a perfectly straight line whose slope is derived from prevailing labour output ratios, and whose position is governed by the overall size of the workforce. Given full employment, output produced is indicated by some point on the line such as C, involving OZ of cloth and OW of wheat. If, subsequently, an opportunity to engage in world trade at prices indicated by the slope of the broken line emerges, production may shift from C to B, involving complete cloth specialisation.[2] In this event, YB of cloth may be exported for YD of wheat to obtain a consumption bundle shown by point D, which represents a larger combination of both commodities compared with the one depicted by point C. Trade gains arise from the fact that the country is enabled to consume aggregate amounts of goods which it is itself incapable of directly producing. Before trade, the country's consumption options were restricted to points along AB, its production possibility curve, but with trade it can consume somewhere along BE, the international exchange curve, and therefore consumption and production points need no longer converge. Consequently, the trade gain potential depends on the extent of the divergence between rates of transformation in production (the slope of AB) and foreign rates of transformation in exchange (the slope of BE). The larger this divergence, the larger are the country's trade gain possibilities.

If the source of trade gains lies in a discrepancy between local and foreign prices, the source of that discrepancy in turn can be traced to international differences in relative labour productivities. In a two good model, demand has no bearing on internal price formation and on determining which good is to be exported. It is of course significant in influencing world prices and trade volumes. When however, the model is extended to a multi-good one, it still remains true that exports all embody lower labour to output ratios than do imports but demand now becomes crucial in determining the cut off point between the two.

A major drawback of the classical model is its one factor assumption. It has been suggested that this was merely intended didactically to illustrate the gains from trade, and that a careful reading of Ricardo reveals that a multi-factor economy was not necessarily precluded.[3] Even so, the classical theory could still be faulted for not posing the question of what might become of the source of comparative advantages if knowledge and skills were to be universalised, thereby eroding the basis for inter-country production function differences.

The Heckscher–Ohlin Theorem

Within the past few decades, the ideas of Heckscher and Ohlin superseded those of Ricardo and have since become synonymous with modern trade theory. By contrast with Ricardian doctrine, the Heckscher–Ohlin (H/O) model assumes two production factors and an internationally uniform production function for each of two industries, the qualities of factor inputs and state of the technical arts being every-where the same. In these circumstances, trade can no longer be regarded as being determined by inter-country differences in relative factor efficiency, instead, relative factor supplies become crucial. This appears evident in noting that the H/O theory's most significant prediction is that a country will export the good that is relatively intensive in the use of its relatively abundant factor.[4] If a country happens to be labour abundant, and if cloth happens to be labour intensive, then that country would export cloth. In a two factor model, relative factor intensity is indicated by the comparative ratio of the two factors (labour and capital) employed by each industry at any set of common factor prices. Relative factor abundance is a little more ambiguous. It can be ascertained by comparing ratios of factors of production measured in physical units, so that if KI/LI > KII/LII, country I is capital abundant (K + L being total quantities of capital and labour, the numerals referring to the corresponding countries) or by relative factor prices, so that if PKI/PLI < PKII/PLII (P standing for price), country I is once again, capital abundant. Only if factor abundance is defined in price terms, are the H/O predictions assured, given of course the maintenance of all crucial assumptions, which, apart from those already alluded to, include: perfect competition, internal but not international resource mobility, full employment, linear homo-geneous production functions and an absence of transport costs or other trade impediments. Sometimes, similar if not identical inter-country taste patterns are also included. In general, all significant differences, except for those pertaining to relative factor endowments, are assumed away. This is done to highlight the significance of relative factor supplies as trade determinants, and for this reason, the H/O model is also known as the factor proportions theory.

That the H/O's postulates are readily derived from the above-men-tioned assumptions, can be seen with the aid of Figure 1.2, in which ww and cc depict the respective isoquants of one unit of wheat and cloth.[5] Within country I, the slope of line AB reflects pre-trade factor costs which will induce product maximising entrepreneurs to produce units of wheat and cloth with input combinations indicated respectively by points E and F. Capital to labour ratios in each industry can be gauged by comparing the slopes of rays from the origin through points E and F (not drawn) which would reveal that wheat is relatively capital intensive. If the unit production costs of each commodity are expressed solely in terms of capital, then both would be equally assessed at OA, with the opportunity cost of 1 wheat equalling 1 cloth.[6] Now assume

Figure 1.2

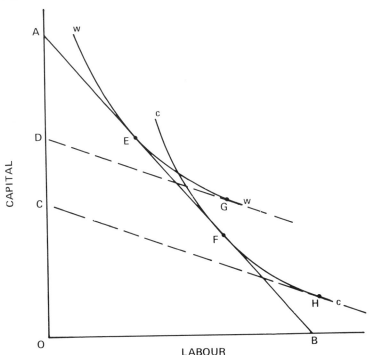

that in country II factor prices are equal to the slope of the broken parallel lines.[7] In this event, the production of one unit of wheat and cloth commands input combinations shown by points G and H, which when valued in terms of capital amount respectively to OD and OC. Since OD > OC, a unit of cloth is cheaper to produce than a unit of wheat, so that bearing in mind the other country's cost ratio, country II would be competitive in cloth and would be inclined to import wheat. [cost of wheat in I/cost of cloth in I < cost of wheat in II/cost of cloth in II]. These results accord with the H/O theory. PKI/PLI < PKII/PLII (line AB is steeper than the broken parallel ones) therefore country I is capital abundant and, as already noted, is likely to export its capital intensive item wheat; similarly, labour abundant country II would export labour intensive cloth.

Within its two factor, two good, two country framework, the H/O model is remarkably neat and precise. Unfortunately, such clarity is gained through the maintenance of what many may regard as an unreasonable set of assumptions. Granted that a theory's predictive power is the touchstone by which it is adjudged, it can still be argued that the H/O model's general usefulness has been vitiated for the sake of analytical rigour. Trade theorists spellbound by the model's elegance and locked into its assumptions have expended prodigious efforts in refining it further. Generations of scholars engrossed in non-operational issues (such as the factor price equalisation theorem) and in otiose welfare considerations, have bequeathed to countless students a very narrow and constricting account of trade determinants. Rigid adherence to what has come to be more aptly described as the H/O–Samuelson theory, forestalled widespread and serious contemplation of the impact on trade of non-competitive markets, product differentiation, economies of scale, multinational corporations, transport costs, industrial location, unemployment, taxes and subsidies, internal factor immobility, money costs and prices, to name but a few factors which common sense would suggest are of relevance. As incredible as it may seem, Ohlin himself actually did take such considerations into account delving into them quite deeply (especially in his work's second edition)[8] affording ironically one of the finest critiques of his much parodied theory. Although Ohlin believed that relative factor proportions are extremely significant in explaining trade flows, he stressed the importance of treating them as but one among many ingredients in a general interdependent model. Since his finer views have habitually been overlooked,[9] it would not be amiss to highlight some of them.

As far as Ohlin was concerned, trade models which do not explicitly incorporate location theory could not adequately explain world trade flows. The question that would-be investigators were invited to pose was not simply why certain countries exchange certain goods but why production is divided among them in a certain way, for in general 'the exchange of goods is determined once the location of production has been fixed'.[10] In this regard, transport costs are crucial and are to be considered not simply as trade inhibitors (the role assigned to them by contemporary economists) but in many instances as trade determinants. To illustrate this point, comparative reference was made to the UK's and the USA'a iron and steel industries, which in the early part of this century were located in regions which involved average haulage distances in attaining necessary inputs and then delivering the steel output to a port of shipment of 30 and 500 miles respectively.[11]

Weight was also attached to the influence of scale economies,[12] for even if factor proportions between countries were originally identical, Ohlin believed that trade could still be profitable if 'the market for some articles within each region is not large enough to permit the most efficient scale of production'.[13] In such circumstances, the specific industries in which countries specialise may be selected on an aleatory basis but upon their establishment, unique demand patterns for factor inputs are likely to emerge, leading to inter-country differences in factor prices thereby providing an additional basis for specialisation. In practice, Ohlin felt that, initially, factor prices were likely to diverge, and that scale economies would complement trade advantages derived from differing factor proportions. However, when the additional impact of both scale economies and transport considerations is acknowledged 'conclusions are reached regarding the location of production and the character and effects of international trade that *deviate considerably* from those that would have been arrived at if only the scarcity of the factors of production has been taken into account'.[14]

The role of innovation, technology and skill differentials was also stressed. Ohlin realised that certain manufactured goods were exported from the US 'simply because by chance some inventions originated there and sustained effort maintained technical superiority'.[15] As for skills, 'a few engineers in one country may have a special knowledge of a particular technical process and may for that reason be able to produce more cheaply than other countries'.[16]

Upon exploring the consequences of relaxing the product homogeneity assumption, it was conceded that issues of 'goodwill, trademarks, exclusive selling rights given to a number of retailers etc.'[17] would be pertinent, and in reference to product differentiation, the phenomenon of intra-industry trade (which only began to receive widespread attention from the early 1970s) was clearly identified. As noted by Ohlin, intra-industry trade was partly due to transport factors and partly due 'to the fact that the imported and exported commodities are of different quality. For instance, before World War I Denmark imported butter from Siberia and exported Danish butter to Great Britain, because of the marked difference in taste. *A study of international trade statistics reveals many similar cases.*'[18]

Endorsing Linder's hypothesis (reviewed below) Ohlin declared that 'the volume of trade is dependent upon the absolute quantity of productive agents in the various regions, not upon the inequality of their endowment'[19] and that 'the best clients of leading manufacturing countries are the other manufacturing countries'.[20] What is more, in relation to trade between industrial and Third World countries we are cautioned to take into account qualitative factor differences as well as differences in public administration, political stability and legal security.[21]

Hopefully, the above discussion absolves the H/O theory's co-founder from responsibility for the model's degeneration into relative aridity.

While qualms about the H/O model's limitations have intermittently been voiced, only fairly recently have serious attempts been made either to construct alternative hypotheses, or to place the theory in proper perspective as just one important but not exclusive trade explanator. An approach typically adopted has been one of attempting to redress glaring deficiencies by modifying the model ever so slightly. In this respect, Bhagwati's strictures are fairly representative.[22] Lamenting that the model had not (at the time he was writing) been extended to a multi-country and multi-commodity framework, Bhagwati envisaged various ways in which a multi-country assumption could be accommodated. Factor proportions could be compared between a given country and the rest of the world, between a country and all its direct trading partners, between a country and all its direct plus indirect trading partners, or between a country and each of those in direct trade with it 'so that the H/O hypothesis would hold for each pair of countries bilaterally'.[23]

With regard to the previous statement, Baldwin maintained that in a multi-country setting, where all goods are traded, the number of products exceeds the number of factors and factor-price equalisation is realised, then although the H/O model would apply for a country's total trade, it 'need not hold on a bilateral basis'.[24] Unfortunately, Baldwin furnished inadequate proof in support of this proposition. A geometric illustration showing how it is possible for say a capital abundant country to import a capital intensive good from a relatively labour abundant partner, while yet globally speaking being a net capital exporter, was provided. Nevertheless, the diagram in question is more akin to a flow chart, indicating the mechanical possibility of bilateral trade diverging from H/O outcomes, with overall trade conforming. What is lacking is an account of the economic bases, motives or incentives for such bilateral trade. Later, Baldwin concurred that in the event of non-factor-price equalisation, the H/O theory would 'hold between any pair of countries', although not necessarily between a given country and all its trading partners.[25]

Baldwin's statement was based partly on work by Caves and Jones whose rather neat and innovative exposition is worth summarising.[26] Assume that a country incapable of influencing world prices produces a number of different products whose representative isoquants are shown in Figure 1.3. Each isoquant depicts alternative input combinations that

Figure 1.3

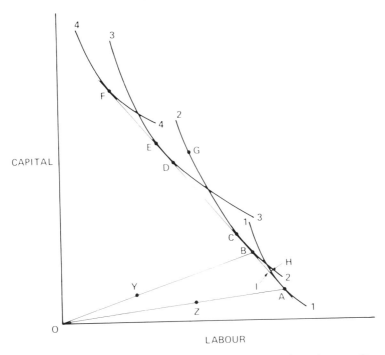

yield products all worth $1 in the international market. At prevailing
prices, some points on each isoquant would be economically unattrac-
tive. Such a point for instance, would be G on isoquant 2, on the
grounds that if, instead, good 3 was produced with inputs represented
by point D, involving less of both inputs, good 2 could be obtained
indirectly by trading good 3. Similarly, point I is economically preferable to point H even though I is not on an isoquant below H. I in fact
indicates an output mix of both goods 1 and 2. Assume that 60 per cent
of good 1 is produced with factors in ratios indicated by the slope of
ray OA and that Z lying 60 per cent along OA (from O) portrays the
actual amounts of factors involved. Now let 40 per cent of good 2 be
produced by combinations of capital and labour shown by point Y. The
linear combination of vectors OY and OZ is OI (not drawn). It should
now be apparent that points along line AB represent varying fractions
of goods 1 and 2 which, in combination, yield $1. Likewise, lines
DC and EF depict alternative mixes of goods 2 and 3, and 3 and 4.
The lines AB, CD and EF are all tangent to the sets of isoquants they

are connecting. If the country's relative factor endowments are indicated by the slope of a ray projecting from O to a point between D and E (not drawn) the country would specialise in good 3 importing the relatively more labour intensive goods 1 and 2 (from more abundant labour sources) and the relatively more capital intensive good 4 (from a more capital abundant country) violating the H/O theory in terms of the country's aggregate though not bilateral trade.

Two versions of the H/O theory have been forthcoming. The first, identified by Baldwin as the 'commodity' version, suggests that a country will export those goods which intensively use its relatively abundant factors. This version is the most widely known and utilised. The second, the 'factor-content' version, 'states that a country will be a net exporter of its relatively abundant factors in the sense that the amounts of these factors embodied in its commodity exports will be greater than the quantities embodied in a representative bundle of import-competing commodities'.[27] This version is said to apply in a multi-country, multi-commodity framework irrespective of whether or not factor price equalisation occurs.

During the 1950s investigations by Leontief indicated that the USA's exports were more labour intensive than its import competing goods. These findings generated numerous forays in attempting either to reconcile Leontief's results with the reigning H/O model, to account for them in terms beyond the model's assumptions or to confirm or confute Leontief's empirical work by replicating it both in the US and elsewhere. The 'Leontief paradox', which will be more extensively treated in the next chapter, undoubtedly created much scepticism with regard to the H/O model and encouraged progress towards its modification. One type of reaction, for example, involved the decomposition of capital into physical and human components, with the contention that when the relative skills of US workers are taken into account, US exports are manifestly more capital intensive than are US imports.[28]

Intra-industry Trade

The general malaise over the capabilities of the H/O model was heightened with increasing observations of intra-industry trade, defined as the 'value of exports of an "industry" which is exactly matched by the imports of the same industry'.[29] On the basis of 1967 trade flows, Grubel and Lloyd estimated that 48 per cent of the average unweighted trade of eleven major industrial countries consisted of intra-industry exchanges. By 1972, intra-industry trade was reckoned to be over 70 per cent for France, the UK, the Netherlands, Sweden, West Germany, Austria, Canada, Italy, Denmark and Belgium. For the US it was 57 per cent.[30]

The concept of intra-industry trade can be problematic in that there are unresolved difficulties in defining an industry. Does the concept focus on the production of a single homogeneous product? If so, would each automobile model constitute an industry in its own right? On the other hand, if goods that are close substitutes (in consumption, or in production?) are designed as comprising an industry, at what degree of substitutability should the line be drawn? In common with others, Grubel and Lloyd decided to 'cease the search for an unambigous definition of an industry at some level of aggregation and instead call each statistical class of internationally traded goods, regardless of the level of aggregation, an "industry" '.[31] Such a procedure allows for 'multi-product' industries which was in fact Grubel and Lloyd's object of special concern, their book being subtitled: 'The Theory and Measurement of International Trade in Differentiated Products'. (In this light, an objection by Lipsey that since there is so much heterogeneity within the commonly used three-digit standard international trade classifications, intra-industry trade is largely a statistical phenomenon, is not a particularly scathing one.[32])

Within multi-product industries, comparative costs are stipulated in terms of individual commodities which may have attained price competitiveness on the basis of scale economies derived from relatively long production runs. Such economies result from 'less frequent halts in production to set or adjust machinery, less "downtime" to move different models or products through production lines, more specialization in labour and capital equipment, and smaller inventories of inputs and output'.[33] Over time, the liberalisation of trade barriers among industrial countries afforded the growing intensity of intra-industry trade (noted above) which in turn gave rise to more intra-industry item specialisation. This process generated mutual trade benefits as prices fell in response to the above-mentioned scale factors.

Trade in functionally homogeneous goods was also considered but Grubel and Lloyd relegated it to a minor role believing it to arise mainly from transport quirks and to be largely confined to a few instances of simultaneous trans-border shipments. For example, a country like China might export rice from one region and import it into another. It is possible that the scope for intra-industry trade in identical commodities is greater than initially realised, for Brander has demonstrated (using a Cournot model) that even in such cases, entrepreneurs might well seek inter-country market penetration.[34] Be that as it may, the pervasive character of intra-industry trade, especially among advanced countries, has called for non-H/O type trade explanations, of which Linder's hypothesis is among the forerunners.

Linder's Hypothesis

While conceding that differences in factor proportions significantly determine trade in natural resource intensive products, Linder maintains that in relation to manufactured goods, the H/O model is found wanting.[35] His disenchantment with that model was engendered by the realisation that 'the factor proportions analysis cannot possibly explain intraregional trade because, by definition, a region has homogeneous factor proportions'.[36] Intra-regional trade must therefore be accounted for with reference to other variables and since intra-regional trade is usually much more intensive than inter-regional trade, Linder concludes that these other variables 'whatever they may be – are more important than factor proportions'.[37] In seeking an alternative hypothesis, Linder contends that a country cannot achieve export competitiveness in any manufactured items which have not originally catered for local needs. He assumes that initially entrepreneurs endeavour exclusively to supply their indigenous clientele and then, as firms grow and home markets become satiated, producers widen their horizons and seek additional outlets abroad. In such a process, the decision to export is the culmination and 'not the beginning of a typical market expansion path'. At first, firms are inward looking because local needs and opportunities are easier to discern, facilitating a relatively more reliable assessment of potential market risks and prospects. However, prior purveyance to the home market is a necessary but not a sufficient condition for export creation. In addition, the product demanded must be 'representative', that is, it must permeate throughout the entire economy. Conceding that his use of the term 'representative demand' is 'deplorably loose', Linder provides a clue as to how it should be construed by mentioning that though Cadillacs are consumed in Saudi Arabia, the overall demand there is insufficient to provide that country with a base from which luxury cars can be exported. Obviously, local demand must be large enough to foster scale economies of some magnitude.

Essentially, Linder's hypothesis amounts to the proposition that the intensity of trade (i.e. trade divided by its GNP)[38] of one country with another, is likely to be greater, the more alike are their demand structures. This is supposed to be the case because countries with similar consumption patterns could readily pool their markets. Entrepreneurs seeking wider trade horizons would be more inclined to encroach upon foreign domains where a significant demand has already been established for the very good which they are seeking to dispose. Linder does not appear to comprehend just why countries might obtain comparative advantages in specific items and readily concedes that his hypothesis merely proffers predictions relating to trade volumes and not patterns. (He suggests that the 'same forces that give rise to trade within each of the countries create trade between them',[39] and that an almost unlimited scope for product differentiation 'makes possible flourishing trade in what is virtually the same commodity. Ships bringing European beer to Milwaukee take American beer to Europe.'[40]

As consumer activities are highly influenced by purchasing power, similarity of *per capita* incomes are taken as an index of similarity of demand patterns, giving rise to the formulation that 'trade between countries will be more intensive the more equal are per capita incomes'.[41] This prediction would be at variance with the H/O's if, as Linder believes, the more factor proportions differ, the greater the chances that *per capita* incomes and hence demand profiles would do likewise. The factor proportions model is not entirely discounted, for it is acknowledged that if a product for which there is a representative demand is intensive in a country's abundant factor, this would indeed increase the possibility of its being an export good, and conversely for products intensive in a country's scarce factors. Nevertheless, it is to be understood that the impact that factor proportions exert is only one among many. Even in situations where countries with divergent *per capita* incomes trade, the goods exchanged are more likely to be selected on the basis of representative demand than on any other consideration. In an hypothetical example, Linder speculates that at one stage Japan might have exported bicycles, for which it had a large representative demand, and imported cars for which because of a limited home market, local production was not warranted. Interestingly, this illustration may accord with the H/O model if, at the time, bicycles were labour and cars capital intensive.

While stressing the importance of *per capita* incomes, Linder recognises that the trade actually realised may 'not be as regular between countries having similar per capita income levels as the trade-creating forces would tend to make it'.[42] Discrepancies may occur largely because of the 'distance factor', a term denoting either outright ignorance on the part of entrepreneurs with regard to foreign markets or narrow trade vistas which recede as the geographic distance between countries widens. In respect to LDCs (Less Developed Countries) Linder argues that since 'many domestic entrepreneurs have never raised their trade horizon very much above the local village market',[42] intra-Third World trade has been meagre. By contrast, the economic interchange between the Third World and advanced countries (in manufactured goods that is) is more intensive than Linder's hypothesis would have us anticipate. This turn of events is accounted for in terms of aggressive advanced country marketing.

Linder's analysis of LDC trade is somewhat flawed. A more convincing explanation of why trade with Third World countries exceeds his model's expectations may be found in the realisation that many LDCs are compartmentalised into two economic subsets, a semi developed urban and a large subsistence or underdeveloped rural sector. Seen in this light, trade between an LDC's modern sector and an advanced economy may accord more with Linder's representative demand notions than with marketing aggressiveness. Linder also asserted that while LDCs had access to foreign capital to develop their primary product industries, no such funds were forthcoming to combine with their cheap labour to yield manufactured exports.[43] Writing in 1961, it might have been too much to expect of Linder that he would have been able to foresee the subsequent involvement of numerous multinational corporations in establishing manufacturing plants in many LDCs, particularly in Asia, specifically to capitalise on available and abundant cheap labour. Considering Linder's reluctance to attribute any strategic importance to factor proportions, at least as far as manufactures are concerned, this lack of foresight is hardly surprising.

Finally, in examining what else besides market risk and awareness prompts producers initially to be parochially orientated, Linder considered the exigencies of the inventive process which usually responds to locally perceived needs, and which depends on swift market feedbacks to eliminate teething problems. Quite independently, a number of other theorists embarked on much more comprehensive and detailed studies into this very issue, and it is to their work that we now turn.

Technology Based Theories

In a seminal paper, Posner was able to illuminate the significance of technology in trade through the device of assuming equal factor

proportions between trading partners and then hypothetically introducing successive technological innovations within various industries in
certain countries.[44] Conceptual problems were encountered in the
attempt to equate relative factor endowments where inputs were not
necessarily meant to be homogeneous and where allowance was explicitly made for diverse production techniques. Two solutions were
forthcoming. Either one assumes factor price equalisation or one
assumes inter-country equality in terms of total capital valuations, even
though momentarily countries' capital stocks are not in physical units
interchangeable. Over time, this lack of interchangeability can be
eliminated by an adaptive process involving learning but since learning
is an investment, an accretion to the capital stock occurs challenging
the equal inter-country capital endowment assumption. Posner sought
to resolve this dilemma by concentrating on a specific or narrow band
of industries, so that in aggregate terms, differences in capital endowments were minimised.

His model assumed: that the same industries exist in all countries,
an absence of tariffs or transport costs, full employment, fixed exchange rates and universally identical consumer tastes. Internationally,
individual industries (identified by their names) need not produce the
exact same products or employ the same production processes, for an
industry is defined as a group of firms capable of easily producing each
other's output, yet being 'substantially less well suited to the production of "outside" commodities'.[45] Not only do we have a multiplicity
of industries but also of factors, or rather subfactors, i.e. subsets of
labour and capital, etc. The latter assumption could favour the circular
argument that a country maintains a comparative advantage in the
production of a certain commodity because it is relatively well
endowed with factors specific to that commodity and it is so well
endowed because its competitive advantage induces the constant
renewal and regeneration of the factors in question.[46] Noting that
machinery designed for particular functions could readily be transferred and installed abroad, Posner rejected the view that factor endowments are the *fons et origo* of trade, and pursued instead, a quest for
the unravelling of alternative explanations as to why a given country
(say Switzerland with regard to watches) maintains competitiveness
over time.

As a preliminary working hypothesis, readers were enjoined to
consider an hypothetical situation within a country where a particular
firm adopts cost reducing measures or alternatively, a new product,
the demand for which displaces those of an industry's more established

items. In these circumstances, firms threatened with displacement would be compelled to emulate the innovator. The need for imitation would be particularly pressing, the greater the initiator's capacity to expand and swamp the market. Two stages are involved in attaining a satisfactory response. First of all, recognition of the need for adjustment must occur (the time taken between the innovation and reaction being deemed 'the reaction lag') and thereafter, the process of assimilating new procedures, 'the learning period' must be completed. The sum of these two periods constitutes the domestic imitation lag. If the innovation stems from abroad, the imitation lag may be extended, as local producers may be less alert to foreign intrusions in comparison with those originating within their midst. (As a corollary, it may also take longer for local consumers to accept a new foreign product.) In the interval between local consumer acceptance and producer imitation, exports flow from the innovating country. Each trade flow 'is in general finite' but the system can yield a constant flow of trade 'if we assume not just a single innovation but a flow of innovations through time, first in one industry, then in another'.[47] Similarly, the importing country may also innovate yielding 'a stable equilibrium of two-way trade'.[48]

Innovations may be concentrated in one or a group of industries on account of any of four factors. There may be a technical linkage between one innovation and another. Alternatively, linkages 'may be induced on the demand side where 'complementarities in consumption' may stimulate changes in products jointly demanded with those recently innovated. An industry may be 'blessed with an excessive quota' of innovators and, finally, an industry may maintain a high rate of expenditure on research and development. Posner made no reference to the characteristics of industries likely to be vested with the latter two attributes. One may however speculate that they are likely to be composed of oligopolists which primarily indulge in non price competition.

Building in part on Posner's work, Hufbauer advanced a slightly more sophisticated explication of what he termed 'technological gap trade'.[49] As a point of departure, Hufbauer also assumed a world of equal factor endowments in which trade is generated by technological innovation, with trade flows limited in duration by the time taken by importing countries' firms to respond successfully to external challenges. The period of the imitation lags would in part vary according to the extent to which foreign innovators are able to maintain scale economy advantages over would-be rivals. Two versions of scale economies were contemplated. One, relating to static considerations, is a function of output magnitudes and the other, a dynamic one, relates to improved performances that accrue over time. Since firms learn by doing, and since learning takes time, a large volume of output achieved in a short timespan would not necessarily elicit the optimal long-term factor deployments and efficiencies. All this implies that even if a defensive firm attains a throughput at least as large as its rival ('and hence as economical from the static scale viewpoint') by virtue of its having set up production at a later period, it would yet be disadvantaged. Fortunately, such disadvantages eventually do in fact wane and unless a new round of innovations is launched, trade flows ultimately discontinue.

Once the equal factor endowment assumption is relaxed, trade flows can no longer all simply be characterised as technologically induced, uni-directional and of limited duration. Assume the existence of both high and low wage countries and that wages are based on productivity levels which in turn are determined by differential applications of science to industrial activity. According to Hufbauer, in such a setting almost all technological improvements, and hence technological gap exports, are likely to be established in high wage economics. If trade is confined to rich countries then the sequence of events would be the same as in the equal factors endowment case but once goods are sold also to low wage countries, a new dimension is added. As the low wage country firms self-defensively produce the importables, not only do exports from the innovator taper off but in due course, specifically on account of their low wage structure, low wage countries acquire comparative advantages in the goods in question and the flow of trade is in fact reversed to move from the poor to the rich economies. Trade flows could be reversed a second time by another round of innovations, or else they could wither as wages rise in low income countries. Whatever the final outcome, initial imitation lags within low income countries are shortened by virtue of their entrepreneurs having access to cheap labour which enables them to offset the disadvantages of not readily being able to capitalise on dynamic scale economies.

Since, in practice, a combination of both technological gap and low wage country exports is likely to occur simultaneously, Hufbauer predicted that the world's latest products would be embodied among the goods offered by rich countries. This was confirmed in his examination of the synthetic materials industry, an ideal case study considering that, in this industry, a stream of new products continually displaces old ones. Hufbauer's study yields one of the earliest accounts of the product cycle theory, a theory which postulates that certain commodities would sequentially be produced in various parts of the world according to the stage, degree of evolution or age of the product in question. In this field, Vernon was likewise a notable pioneer. An outline of his views follows directly.

Vernon divaricates from Hufbauer in yielding a more solid understanding of the high wage-product nexus.[50] While he assumed that all advanced country entrepreneurs are equally capable of absorbing and utilising the latest scientific knowhow, Vernon believed that the probability of their doing so varies according to perceived profit opportunities revealed through appropriate channels of communication, in which regard local markets are of prime importance. Since the US market is one in which there are very large average incomes, high labour costs and a relatively abundant capital supply, Vernon would expect US manufacturers to be among the forerunners in founding product or production processes suitable to such a milieu.[51] Not only would US producers constitute a vanguard in pursuing new technological trends but they would also tend to locate their pathbreaking production ventures within the US itself even if available inputs are not necessarily the cheapest. This is explained in terms of the need, during the product's chrysalis, to be in immediate reach of likely clientele as the commodity's ultimate standardised form as well as those of its manifold inputs is realised through a process of experimentation and adaptation in which rapid market feedbacks are critical. At any rate, since producers can entertain some early monopoly power because of product differentiation, at first, 'small (input) cost differences count less in the calculation of the entrepreneur than they are likely to count later on'.[52]

Once some basic product standardisation is attained, the need for production flexibility is somewhat obviated. The product is deemed to have entered its 'maturing phase' where concern for input cost minimisation grows. Eventually, assuming high income elasticities of demand, markets within other advanced economies beckon and exports begin to flow from the US. Shortly thereafter, an option of transferring production abroad is likely to be considered in the light of a near or complete exhaustion of scale economies (within the US), the threat of foreign competition, the need to jump actual or impending tariff barriers and the financially attractive prospect of locating in lower labour cost economies. If overseas production does occur, export flows from the US to other advanced countries would begin to ebb, and new export streams might emerge, say from Europe and the US, to the Third World.

When all residual development problems are resolved, the product's third and final stage, the 'phase of complete standardization', is attained. Henceforth the allure of cheap Third World labour becomes overwhelming, especially in instances where a large body of unskilled workers can undertake specialised tasks decomposed into simple repetitive procedures. Although LDCs manifest capital shortages, this would impose no serious obstacle to advanced country firms, who could and would transfer funds provided other conditions attracting them to the LDCs prevail. Vernon predicts that in this third phase export flows from the US to the LDCs would be reversed as production advantages emanating from LDC labour overwhelm those that may be directly obtained in the US.

Although the product cycle thesis is couched in terms of technological developments and is explicitly dynamic, it can be reconciled with the essence of the more static H/O theory. In the first phase of the production cycle, products which incorporate advanced scientific inputs tend to be devised in the US where not only market considerations but also input availabilities (the skill abundance?) yield regional manufacturing advantages, whereas in the third phase, plants relocate to LDCs on account of their low wage levels. Between production phases one and three, something akin to factor intensity reversals occurs. Strictly speaking, factor reversals occur at a given moment of time when factor intensities diverge internationally because of a combination of widely disparate factor costs and elasticities of factor substitution. In the product cycle case, 'reversals occur over time with entrepreneurs not really facing significant options of varying capital labour ratios in any given period. It has been argued that much of the Leontief paradox and hence the standing of the H/O theory, is reconcilable in terms of the product cycle model.[53] Hirsch felt that since products at early development stages require relatively large research and development and skill inputs, of which the US has a relative abundance, the US naturally exports such items in exchange for products which have reached maturation and which, although relying on a fair amount of unskilled labour, also embody large quantities of internationally mobile capital.

The product cycle theory, drafted as it is in such loose terms, has generally not evoked theoretical criticism save those relating to its vagueness and lack of vigour. A critique advanced by Finger censored the literature for not recognising that the product cycle hypothesis should really be seen in the context of attempts at incorporating the phenomenon of non price competition as a trade explanator.[54] According to Finger, non price competition occurs when manufacturers of differentiated goods attempt to retain existing or capture new markets by devising new products. The pace of product development indicates the relative intensity with which an industry indulges in such competition. It can be identified by the rate of product turnover or more specifically 'the rate of change of the list of products offered for sale in a given market'. Finger claims that this variable 'provides a much more satisfactory basis than any previously offered'[55] in accounting for non factor proportions based trade. The importance of technological breakthroughs as sources of comparative advantage is downgraded in favour of the rapid generation of new goods as such. To exemplify this, the frequent style changes (which in Finger's opinion are proxies for product turnover rates) that dominate the ladies' garment and leather footwear industries are cited as instances of non price competition which do not necessarily involve new production techniques. While conceding that 'the technology gap and the product turnover views of competition by product development are conceptually distinct', Finger submits that his approach adds to the technology gap theorising by embracing both aspects. The hypothesis that exports are a function of product turnover rates was tested by Finger who, for various years, regressed either US or Japanese exports, imports or net exports (of specific industries) on capital per man, labour skills, a scale economy variable, rates of product turnover, average produce age and a concentration proxy. Despite the fact that in only one of 13 separate regressions was the rate of product turnover variable statistically significant at the 5 per cent level, and that other key product cycle theory variables such as income elasticities or rates of growth of value added were omitted, Finger did not balk in concluding that his results confirmed that product turnover rates are ingredients in determining US and Japanese trade positions.[56] By highlighting fashion goods, Finger's attention seems to be more on style changes than in the generation of new products as such, for as the term 'new product' is generally understood, either input or the consumer utility afforded is appreciably changed. The ambiguity in Finger's study clearly emerges when in one statistical series items that 'changed' over a period were enumerated while in another, only items 'newly established' were included.

Thus far we have partly reviewed some of the major trade determination theories. Not all relevant hypotheses or ideas have been touched upon. Further concepts bearing on the issue will be dealt with later but at this stage it might be worthwhile enquiring how the above described theories stand in the light of empirical investigations; the subject matter of the following chapter.

Notes

1. It can henceforth be assumed that standard cloth and wheat units are considered.

2. The country in question is taken to be incapable of altering international terms of trade.

3. See for instance: J. Bhagwati, *Trade, Tariffs and Growth* (Weidenfeld and Nicolson, London, 1969), p. 7.

4. Factor reversals do not occur, i.e. if one commodity is labour intensive at one set of relative factor prices, it continues to be so at all others.

5. Since each industry isoquant, in a map of linear homogeneous ones, is a mirror image of those above and below it, any one can be arbitrarily chosen as being representative of them all.

6. With the slope of the line AB, the combinations of capital and labour at either E or F can both be exchanged for, or are equivalent in value to OA of capital.

7. Since we are primarily interested in factor prices and not in total resources, only the slope and not the actual position of such lines is relevant.

8. B. Ohlin, *Interregional and International Trade,* 2nd edn (Harvard University Press, Cambridge, 1967).

9. They certainly are not cited in the overwhelming majority of undergraduate trade textbooks.

10. Ohlin, *Interregional and International Trade,* p. 307.

11. Ibid., p. 178.

12. These were ascribed mainly to factor indivisibilities but possibilities of learning by doing were not discounted. See, for example, p. 85.

13. Ohlin, *Interregional and International Trade*, p. 38.

14. Ibid., p. 312, italics added.

15. Ibid., p. 184.

16. Ibid., p. 64.

17. Ibid., p. 175.

18. Ibid., p. 66, italics added.

19. Ibid., p. 118.

20. Ibid., p. 219.

21. Ibid., pp. 309 and 316.

22. See Bhagwati, *Trade, Tariffs and Growth,* pp. 267–31.

23. Ibid., p. 27.

24. R. Baldwin, 'Determinants of the Commodity Structure of U.S. Trade', *American Economic Review* (March 1971).

25. R. Baldwin, 'Determinants of Trade and Foreign Investment: Further Evidence', *Review of Economics and Statistics* (Feb. 1979). The question of non or actual factor price equalisation is contentious. If its presence is postulated as a pre-trade occurrence, then factor proportions do not diverge in price terms, the only meaningful criterion. Is the non-occurence of factor price equalisation a pre- or post-trade phenomenon? If it's a pre-trade condition, this is fairly standard. If it's a post-trade condition, some market failure may be implied. Presumably, in this case, it's a pre-trade condition.

26. R. Caves and R. Jones, *World Trade and Payments* (Little Brown and Co., Boston, 1977), p. 121.

27. Baldwin, 'Determinants of Trade and Foreign Investment'.

28. See for instance, P. Kenen, 'Nature, Capital and Trade', *Journal of Political Economy* (Oct. 1965), pp. 437–60.

29. H.G. Grubel and P.J. Lloyd, *Intra-Industry Trade* (Macmillan, 1975), p. 20.

30. See A. Aquino, 'Intra-Industry Trade and Inter-Industry Specialization as Concurrent Sources of International Trade in Manufactures', *Weltwirtschaftliches Archiv,* vol. 114 (1978), pp. 275–96.

31. Grubel and Lloyd, *Intra-Industry Trade,* p. 4.

32. See R. Lipsey's review of Grubel and Lloyd's book, *Journal of International Trade,* vol. 6 (1976), pp. 312–14.

33. Grubel and Lloyd, *Intra-Industry Trade,* p. 8.

34. J.A. Brander, 'Intra-Industry Trade in Identical Commodities', *Journal of International Economies,* vol. 11, no. 1 (Feb. 1981), pp. 1–14.

35. S.B. Linder, *An Assay on Trade and Transformation* (Almqvist and Wiksell, Uppsala, 1971).

36. Ibid., p. 85.

37. Ibid., p. 85.

38. Intensities of trade are supposed to indicate propensities of countries to trade with one another.

39. Linder, *An Essay on Trade and Transformation,* p. 102.

40. Ibid., p. 102.

41. Ibid., p. 17.

42. Ibid., p. 108.

43. Ibid., p. 93.

44. M.V. Posner, 'International Trade and Technical Change', *Oxford Economic Papers* (Oct. 1961).

45. Ibid., p. 326.

46. In this regard, it is worth noting Corden's contention that the factor proportions theory refers only to factors of production that are generally available for many different products. 'It does apply to factors specific to one activity'. See M. Corden, 'Intra-Industry Trade and Factor Proportions Theory' in H. Giersch, *On the Economics of Intra-Industry Trade* (Mohr, Tubingen, 1978), p. 5.

47. Ibid., p. 335.

48. Ibid., p. 336.

49. G.C. Hufbauer, *Synthetic Materials and the Theory of International Trade* (Harvard University Press, Cambridge, Mass., 1966).

50. R. Vernon, 'International Investment and International Trade in the Product Cycle', *Quarterly Journal of Economics* (May, 1966).

51. Vernon is careful to stress that he is not claiming that all or even most innovations originate in the US but rather that those appropriate to the pecularities of the US economy are likely to be established there. Morrall, for instance, incorrectly interpreted Vernon in suggesting that readers could reasonably conclude that only the US would innovate (see J. Morrall, *Human Capital, Technology and the Role of the U.S. in International Trade* (University of Florida Press, Gainsville, 1972).

52. Vernon, 'International Investment', p. 195.

53. See for example, S. Hirsch, 'The United States Electronics Industry in International Trade' in L.T. Wells Jr. (ed.), *The Product Life Cycle and International Trade* (Harvard University Press, Boston, 1972), pp. 49, 50.

54. J.M. Finger, 'A New View of the Product Cycle Theory', *Weltwirtschaftliches Archiv,* band 111 (1975c), pp. 79–98.

55. Ibid., p. 81.

56. Ibid., p. 96.

2 TRADE THEORIES EMPIRICALLY ASSESSED

In keeping with the tendency to subject economic hypotheses of all kinds to statistical scrutiny, those relating to trade have ever increasingly been investigated. An enormous number of empirical studies has burgeoned, most of which are of interest and relevance. To discuss or even mention all of them would take us far beyond the scope of this book. For our purposes, a summary of some of the major research work will suffice.

We still start with probes into the Ricardian theory, will wend our way through controversies in the H/O model and we will then note how post H/O theories stand in the light of empirical research recently conducted.

The Ricardian Theory

One of the most celebrated attempts at testing the Ricardian theory was undertaken by MacDougall, who in noting that before World War II, 'American weekly wages in manufacturing were roughly double the British', concluded that the US ought to have then had a comparative advantage in industries where output per worker was more than twice the British.[1] An examination of 1937 trade data disclosed that, in the main, the US industries in question upheld a larger share of the world export market than did its UK competitors. On the strength of these results MacDougall considered the Ricardian theory to be validated, especially since his figures revealed that where US labour productivities were less than double those of the British, UK exports exceeded American ones by very large margins. While not questioning the accuracy of MacDougall's observations, it is not clear that the inference he draws is consonant with the theory's essence. The theory is usually formulated in terms of bilateral trade, where one country exports to the other, goods in which its labour force is comparatively more efficient. While no allowance is made for the same goods to be exported simultaneously by both countries, MacDougall's approach is cast in terms of comparative export market shares sustained in third party economies. This is supposedly justified on the grounds that in the review period, trade between the US and UK was severely restricted because of inordinately high tariffs. Although there appears to be no theoretically sound basis for such a procedure, it has been accepted by many as 'a valid translation of the classical comparative costs model into a multi-country setting'.[2] MacDougall recognised that, theoretically, if either the US or UK 'had any comparative advantage, however small, she would get the whole export market'.[3] That in practice, both had at least some share, even if labour productivity ratios diverged from relative wages ratios, is accounted for by the existence of imperfect markets, non-homogeneous products and transport costs. None the less, MacDougall felt reassured that the labour theory was indeed confirmed since there was a clear 'tendency for each country to get a larger and larger share of the market the greater its comparative advantage'.[4]

As opposed to a large number of economists who have accepted the validity of MacDougall's test, Bhagwati advanced some pointed criticism.[5] His disinclination to endorse MacDougall's findings is based primarily on two considerations. In the first instance, Bhagwati maintains that a test relating relative labour productivities to relative export shares is not in keeping with the Ricardian hypothesis. (In this regard, his reservations appear to have been shared by Caves. On recording MacDougall's amazement that in instances where US labour productivity advantages had barely offset higher wage rates, US and UK exports were not on average equal, Caves declared that 'actually, theory reveals no reason cost parity should go hand in hand with parity in export quantities' and 'where costs are not identical, many variables are relevant which MacDougall does not mention'.[6]) The second pillar on which Bhagwati bases his dissension is perhaps even more damning. Marshalling MacDougall's data, as well as figures provided in supplementary papers by Stern and Balassa, Bhagwati regressed export price ratios on labour productivity ratios and found the results to be 'almost entirely hopeless'. Likewise, the relationship between comparative unit labour-costs and export price ratios was seen 'to be equally disappointing'. Accordingly, Bhagwati concluded that contrary to general belief 'there is as yet no evidence in favour of the Ricardian hypothesis'.

Somehow, Bhagwati's verdict has received little endorsement.[7] Caves and Jones, for example, recently upheld the view that MacDougall's study demontrates 'that American and British trade patterns have been found broadly consistent with its (i.e. the Ricardian) predictions'.[8] They dismissed Bhagwati's disclaimers on the grounds that in a purely perfectly competitive market, American and British exports would sell at the same price and hence they describe Bhagwati's efforts in comparing export price and labour productivity ratios as being meaningless. This is somewhat surprising considering Caves' clear awareness that MacDougall operated in a non-perfectly competitive environment.[9] In his earlier monograph, Caves referred to MacDougall's assertion that if perfect competition prevailed, 'one would expect that the ratio of United States to United Kingdom exports for homogeneous product groups would be either zero or infinity, as United States wage productivity does or does not fail to offset the United States wage disadvantage'.[10] By contrast, in their textbook, Caves and Jones maintained that in a purely competitive market, one country 'could have a productivity advantage and *hence a larger market share*'.[11]

Rebuffs to Bhagwati's challenges of the kind described above, are not very convincing, and in the absence of a more forceful defence of MacDougall's approach, Bhagwati's reservations merit consideration. Whatever the case, lack of any conclusive confirmation of the Ricardian hypothesis may not be unduly disturbing considering the hypothesis' limited practical usefulness, for the reliance of a prediction based 'on labour productivity unaccompanied by any explanation of why the labour productivity is what it is, and how therefore it may be expected to change, restricts the utility of the prediction'.[12]

The Leontief Paradox

Leontief's investigative foray into the factor intensity composition of US trade unleashed a frenetic controversy, in which the empirical validity of the H/O theory was vigorously contested.[13] This was so since Leontief's research indicated that, contrary to general expectations, US imports appeared to be more capital intensive than US exports. Such a conclusion was derived by comparing, with the aid of a 1947 input-ouput table, relative quantities of capital and labour needed (in that year) to produce representative samples (equal to a million dollars each) of US exports and import competing goods. Exports required $2,550,780 of capital and 182,213 labour man years, whereas import competing goods utilised $3,091,339 of capital and 170,004 labour man years. On the basis of these observations, Leontief concluded that 'America's participation in the international division of labour is based on its specialization on labor intensive, rather than capital intensive, lines of production'. Leontief's proposed resolution of this apparent paradox is based on his assumption that 'one man year of American labor is equivalent to, say, three man years of foreign

labor'. With this in mind, the reader is called upon to accept the proposition: that to obtain a true measure of the US' relative labour
endowment, 'the total number of American workers must be multiplied
by three'. If this is done, then it would seem that the US is indeed
relatively labour abundant and that its trade pattern conforms to
standard H/O predictions.

Leontief aggregated labour in physical and capital in value terms,
a justifiable procedure where labour units are actually homogeneous
but in practice they are fairly differentiated, a fact on which much
of the subsequent criticism of Leontief's paper hinges. If both production factors are heterogeneous, then both should be measured in
dollars, in which case, it is not clear from the information contained in
Leontief's paper, whether or not US exports are relatively labour intensive. Leontief was unable to provide an adequate explanation for the
supposed superior productivity of US labour. He dismissed the possibility of its being due to US workers combining with technologically
advanced equipment, on the grounds that if such combinations were
profitable in the US, they 'would in general be profitable also in the
corresponding industries abroad'. Instead, he subscribed to the belief
that absolute US labour advantages were explicable in terms of better
entrepreneurship and a generally more auspicious economic environment. His initial attempts in interpreting his findings have not been well
regarded and in turn, numerous alternative accounts as well as further
empirical assessments have been advanced.

Before dealing with some of the ideas and contributions subsequently proposed, two points relating to Leontief's statistical procedure may be noted. His calculations were based on both direct and
indirect input coefficients. However, since many inputs are tradable,
it might be argued that only the direct coefficients are appropriate.
Needless to say, this does not necessarily follow; for in the instances
where inputs are not traded, use of direct coefficients only would tend
to cause factor intensity mis-specifications and where inputs are traded,
Leontief's procedure nets out factor flows. Secondly, aggregations in
input-output tables could be misleading, for it is possible that some
capital intensive exports may have been aggregated with 'similar' non-
export labour intensive activities.[15] While no evidence is on hand to
substantiate this, lingering doubts have not entirely been dispelled.

Let us now mention some of the other solutions forwarded in
resolving the Leontief paradox. One line of enquiry reveals that US
exports require relatively more skilled inputs than do US import
competing industries. If labour skills are regarded as production factors

in their own right, then given that the US is relatively skill abundant, its trade flows would then be harmonious with H/O expectations. Alternatively, on estimating values of human capital stocks (by taking into consideration enhanced earnings that result from extra education) and adding such values to these associated with physical assets, US exports may very well exhibit relatively high capital intensities.[16] Unfortunately, most human capital calculations are flawed because of the assumption that all income disparities reflect differences in education. In reality, market imperfections, social factors and innate differences in ability also determine earning differentials. Furthermore, where formal education expenses are taken as a basis for measuring human capital investments, the acquisition of skills through on the job training would needlessly be overlooked.[17] Allied to the subjects immediately under discussion, are research and development activities which are highly visible in US export industries. Considering that the US expends relatively large sums in this sphere, its export pattern could accord with the H/O theory if research and development, like skills, are treated as factor inputs.

It has been alleged that since World War II, the US has become increasingly dependent on non-agricultural resource intensive imports. If, by and large, natural resources can only be extracted and processed by capital intensive means, then an adverse imbalance in natural resource trade could in itself be an important ingredient in generating the Leontief result.[18] When, in a subsequent paper, Leontief excluded from the input-output matrix, 19 natural resource based industries, a standard H/O outcome was realised.[19] On a theoretical plane, where factor price equalisation is realised, trade in natural resource intensive goods cannot account for the paradox. To achieve factor price equalisation (assuming equal tastes and that all goods are traded), factors must indirectly be consumed by each country in equal proportions,[20] a state of affairs which can only be achieved if the capital abundant country is a net exporter of capital intensive goods. Since the conditions for complete factor price equalisation are unlikely ever to be fulfilled, the natural resource solution remains one meriting close attention.

The US tariff structure has also been singled out as an ingredient which tends to distort that country's trade pattern, especially since labour intensive industries, in particular, are highly protected. Strictly speaking, in terms of a two good, two factor, two country H/O model, tariffs can only restrict trade volumes. They cannot, for example, induce a capital abundant country to export labour intensive goods. On the other hand, if one accepts the proposition that even though a country's aggregate trade flows comply with the H/O theory, individual flows need not, then tariff barriers could be consequential. If, for instance, in the absence of tariffs, capital abundant country A exports labour intensive goods to B in exchange for capital intensive ones, and capital intensive goods to C for labour intensive ones, and if its trade with C just enables it to be a net capital exporter, then tariffs inhibiting bilateral trade with C may induce the Leontief paradox. However, from the discussion in the previous chapter, the reader may recall that the conditions required to allow global trade to conform, while bilateral trade diverges from H/O forecasts, are far too stringent to allow us to consider the tariff solution with confidence.

As a last resort, Leontief's results might be taken to reflect a theoretical shortcoming in the H/O model, for although it is assumed that goods designated as being of a certain factor intensity in one country are similarly designated abroad, it may well be the case that a good which is capital intensive in the US, is labour intensive elsewhere. If so, it would then be impossible for *both* the US and its trading partners to export only those items which are intensive in their abundant factors. By comparing the rankings, by capital intensity, of 20 US and Japanese industries, Minhas tried to assess the likelihood of factor intensity reversals actually occurring.[21] Classifying products on the basis of both direct and indirect inputs, the rank correlation coefficient between the two series was found to be .328, but when the calculations were based on direct inputs only, the coefficient rose to .730. Even so, Minhas was not convinced that factor intensity reversals were improbable. On reappraising Minhas' work and utilising his figures, Hufbauer and Ball both concluded independently of one another, that if comparisons are limited to manufacturing industries and only direct inputs are considered, then since the rank correlation coefficient then rises to .833, reversals could safely be ruled out.[22] By now, most economists would endorse Hufbauer and Ball's conclusions. Nevertheless, taking into account the fact that Leontief's study was based on both direct and indirect inputs and that all US trade (not just manufactures) was being investigated, the prospect of factor intensity reversals explaining the paradox cannot entirely be dismissed.

Among the numerous contributions to the Leontief debate, Baldwin's features as one which not only addresses itself to all of the above-mentioned issues, but which extensively re-examines the US trade pattern with updated data; 1962 trade flows are analysed by means of 1958 input-output coefficients, as opposed to the 1947 vintage figures that Leontief originally used.[23] Replicating Leontief's method, the paradox was still manifest, even where natural resource industries were excluded. Only on melding human and physical capital and omitting the natural resource industries, did the expected H/O outcome eventuate. Some eight years later, using the 1963 US input-output table applied to 1969 trade data, Baldwin once again disclosed the paradox (although not when natural resource products were left out).[24] The ratio of capital per worker in import competing industries to capital per worker in export industries (calculated on the basis of US coefficients) was also seen to be greater than unity 'for such other capital abundant countries as Germany, France, the United Kingdom, Belgium–Luxembourg, Sweden and Switzerland'.[25] This tends to concur with Hufbauer's findings, which show that in 1965, for the US, Germany, France and the UK, the capital per man embodied in import competing industries exceeded the capital per man embodied in exports.[26] For Belgium and Sweden, the situation was reversed, whereas Switzerland was not considered.

Dissatisfied with the methodology of Baldwin and others, Harkness and Kyle decided to test whether one could 'explain' a binary dependent variable (which takes a value of one where an industry is a net exporter and nought where it is a net importer) in terms 'of industry characteristics suggested by a modified multi-factor-proportions model'.[27] Fifty-eight of the 79 industries represented in the 1958 US input-output table were divided, in terms of 1962 trade flows, into either net exporters or importers.[28] These binary variables were then related to physical capital/labour ratios and the proportions within an industry of: scientific and engineering manpower, non technical professionals and other skilled personnel, unskilled workers and, finally, farmers. Dummy variables in the case of resource intensive industries were also incorporated. Since binary dependent variables preclude the use of ordinary least squares and as generalised least squares were, for other reasons deemed invalid, Harkness and Kyle employed logit analysis which was reputed to provide 'a close analogue to the standard regression model'. Their results showed that in non-resource industries, there is a statistically positive link between physical capital intensity and skilled labour of all types on the one side, and net exports on the other. Accordingly, Harkness and Kyle believed the H/O theory to be confirmed and that capital intensity does 'have a significantly pronounced impact, ceteris paribus, on the comparative advantage of resource exclusive U.S. industries'.[29]

Harkness and Kyle accounted for the divergence of their result from those that supported the Leontief paradox, in terms of their specifically chosen binary dependent variable. They argued that the H/O model 'simply predicts that industries with relatively high capital-labor (K/L) ratios will tend to be exporters', and that it does not suggest that 'across industries, either the relative or absolute share of net exports will be monotonically increasing with the K/L ratio'. In their opinion, previous studies resorted to an ill-conceived use of the share or volume of net exports as a measure of an industry's comparative advantage and, therefore, results so obtained were deemed invalid. However, as indicated in the previous chapter,[30] Caves and Jones, among others, demonstrated that theoretically within a multi-country setting, a country in aggregate terms may not necessarily import only those items which are intensive in its scarce factors. Noting this, particularly with Harkness and Kyle's paper in mind, Baldwin maintained that as a consequence, 'tests of the Heckscher–Ohlin theory based simply on whether an industry using a particular abundant factor is a net exporter or importer of its product are not appropriate'.[31] Harkness and Kyle were also criticised by Balassa 'in part because of the error possibilities involved in a binary classification and in part because large and small export-import balances are given equal weight'.[32]

Interestingly, Branson and Monoyios, by means of probit analysis, a technique which provides virtually the same outcome as logit analysis, tested Harkness and Kyle's binary variable against 1963 and 1967 US data to find, in both instances, negative coefficients in terms of physical capital intensities.[33] While conceding that additional data samples would help to resolve the issue, Branson and Monoyios declared that their 'interim conclusion would be that the presumption of no sign reversal should stand', i.e. the Leontief paradox still holds. This view was reinforced by their running of standard regressions of net exports on physical and human capital respectively as well as on total labour intakes.[34] (Other tests that were undertaken indicated that 'scaling' the data to industry size had no noticeable effect,[35] that it is unclear whether human capital is better represented by discounting wage differences between the average wage in each industry and the median wage earned by men with only eight years of education or by the fraction of workers in skilled categories, and that as the human and physical capital independent variables significantly exhibited opposite signs, they should not be aggregated in explaining US trade.)

A few years later, Leamer, who adopted Vaneks' extension of the H/O theorem to cope with multi-commodity and multi-factor cases, claimed to have dispensed with Leontief's paradox.[36] To enable readers to appreciate Leamer's somewhat convoluted approach, part of his paper is hereby paraphrased. Given the usual strict H/O assumptions, including factor price equalisation and identical homothetic consumer preferences, the following relations were derived:

Country i's trade is $T_i = Q_i - C_i$

where: T_i is a country's net export vector
        Q_i is a country's output vector
        C_i is a country's consumption vector

Factors embodied in country i's trade are
$$
\begin{aligned}
AT_i &= A(Q_i - C_i) \\
&= AQ_i - AQ_w\alpha_i \\
&= \underline{E_i - E_w\alpha_i}
\end{aligned}
$$

(Equation One)

where: A is a matrix of factor requirements
        E_i is a country's factor endowment vector
        E_w is the world's factor endowment vector
        α_i is a set of positive scalars
        $C_i = Q_w\alpha$ (because of homothetic preferences)
        $AQ_i = E_i$

From Equation One: $K_t = K_i - \alpha_i K_w$
                          $L_t = L_i - \alpha_i L_w$

where: K_t and L_t are capital and labour in net exports
        K_i and L_i are country i's factor endowments
        K_w and L_w are the world's factor endowments

Country i is defined to be capital abundant 'if and only if the share of the world's capital stock located in i exceeds the share of the world's labour force: $K_i/K_w > L_i/L_w$'.

From the above, country i is revealed by trade to be relatively capital abundant if: $K_i/(K_i - K_t) > L_i(L_i - L_t)$

(Inequality One)

Given that $K_c = K_i - K_t$
             $L_c = L_i - L_t$

where: K_c is capital embodied in i's consumption
          L_c is labour embodied in i's consumption

Inequality One can be written as:
$$K_i(L_i - L_t) > L_i(K_i - K_t)$$
or $- K_i L_t > - L_i K_t$
or $- K_c L_t > - L_c K_t$

and finally as $K_t/L_t > K_c L_c$,[37] that is, a country 'is capital abundant if the capital intensity of net exports exceeds the capital intensity of consumption'.

On examining 1947 US data (the year on which Leontief's original paper centred) Leamer discovered that the US was indeed a net exporter of labour and capital services. In addition, as capital per man in net exports, estimated at $11,783, exceeded the capital to man ratio of $6,737 in consumption, Leamer concluded that the 1947 trade figures were consistent with the US being relatively capital abundant. Considering Leamer's reliance on the unsatisfactory quantity as opposed to price definition of factor abundance, and the fact that his empirical observations are interpreted against a framework based on the extremely dubious (to say the least) factor equalisation and equal homothetic taste assumptions, his conclusions can at best be regarded as being highly tentative.

Finally, Stern and Maskus in attempting to redress the fact that most studies have focused on events in only a single year, regressed, for every year over 1958–76, US exports on physical and human capital (direct inputs only) as well as on total industry employment (L).[38] In each regression, the physical capital and employment coefficients were negative while those of human capital were both positive and consistently significant at the 1 per cent level. Next, they conducted a probit analysis for each year, and found that without exception, net exports were negatively related to either physical capital (K) or K/L. When the figures were re-computed with the exclusion of natural resource industries, the capital to labour coefficients were consistently positive, but not statistically significant. From all this Stern and Maskus inferred that Branson and Monoyios' work reflected the presence of natural resources, and that while Harkness and Kyle's empirical results might be matched in other years, since Baldwin's theoretical objections were accepted, Harkness and Kyle's approach was not endorsed.

Two other aspects of Stern and Maskus' paper are pertinent to the issues at hand. In the first instance, they duplicated Leontief's method using 1958 and 1972 data. In the earlier year, the gross physical capital to labour ratio of imports over exports was found to be 1.07 but by 1972 the ratio declined to .95 in line with normal H/O expectations.[39] Complementing this procedure, the pair of ratios that served as Leamer's litmus test were also calculated for the same two years. For the prior period, when the US happened to be a net exporter of both capital and labour services, the capital to labour ratio of net exports fell short of the capital to labour ratio in consumption, a result discordant with Leamer's. Later, the absolute value of the net exports of capital to labour ratio again exceeded the factor ratio in consumption but as on this occasion the US had become a net importer of capital and labour services, this heralded an absence of Leontief's paradox.

Only a handful of contributions to the Leontief controversy have thus far been reviewed. The debate is likely to continue ad nauseam without any definitive resolution. This is probably due to the fact that other non H/O type variables affect trade flows. An outline of some of the efforts to capture these, empirically speaking, is provided in the section that follows.

The H/O Model and Some of its Rivals

In keeping with the budding awareness of the need to evaluate new hypotheses, Hufbauer undertook a wide ranging statistical analysis involving a number of alternative trade theories being 'pitted against one another on common commodities and countries'.[40] His enquiry also delved into the 'links between characteristics embodied in trade and national attributes'. 1965 data sources were used for a 24 country sample which accounted for approximately 90 per cent of all non-Communist manufactured trade.

As a prelude to his major assignment, the strength of association between and within elements of three sets of variables were measured. Rank correlations were calculated between variables relating to the commodity characteristics of total manufactured exports of each country and those depicting national characteristics. The former set contained industry averages of; capital per man, skill ratios, wages per man, a scale economy proxy, a consumer to capital goods ratio, the first trading date of products and a measure of product differentiation. National features were reflected by: fixed capital per manufacturing employee, the proportion of skilled to total employees, total manufacturing output and GDP *per capita*. In all instances, the correlation coefficients were high (no less than .6) and significant at the 1 per cent level, suggesting that manufactured export attributes do indeed correspond to specific country ones. For example, exports embodying a high average of capital per man tend to be associated with economies endowed with large quantities of fixed capital per manufacturing employee, etc. The second set of calculations involved measurements of the associative strength among export commodity characteristics. Here the results were varied. Weak and statistically insignificant rank correlations were reported for some combinations (such as for product differentiation and wages per man) but in most cases the connections were close enough to warrant the suspicion that one theory's good performance might simply be due to another's. Finally, rank correlations among the national features were derived. With the exception of total manufacturing output, 'a considerable interrelationship' was exhibited, prompting Hufbauer to remark that 'for practical purposes a composite attribute might perform almost as well, or as poorly, in explaining different export characteristics'.

Upon dealing with the theories under review, the operation of the Leontief paradox was (as already mentioned) seen to be upheld.[41] Accordingly, one might reasonably conclude that the H/O theory was statistically unsubstantiated. None the less, Hufbauer felt that the 'factor proportions theory performs surprisingly well when applied to the exports alone of the twenty-four nation sample',[42] the rank correlation between relative capital endowments and capital labour ratios embodied in exports being .704. Unfortunately, the relation between endowments and imports was not explored. The other body of theories surveyed were those that stress the importance of human skills, scale economies, stages of production (measured by the consumer to capital goods ratio) the technological gap (shown by the first date a good is traded) and the product cycle (indicated by the degree of product differentiation). All of these theories were thought to be operable given that exports manifesting the characteristics these theories postulated correlated strongly with appropriate national attributes. As a result of this plethora of confirmations, Hufbauer concluded that 'it must be conceded that many different characteristics express themselves in export patterns. No theory monopolizes the explanation of manufactures trade.'[43] One glaring weakness of Hufbauer's study and one which Hufbauer himself highlights, is the fact that US data sources were virtually exclusively relied upon to depict commodity characteristics. If, as is generally believed, skill and other factor intensity reversals are not widespread, this deficiency would not necessarily impair the value of Hufbauer's research.

Of the prodigious comparative studies of the H/O and product cycle theories, Morrall's was fairly wide-ranging.[44] Encompassing the entire range of two-digit US manufacturing industries, Morrall, for the years 1958, 1960, 1965 and 1966, correlated net exports, or net exports as a percentage of industry shipments with variables appropriate to the models considered. Looking at the H/O model, the variables selected included: labour skills, wages per employee, non-wage value added per employee and degree of worker education. By and large, the correlation coefficients between each pair of dependent and independent variables supported the H/O theory, especially when net exports as a percentage of shipments were involved. Of all the independent variables, labour skills seemed the most relevant. The proxy for the capital to labour ratio, i.e. non-wage value added per employee, did not appear statistically significant until 1966. However, since over time, the size of its correlation coefficient steadily increased, Morrall speculated that repetitive Leontief type tests 'may not show the same results as before'.[45] (Our discussion above has already mentioned that Stern and Maskus found that by 1972, the paradox no longer held.)

With regard to the product cycle theory, the independent variables used were: scientists and engineers as a percentage of the workforce, the percentage change of value added between 1947 and 1965,[46] an index of the relative growth of labour efficiency (innovations are likely to be labour saving) and an index of profit rates.[47] Except for labour efficiency, rank correlations between dependent and independent variables were all generally close and significant, even more so than within the first battery of tests.

On resorting to multiple regression analysis in which the two models were either combined or treated separately, the explanatory power of a composite model was seen to be superior. This is not surprising considering that both sets of models are credited with some ability in aiding our understanding of trade flows.

Perhaps the most challenging aspect of Morrall's work lies in his insistence on adhering to the price definition of factor abundance (an omission practised by virtually all other researchers) and on his assertion that contrary to general belief, the US (on price criteria) has a relative shortage of skilled manpower. Since the US is, even by Morrall's account, physically well endowed with labour skills, an observation of relative scarcity in price terms, hinges on the US' demand for skills being exceptionally high. In this sphere, Morrall's evidence is shaky. Because his data were not internally comparable and because Morrall had not calculated the costs of skilled inputs relative to returns on capital, his claim does not appear to be vindicated.

Morrall's monograph has been subjected to a fair amount of criticism. In some cases, as by Goodman and Ceyhun, his study has been brusquely dismissed 'because of the inherent limitation of the methods used'.[48] In others, as by Stern, he has been taken to task for discriminating between two sets of theories on the grounds that the existence of high correlations between labour skills and value added, and labour skills and scientists and engineers, vitiate interpretation of the statistical findings.[49] Interestingly, some complaints seemed to be diametrically opposed. For instance, Stern admonished Morrall for keeping human and physical capital separate. 'If instead he had treated them jointly, the United States would appear to be capital abundant'.[50] By contrast, Branson asserted that Morrall accepts without critical comment the notion 'that physical and human capital can be aggregated in a demonstration that U.S. trade is capital intensive'.[51]

Shortly after Morrall's book appeared, Hirsch published the first of two papers evaluating as trade determinants, the relative performance of H/O and technological type variables.[52] His initial venture based on 1970 data involved 25 industries and spanned 29 countries. Utilising Balassa's revealed comparative advantage index (discussed below), export performance indices for every industry in each country sampled were calculated. Then, for every industry, the simple correlation coefficient between its export performance in a country and that country's average value added per employee (taken as a measure of capital endowments) was obtained and ranked from high coefficients downwards. Next, the industry characteristics: research and development expenditures, proportion of skilled labour and average wages representing the neo-technology school, as well as physical and overall capital intensity (indicated respectively by non-wage and total value added per employee) representing the H/O theory, were used to generate five additional rank sets which were sequentially correlated with the industry ranking initially obtained. The results yielded significantly higher rank correlation coefficients for the neo-technology variables, with research and development displaying the strongest association (a coefficient of .76, or .84 when drugs and non metallic minerals were excluded). By contrast, the correlation coefficient of physical capital intensities with the above ranked industries was the lowest (.46 and not significant, or .62 with the exclusion of drugs and non metallic minerals). In other words, industries whose export performances were positively associated with large capital endowments were more likely to be research and development rather than capital intensive.

The above described tests were complemented by 29 multiple regressions, one for each country, in which industry export/output ratios were run on: skills, capital and scale variables as well as on a dummy for resource intensive products. As before, the 'skill variable conformed to expectations but the capital variable was perverse, displaying a negative sign for almost all advanced economies. On the basis of these general statistical findings, and particularly since skill and capital coefficients frequently exhibited opposite signs (testifying to the fact that these two factors cannot legitimately be aggregated), and as capital is fairly mobile internationally, Hirsch concluded that the neo-technology approach is more useful in both understanding and predicting aspects of a country's comparative advantage.

A year later, Hirsch's other study, which likewise sought to gauge the relative explanatory power of the two models in question, was released.[53] On that occasion, using 1969 data, he computed simple linear regressions (over a cross section of 28 countries) of an industry's share of a country's exports on *per capita* income (a proxy for relative capital abundance). Eight separate industries were involved, classified into four sections: high skill industries divided into labour or capital intensive ones and low skill industries similarly subdivided. In essence, it was argued that in the case of industries which were skilled yet labour intensive, a negative slope coefficient would be accepted as evidence in favour of the H/O theory and a positive one in favour of a product cycle model. As it turned out, the data supported the product cycle paradigm but only if one accepts that the H/O model merely relates to two factors — labour and physical capital; whereas the product cycle theory (in its mild form) relates to three. Hirsch claimed 'that skill intensity as such has no bearing on trade in the H/O model'. Many would disagree, for numerous efforts have been made in presenting skills as an independent factor, whose relative availability has a direct bearing on trade flows.

Skills and Technological Factors

Donald Keesing has probably done as much as anyone in bringing to the fore the importance of skills in trade. In a paper delivered in the mid-1960s,[54] Keesing identified the skill needs of the 1972 export and import commodities of some 14 different economies.[55] At one extreme, the exports of countries like India and Hong Kong required relatively few skills, while at the other, the US had the most skill intensive exports as well as showing 'signs of having the greatest relative abundance of hard to acquire skills'. Realising that his particular comparisons could be deceptive, given that US industry sources were relied upon to identify product skill coefficients, Keesing correlated the skill requirements of US goods with an index of those goods' export competitiveness. The correlations showed 'that U.S. comparative advantage centers in industries involving a high percentage of professional labor and a low percentage of unskilled labor'. It would seem that Keesing was unduly cautious, for shortly thereafter, he was able to demonstrate 'that the relative skill intensity of other trade flows, as measured in previous studies using U.S. coefficients, would also be roughly duplicated if coefficients from any other leading industrial country were used instead'.[56]

Baldwin had also pondered the importance of skills in explaining US trade.[57] In his enquiry, he observed a higher ratio of workers with 13 or more years of education, in export rather than import competing industries. Furthermore, the export industries employed relatively more scientists and engineers and expended proportionately more in research and development. Reviewing the evidence, Baldwin was convinced that it is necessary 'to discard simple, single-factor (e.g. capital per worker) trade theories in favor of multi-factor models. In particular, the labor force must be divided into various skill groups and the notion of relative differences in human capital taken into account.'

On a somewhat different yet related plane, Gruber and Vernon delved into the various factors that determine comparative advantage mainly in order to assess the role of technology.[58] In the process they analysed the '1964 exports of specified manufactured goods, broken down into twenty-four categories from each of ten exporting areas'. To establish the relations, if any, between industry export performance and product characteristics, each area's relative export share within each industry, was regressed on six industry attribute variables. Ten regressions (one for each exporter) were thus obtained. The six independent variables were: raw labour, technology intensity, capital intensity, intermediate good specialisation, industry concentration and the ratio of crude material inputs to total output. Only direct inputs were considered and US industry data were used. As it turned out, only three of the ten multiple regressions yielded high R^2s, i.e. those relating to the US, Japan and Mexico. The results for the US strongly indicate a

positive association for *that* country, between exports and high technology intensity and a negative one between exports and both raw labour
and capital intensity. As the authors acknowledged, 'the capital result
would probably have been resisted before the Leontief paradox was
exposed, but perhaps, by now, it is part of conventional wisdom'.[59]
With respect to the technology nexus, which basically revolved around
the percentage of scientists and engineers that constituted an industry's
workforce, Gruber and Vernon felt that their analysis clearly warranted
regard of the technology (or the human skill) factor as a distinct trade
variable. (The remainder of their paper concentrated on factors affecting bilateral trade. Of a number of variables tested, 'the distance factor'
emerged as a powerful explanator, even for seemingly low transport
cost goods such as drugs, in which case the significance of other trade
impediments associated with distance such as foreign market ignorance
may also be crucial.)

Thereafter, research into the relation between trade and technology
intensified. A fairly comprehensive investigation dealing specifically
with US manufactured exports was presented by Goodman and
Ceyhun.[60] As a working model, they assumed that export performance
(indicated by a geometric average of export growth rates and export
shares in total sales) was a function of: technological innovation (given
by proportions of R & D expenditures as well as scientists and engineers), industry concentration, industry growth, sales promotion,
a labour skills ratio, unit labour costs, scale economies and the capital
to labour ratio. On the grounds that ordinary least squares were un-
suitable because of collinearity among the independent variables, a
principal components regression method was employed. Both time
series covering the period 1956 to 1968 and cross section calculations
were undertaken, with the variables being appropriately lagged.

We will concentrate on the time series regressions. Industries were
divided (according to ratios of R & D expenditures to total revenue)
into two groupings of: five new and seven standard or old ones. Goodman and Ceyhun anticipated that the new industries would exhibit
a strong and positive relation between export performance and technological progress as reflected by high: R & D ratios, market concentration, increases in output, advertising expenses, skill ratios and unit
labour costs. The old industries were expected to comply more with
the factor proportions hypothesis whereby exports would be determined by relative cost considerations. With this in mind, high:
scale economies and capital labour ratios along with low: per unit
wage costs, skill ratios and market concentrations were expected.

Remarkably high R^2s were obtained. In nine of the 12 regressions, an R^2 of .80 and above was reported. This compares very favourably with studies primarily focusing on H/O variables. For example, the *highest* R^2s obtained by Branson and Monoyios, Stern and Maskus, and by Baldwin were .67, .43 and .51 respectively.[61]

Predictions with regard to new industries were realised in the cases of R & D ratios and industry concentration. The capital labour ratios and industry growth variables were not statistically conclusive; whereas the signs of the four remaining determinants varied from industry to industry; with labour skills frequently being negative. In the case of the old industries, while labour skill and wage cost variables lived up to expectations, the capital to labour ratio, though not significant, was habitually negative. Surprisingly, the R & D ratio was almost always positive.

Considering that their regressions had such strong explanatory powers and that the R & D factor was so prominent (it was positive and significant at the 1 per cent level in ten out of 12 cases) Goodman and Ceyhun's paper provides a weighty endorsement of the importance of technology in trade. Under the circumstances there may be valid grounds for their concern that trade theory can be characterised by 'an unwarranted underemphasis of non-price factors'.

The Product Cycle Theory

Because US incomes have been high and because innovators are thought to pander, at least initially, to local markets, Wells' interpretation of the product cycle theory leads to the predication that within the US, high income products would sustain above average export growth rates.[62] To test this proposition, Wells would have preferred to have regressed export growth rates on income elasticities of demand but for want of information, income elasticities of ownership were used. From a 20 industry sample, relying on 1961 figures for the dependent variables, and the years 1952-3 and 1962-3 for deriving export growth rates, a correlation coefficient of .896 was attained. Two minor quibbles may be raised in connection with the above procedure. For one thing, Wells may be chided for accepting export growth rates as a measure of comparative advantage, a charge which could of course equally be levelled against scores of others. For another, while the US may, because of large R & D investments, be a leading innovator, it does not necessarily follow that all or even most innovations would be devised solely to meet the needs of more opulent consumers.[63] Hirsch's approach, which assumes that goods that experience high value added growth rates (and therefore identified as being within an early product cycle stage) achieve exceptional export performances, meets these two objections.[64]

In considering other trade determinants, Wells reasoned that where scale economies prevail, exports would be more pronounced. Alas, as he resorted to a 'crude measure of economies of scale' and drew conclusions merely from the appearance of scatter diagrams, it would seem that there is some substance to Stern's stricture that 'Wells' formulations are unfortunately rather vague and his empiricism so casual that his results do not seem well grounded'.[65]

Mullor-Sebastian attempted to improve on Hirsch's study by covering, over a longer time span, more products at a less aggregated level.[66] She pointedly remarked that since new products are not necessarily synonymous with research intensive ones, international competitiveness in R & D goods 'does not necessarily amount to providing evidence in favor of the product cycle theory'. Unfortunately, she relied on world production growth rates as an indicator of a product's maturity; even though only US trade was scrutinised. As a result, her correlations of world production growth rates and US trade balances may simply have shown that US net exports were high in areas where world demand was similarly so. Inclusion of resource based industries, such as wood and cork products, also diluted concentration on strong product cycle theory industry candidates.

An implicit warning against an unqualified acceptance of certain aspects of product cycle or technology based trade theories is contained in Mansfield *et al.*'s paper.[67] Examining a 1974 sample of 23 US firms, they observed, especially among large firms, a growing tendency for updated technology relating to the creation of new goods or product improvements 'to be transferred directly to overseas subsidiaries' or 'to be transferred more quickly to them (in part because more subsidiaries already exist)'. This suggests that successive product innovations need not necessarily engender exports or that their impact may currently be somewhat less than writers such as Vernon or Posner would originally have envisaged.[68] Alternatively, where breakthroughs occur in processing, the predicted export turn around effect, when new technologies are assimilated (with lags) by lower wage countries, may be partly, or constantly postponed, depending on the ability of the original innovator to maintain a stream of process improvements.

Mansfield's revelations are bolstered by an article of Dunning and

Buckley who, in employing a two country model, discovered a fairly strong link between the ratio of: US to UK foreign investment in particular industries, and the R & D and skill characteristics embodied in them.[69] Their research indicated that 'R. and D. performs better as a determinant of international production than of trade', and that the prevalence of technologically intensive international firms weakens 'the explanatory power of hypotheses based solely on location specific endowments'. For example, although the US may have an advantage in the production of knowledge, 'when this can be transmitted to other countries within US enterprises, what would otherwise be a location specific advantage becomes an ownership specific advantage'. Such a conclusion was partly derived by observing that the trade explanatory power of R & D and skill intensive variables is enhanced when the dependent variable is formulated in terms of US/UK exports by locally owned firms only, as opposed to US/UK exports in general. Finally, Dunning and Buckley established that where *plant* economies are significant, firms would be predisposed to utilise their home facilities to the full rather than to transfer output abroad. This tends to reinforce the importance of improvements in processing as an inhibitor of production relocation.

As it happens, such developments were contemporaneously perceived by Vernon himself; for he was cognisant of the fact that multinational corporations (MNCs) were tending to transfer production abroad at increasingly short post-innovation intervals.[70] Judging from a sample of 57 US based MNCs, it would seem that whereas between 1946 and 1950, 8.1 per cent of new products were manufactured within a year of innovation by foreign based subsidiaries, by 1971-5, 35.4 per cent were. This trend was influenced by, among other things, the growing dispersion of subsidiaries. In 1950, only 43 of 180 leading US manufacturing companies maintained foreign branches in at least six but no more than 20 countries (none were in excess of 20); yet by 1975, 128 reached into 6-20 different countries, with 44 embracing more than 20. Not only had the MNCs enchanced their worldwide network but as individual firms accrued experience in transferring technology abroad, they 'were quite consistently quicker off the mark with any new product than were firms with fewer prior transfers'.[71]

Additional considerations, which tended to attentuate the product cycle theory's predictive ability with regard to US trade, were taken into account. *Per capita* income differences between the US and European countries narrowed appreciably, thus weakening the model's 'critical' assumption, 'that entrepreneurs of large enterprises confronted markedly different conditions in their respective home markets'. Furthermore, Vernon conceded that with many firms currently on the threshold of catering directly for the world rather than local markets or with enterprises integrating their global production facilities in both advanced and less developed countries and engaged in crosshauls between plants in assembling final products, the cause and pattern of trade, 'will be at variance with product cycle expectations'.

On the other hand, influences are at work which at least permit the product cycle theory 'to provide a guide to the motivations and response of some enterprises in all countries of the world'. These relate to: the advent of smaller innovating firms which have not yet established foreign subsidiaries, innovations originating in Europe and Japan which economise on material and capital (e.g. small cars), the continued trade between advanced and less developed countries, and, finally, some LDC firms which are beginning to promote new products appropriate to their milieu and which allow them to generate their own export and investment cycle in relation to other even less industrialised LDCs.

'Revealed' Comparative Advantage

Instead of relying on standard statistical analysis to unravel the various causes of trade, Balassa devised and employed a technique to investigate the extent to which countries maintain comparative advantages in manufactured goods in general, and in research intensive ones in particular.[72] For the years 1953, 1962 and 1971, he compiled 'revealed' comparative advantage indices for each of 73 product classifications exported by each of 13 countries. The indices were 'calculated by dividing a country's share in the exports of a given commodity category by its share in the combined exports of manufactured goods of all the thirteen industrial countries under consideration'. For each country, products were then arranged in descending order of index magnitude and assigned cardinal numbers from one onwards. The lower a good's number, the more competitive it is internationally.

Of the 73 product categories listed, nine, using 1967 US data, were deemed research intensive on the basis of both research and development expenditures exceeding 3.5 per cent of total revenue, and of scientists and engineers accounting for more than 3.5 per cent of all employees.[73] By making internal comparisons of changes in the average ranking of the nine technology based industries, movements in each country's relative ability to export such industries were assessed. For instance, since in the US the average ranking of research intensive products rose from 18 in 1953 to 10 in 1971, Balassa concluded that 'the evidence provided points to the strong, and increasing, comparative advantage of the United States in research intensive products'.[74] Balassa's procedure in determing goods for which a country has a comparative advantage is simple yet ingenious; for the mere fact that a country exports a particular commodity cannot be taken as proof that that is where its advantages lie. His approach allows one to avoid the pitfall of equating an industry's absolute or relative export level within a country, with a measure of comparative advantage. This is especially so where intra-industry trade prevails. Use of his index as the dependent variable in regressions on product characteristics, etc. would appear to be promising. None the less, some minor misgivings relating to Balassa's methodology may be harboured.

As already mentioned, because the average ranking of the nine research intensive industries had risen, this was regarded as an indication of US improvements in this area. This may well be the case but since not every industry recorded gains and *since weights linked to export values were not used*, misleading results are quite feasible. Furthermore, the use of broad commodity classifications is fraught with shortcomings. A country may in practice maintain a significantly large market share of a small subset of a product grouping, yet its overall share may be low; thus incorrectly indicating an inability to compete. More care in making inter-country comparisons is warranted. A good leading, say, country A's 'revealed' comparative advantage ranking is presumably one in which that country is *relatively* most successful *vis-à-vis* its rivals. However, even if the same good is ranked as country B's fifth best good, it does not follow that in this instance B is less competitive than A. While the issue can be resolved by comparing absolute index magnitudes, Balassa's data were depicted in terms of index rankings only.

The Linder Hypothesis

Linder's hypothesis that countries with similar living standards tend to trade relatively more intensively with one another, has been subjected to several empirical enquiries.[75] For illustrative purposes we refer to the papers by Fortune, and by Sailors *et al.*[76]

Accepting Linder's recommendation that the average propensity to import be taken as a measure of the intensity of trade between countries, and that country j's exports to i, rather than i's imports from j be utilised, Fortune, on the basis of 1967 trade flows, regressed (for each of 23 separate economies) average import propensities of manufactures onto dissimilarities of *per capita* incomes and distances between trading partners. Absolute *per capita* income differences served as indices of dissimilarity, while distances were measured in miles between countries' major cities. In general, very low R^2s were obtained; suggesting the omission of other crucial explanators. Although the distance variable was significant at the 5 per cent level in only eleven of the 23 regressions and the income variable on only nine occasions, Fortune contended that his results 'give some support to the Linder hypothesis'.

Sailors *et al.* calculated rank correlation coefficients between income differences and 1958 import propensities, for 31 countries. That is, each correlation matched one country and its relations with the rest. If the country was Sweden for example, then income differences between it and all others would be calculated and ranked. Similarly the propensity of each to import from Sweden would be calculated and ranked and then the two rankings would be correlated. Sixteen of the 31 correlations were significant at 5 per cent. As a further refinement, six countries either relying excessively on non-transportable natural resource inputs or whose manufactured exports constituted a small proportion of total exports, were excluded. Given that 14 of the remaining 25 correlations were significant, Sailors *et al.* were inclined to accept Linder's viewpoint.

As may be recalled, Linder also argued that a country is likely to possess comparative advantages in commodities for which local demand is fairly substantial. Consumer spending patterns in turn were thought to be primarily governed by *per capita* income levels. This hypothesis has been tested by Blejer, who relied on income and elasticity of demand measurements to identify the manufactured goods most likely to be purchased at various income ranges.[77] More specifically, industries were divided into three groups; those with income elasticities of demand less than 1.0, those between 1.0 and 1.8 and those greater than 1.8. Capital goods were included in the third group, on the assumption that high incomes are likely to be associated with a larger proportion of capital good creation. Blejer felt that if Linder's views were valid, one should be able to discern 'a positive relationship between income per capita and the share in total industrial exports of high income elasticity commodities and a negative relationship for low income elasticity goods'. In this light, he separately regressed the 1970 export shares of each of his three product divisions (from a 30 country sample) on *per capita* incomes (none of which were less than US $500). The results obtained were consistent with the hypothesis under review.

Using the same data, the performance of the H/O model was then compared. To do this, manufactured goods within each country were divided into three categories according to whether they were relatively intensive in: unskilled labour, human or physical capital. Each category's relative export shares were then regressed against *per capita* incomes giving rise to a negative coefficient in the case of the labour intensive goods and a positive one with regard to human capital. The regression involving physical capital registered positive significance only upon the exclusion of natural resource intensive items.

Since at that stage, both models appeared to be equally reliable, Blejer tried to discriminate between them by proceeding further. Where data sources permitted, each unit of the two three-member class sets was subdivided on the basis of attributes belonging to the alternative set. For example, labour intensive goods were broken down into those with an income elasticity of demand; of less than 1.0, of between 1.0 and 1.8 and in excess of 1.8. Keeping the intensity of the goods constant and thereby isolating H/O type considerations. the shares of each subdivision's exports were regressed on *per capita* incomes and, once more, the Linder hypothesis was substantiated. However, when income elasticity of demand was kept fixed and products were classified on the basis of factor intensities, the export shares of each factor intensity group when regressed on *per capita* incomes, did not support the H/O model. In which case, it would seem that empirically speaking, Linder's theory is more appealing.

The 'Stages' Approach to Comparative Advantage

In the latter part of the 1970s, Balassa tried to determine the expected export structure of economies at alternative levels of development.[78] Within each of his 36 country samples (equally divided into developed and developing countries), he regressed 1972 'revealed' comparative advantage indices of 184 product categories, on factor intensities (variously defined). The regression coefficients thus obtained, were in turn correlated with country characteristics, to ascertain the effects of these on international specialisation. Drawing on his results, Balassa concluded 'that intercountry differences in the structure of exports are in a large part explained by differences in physical and human capital endowments'. As countries attain economic growth, their exports become less labour intensive, enabling LDCs at relatively low levels of development to expand their exports by taking over from those graduating to more capital intensive ones. In so doing, 'the foreign demand constraint under which developing countries are said to operate' is partly overcome. This has interesting implications with regard to trade induced structural adjustments within developed economies. Conventional wisdom foresees inexorable pressures on advanced countries' labour intensive industries as Third World countries intrude in this area. If, in fact, LDCs progressively slough off their labour intensive exports, then the requisite adjustments required by developed countries would not be quite as severe as originally foreshadowed. More adaptations than expected would need to occur within capital intensive sectors but since increases in intra-industry trade is very likely, the employment consequences of such changes need not be too drastic. At this point, we seem to be running ahead of ourselves, for these issues will be explored in detail in a subsequent chapter.

Returning to Balassa's paper, it should be noted that as in other studies of a similar nature, US data were exclusively relied upon to determine factor intensities, and that only direct inputs were taken into account. Capital intensities were calculated in terms of aggregate as well as physical and human components. In each case, measures were alternatively devised on the basis of stock and flow concepts. (See Appendix at the end of this chapter.) When comparative advantage indices were regressed on aggregate capital intensities based on stocks, only 22 of the 36 separate regressions were significant at 5 per cent, and of these, 15 were LDCs but when calculations were based on flow variables, 29 regressions registered significance. As the signs were generally in the expected direction, negative for almost all LDCs and positive for most developed economies, the results appear to be in keeping with the H/O theory. However, if one focuses on the set of stock variable regressions, which Balassa would have liked to have done,[79] then the endorsement is hardly overwhelming. Although Balassa acknowledged the merits of technology based theories, he felt that they related mainly to intra-advanced country trade, and that given that the H/O model is generally assumed to be helpful in analysing trade between LDCs and developed economies, he accepted it as the underpinning for his study. Nevertheless, since bilateral trade between LDCs and developed economies was not specifically considered, and since rather a few advanced countries appeared to conform to H/O patterns, it might have been more appropriate to have considered a sample of LDCs only.

Determinants of LDC Trade

Using Lary's criteria for determining factor intensities, as well as his 1965 data, which was also updated to 1975, Tuong and Yeats tested the proposition that LDCs are likely to improve their relative manufactured export performance by concentrating on the most labour intensive products.[80] Separately correlating both the level and change in LDC import shares within the US with an index of value added per employee (measuring capital intensity), significant coefficients of −.539 and −.435 were respectively obtained. From this, they maintained that 'LDC performance is influenced by the *degree* of labour intensity of individual products'.[81] However, as the authors themselves acknowledged, some LDCs, especially within South East Asia, have begun 'a transition from labour to semi-capital intensive production', which would seem to impart more relevance to Balassa's 'Stages Approach' than to theirs. Four years earlier, in seeking 'to identify those industries in which the less developed countries were likely to be most competitive', Helleiner discovered that 'wage levels, technological characteristics and the degree of standardization seem to provide the best broad guides to the identification of developed country sectors and the industries which can expect the greatest competition from the less developed countries'.[82] Unlike Tuong and Yeats, Helleiner found that in his analysis, involving the 1972 LDC import shares of 106 different goods within the US, Canada and other OECD countries, 'value added per employee', particularly in the US, was not consistently 'a good explicator of less developed countries' "competitiveness" in manufactured goods trade'. Only in terms of human capital (shown by wages per employee) was a strong and negative relation with LDC import penetration discerned. Furthermore, LDC exporters did better where scale economies were not of consequence and where products were fairly standardised. Other variables 'tried' and found wanting were: market concentration, firm size, product age or 'maturity' and the ratio of advertising expenditures to gross sales.

Conclusion

In briefly taking stock of all the above reviewed work, one thing is perfectly clear; no single trade theory or model has a monopoly in predictive power. While the H/O theory is still dominant (almost to the exclusion of others) within the realm of the typical undergraduate textbook, its empirical standing is not above reproach. Aside from the ambiguities in the Leontief debate, in almost all cases where physical capital intensities are involved, the results are either perverse or indecisive. Only when capital is decomposed into physical and human components, is the model redeemed. On contrasting the H/O model's performance with technology or Linder based models, it not infrequently shows up as a poor second. By persistently maintaining it in the *foreground*, the economic profession brazenly displays an inertia and conservatism which appears to flout the open mindedness and impartiality which they would have us believe they profess. As to the other models, once again, Hufbauer's embarrassment of riches emerges. Considering that in manufactured goods alone, there is such a diversity of product characteristics, it is not surprising that various alternative hypotheses each have a glimmer of truth. Given that so many factors (of which some may be vague yet important, e.g. promptness, reliability, reputation for quality, after sales services, cultural-political ties, etc.) influence export performance, it would seem that the search for *the* solitary yet comprehensive theory is a chimera which should be abandoned. The pragmatic and eclectic approach, although not aesthetically satisfying to our mathematical and general equilibrium purists, is the only means by which we are likely to gain any practical and meaningful insights into the nature of contemporary trade flows.

Appendix: A Note on the Derivation of Capital Intensities

Capital intensities may be calculated on the basis of either stock or flow variables. The flow variable method, pioneered by Lary,[83] takes value added per man as a measure of overall capital intensity, with *per capita* non-wage value added and wage value added as indicators of physical and human capital intensities respectively. In general, estimates derived from stock concepts take capital stock values divided by the number of workers plus the discounted value of the differences between an industry's average wage and the unskilled wage, as a joint measure of overall capital intensity. The first part obviously deals with physical capital alone and the second with human capital. There are pitfalls in using either the flow or stock approach. These have been summarised by Balassa[84] who, in regard to flow measures, refers to: the existence of market imperfections, inter-industry differences in risk (and therefore, acceptable profit levels), the inclusion of items other than capital's remuneration in non-wage value added (e.g. advertising), as well as the inclusion of unskilled wages in wage value added, as all being factors which impede accuracy. In turn, inter-industry differences in depreciation rates as well as the use of historic rather than replacement values were rated as disadvantages arising from stock measures. To these should be added the problem of gauging the true value of human capital, when reliance is placed on earnings as an indicator. (This has partly been aired early on in the chapter.)

The case in favour of the flow approach has been presented by Lary as being one which facilitates a unified treatment of both physical and human capital, which enables a rich data source in the form of various national manufacturing censuses to be tapped and which 'fits better with the notion of factor inputs into production and with the theory of production functions'.[85] Since value added consists of the sum of employment and capital expenses, non-wage value added represents a reasonable measure of capital. Depreciation, profits and interest payments are automatically incorporated. 'When depreciation is too large by a certain factor, profits are understated by exactly the same factor.'[86] On the other hand, abnormal profits within a given year distort capital intensity measures.

Notwithstanding the snags associated with either method, Balassa, relying on a US sample, obtained a rank correlation coefficient of .782 between the two measures of aggregate capital intensity. Similarly, Lary found a meaningful association 'between non-wage value added per employee and physical assets per employee, with assets measured either gross or net'. From a 276 four-digit industry sample, he derived correlation coefficients of .81 and .80 involving in turn gross and net measures.

Notes

1. G.D. MacDougall, 'British and American Exports: A Study Suggested by the Theory of Comparative Costs', *Economic Journal* (Dec. 1951).

2. R.E. Caves, *Trade and Economic Structure* (Harvard University Press, Cambridge, Mass., 1967), p. 269.

3. MacDougall, 'British and American Exports'.

4. Ibid.

5. J. Bhagwati, 'The Pure Theory of International Trade: A Survey' in J. Bhagwati, *Trade, Tariffs and Growth* (Weidenfeld and Nicolson, London, 1969).

6. Caves, *Trade and Economic Structure*, p. 259.

7. Support of a kind is provided by Stern who believes that the empirical testing of the Ricardian model has foundered over the issue of whether comparative labour productivities can serve as proxies for comparative costs, 'given the existence of other productive factors and the fact that, in actuality, trade is determined by differences in absolute money prices'. See R.M. Stern, 'Testing Trade Theories' in P. Kenen (ed.), *International Trade and Finance: Frontiers of Research* (Cambridge University Press, Cambridge, 1975), p. 4.

8. R. Caves and R. Jones, *World Trade and Payments* (Little Brown and Co., Boston, 1973), p. 191.

9. Caves, *Trade and Economic Structure*, p. 269.

10. Ibid., p. 269.

11. Caves and Jones, *World Trade and Payments*, p. 191, italics added.

12. Bhagwati, 'Pure Theory of International Trade', p. 23.

13. W. Leontief, 'Domestic Production and Foreign Trade: The American Capital Position Re-examined', *Economia Internazionale*, vol. II, no. 1 (Feb. 1954).

14. Non competitive imports were accordingly left out of consideration. This could of course influence the results but 'given the fact that these imports constitute only 8 percent of total U.S. commodity imports' and 'on the basis of a rough survey' of their factor intensities, Baldwin concluded that it is most unlikely that their exclusion would account for the results that Leontief actually obtained. See R.E. Baldwin, 'Determinants of the Commodity Structure of U.S. Trade', *American Economic Review* (March 1971).

15. See Bhagwati, 'Pure Theory of International Trade', p. 28.

16. See P. Kenen, 'Nature, Capital and Trade', *Journal of Political Economy* (Oct. 1965).

Baldwin (in 'Determinants of the Commodity Structure of U.S. Trade') has questioned the propriety of combining estimates of human and physical capital, especially in LDCs, where market imperfections even 'make it difficult to regard all physical capital as fungible in the long run'. The problem with this objection is that if LDC physical capital is indeed industry specific (possibly even in the long run) it would not be possible to aggregate capital into one homogeneous category, thus complicating the analysis of LDC trade in H/O terms. (As shown later, the H/O theory is adept in explaining a large part of LDC manufactured trade.)

17. For a further discussion of problems associated with measuring capital, see the appendix to this chapter.

18. Capital intensive processing may profitably be undertaken within capital scarce countries where the costs of transporting bulky, unrefined raw materials is prohibitively expensive.

19. W. Leontief, 'Factor Proportions and the Structure of American Trade: Further Theoretical and Empirical Analysis', *Review of Economics and Statistics* (Nov. 1956).

20. See Baldwin, 'Determinants of the Commodity Structure of U.S. Trade'.

21. B.S. Minhas, *An International Comparison of Factor Costs and Factor Use* (North Holland, Amsterdam, 1963).

22. As reported by H. Lary, *Imports of Manufactures from Less Developed Countries,* National Bureau of Economic Research, New York (1968), pp. 55–68.

23. Baldwin, 'Determinants of the Commodity Structure of U.S. Trade'.

24. R.E. Baldwin, 'Determinants of Trade and Foreign Investment: Further

Evidence', *Review of Economics and Statistics* (Feb. 1979).

25. Baldwin, 'Determinants of Trade and Foreign Investment'.

26. G.C. Hufbauer, 'The Impact of National Characteristics and Technology on the Commodity Composition of Trade in Manufactured Goods' in R. Vernon, *The Technology Factor in International Trade* (National Bureau of Economics Research, New York, 1970).

27. J. Harkness and J.F. Kyle, 'Factors Influencing United States' Comparative Advantage', *Journal of International Economics* (May 1975).

28. Baldwin provided them with the data, which referred to both direct and indirect factor inputs. For sources and definitions, see Baldwin, 'Determinants of the Commodity Structure of U.S. Trade'.

29. Harkness and Kyle, 'Factors Influencing United States' Comparative Advantage', p. 163.

30. See pp. 8–10.

31. Baldwin, 'Determinants of Trade and Foreign Investment', p. 41. Incidentally, Baldwin felt that if the H/O factor content version held (for an explanation see page 10 then a 'regression relating net exports to capital/labor intensity ratios by industry will yield the appropriate positive (though not necessarily significant) sign', ibid., p. 41.
Choudri also tried to determine whether particular products are likely to be exports on the basis of product characteristics, and using a linear probability regression model, he too yielded empirical findings favouring the H/O model. See E.U. Choudri, 'The Pattern of Trade in Individual Products: A Test of Simple Theories', *Weltwirtschaftliches Archiv*, band 115, heft 1 (1979).

32. B. Belassa, 'A "Stages" Approach to Comparative Advantage', *World Bank Staff Working Paper,* no. 256 (May 1977a).

33. W.H. Branson and N. Monoyios, 'Factor Inputs in U.S. Trade', *Journal of International Economics* (May 1977), pp. 111–31.

34. Discounted wage differences served as a proxy for human capital.

35. According to Stern and Maskus this is not strictly correct as standard errors in their own work were 'noticeably higher in the scale regressions'. See R.M. Stern.and K.E. Maskus, 'Determinants of the Structure of U.S. Foreign Trade, 1958–76', *Journal of International Economics* (1981), pp. 207–24.

36. E.E. Leamer, 'The Leontief Paradox Reconsidered', *Journal of Political Economy* (June 1980).

37. Assuming both K_t and L_t are positive.

38. Stern and Maskus, 'Determinants of Structure of U.S. Foreign Trade'.

39. By comparison, Baldwin (1971) obtained for 1962 a ratio of 1.27, using net flows. Goodman and Ceyhun obtained ratios of 1.40 and 1.29 for 1958 and 1966 data, although they based their work on total trade flows rather than on a million dollars' worth of imports and of exports. See B. Goodman and F. Ceyhun, 'U.S. Export Performance in Manufacturing Industries: An Empirical Investigation', *Weltwirtschaftliches Archiv* (1976), pp. 525–54.

40. Hufbauer, 'Impact of National Characteristics and Technology'.

41. Interestingly, H. Lary taking value added per employee as an index of physical *and* human capital and applying these indices to Hufbauer's data determined that 1965 US exports were distinctly more capital intensive than imports. Lary argued that 'a basic flaw in the Leontief paradox was reliance on an inadequate physical concept of capital'. See H. Lary in 'Comment on Hypotheses and Tests of Trade Patterns' in R. Vernon (1970), pp. 298–301.

42. Hufbauer, 'Impact of National Characteristics and Technology', p. 171.

43. Ibid., p. 194.

44. J.F. Morrall, *Human Capital, Technology and the Role of the United States*

in International Trade (University of Florida Press, Gainesville, 1972).

45. Ibid., p. 40.

46. Based on Morrall's belief 'that the most rapidly growing industries are likely to be industries that are in the new product stage'.

47. New products may, because of temporary monopoly advantages, be highly profitable.

48. Goodman and Ceyhun, 'U.S. Export Performance in Manufacturing Industries', p. 551.

49. Stern, 'Testing Trade Theories', p. 28.

50. Ibid., p. 28.

51. W. Branson's review of Morrall's book, *Journal of International Economics* (1975), p. 300. Branson provided an accurate and comprehensive account of the entire book. In the quote above, he was referring to Morrall's initial literature review.

52. S. Hirsch, 'Capital or Technology? Confronting the Neo-Factor Proportions and Neo-Technology Accounts of International Trade', *Weltwirtschaftliches Archiv*, bd CX (1974a), pp. 534–63.

53. S. Hirsch, 'The Product Cycle Model of International Trade – A Multi-Country Cross-Section Analysis', *Oxford Bulletin of Economics and Statistics*, vol. 37, no. 4 (1975), pp. 305–17.

54. D.B. Keesing, 'Labor Skills and Comparative Advantage', *American Economic Review* (May 1966).

55. Based on 46 manufacturing industries.

56. D.B. Keesing, 'Different Countries' Labor Skill Coefficients and the Skill Intensity of International Trade Flows', *Journal of International Economics* (Nov. 1971).

57. Baldwin, 'Determinants of the Commodity Structure of U.S. Trade'.

58. W.H. Gruber and R. Vernon, 'The Technology Factor in a World Trade Matrix' in R. Vernon (ed.), *The Technology Factor in International Trade*.

59. Ibid., p. 254.

60. Goodman and Ceyhun, 'U.S. Export Performances in Manufacturing Industries'.

61. Branson and Monoyios, 'Factor Inputs in U.S. Trade'; Stern and Maskus, 'Determinants of Structure of U.S. Foreign Trade'; and 'Determinants of the Commodity Structure of U.S. Trade'.

62. L.T. Wells, Jr, 'Test of a Product Cycle Model of International Trade: U.S. Exports of Consumer Variables', *Quarterly Journal of Economics* (Feb. 1969).

63. Of course there is a reasonable presumption that this would be so and, to a large extent, the regression results support such a view.

64. S. Hirsch, 'The United States Electronics Industry in International Trade' in L.T. Wells, Jr (ed.), *The Product Life Cycle and International Trade* (Harvard University Press, Boston, 1972).

65. Stern, 'Testing Trade Theories'.

66. A. Mullor-Sebastian, 'The Product Cycle Theory: Empirical Evidence', paper presented at the 44th Annual Meeting of the American Economic Association, Washington, DC (28 Dec. 1981). Mullor-Sebastian's paper represents one of the most recent attempts in evaluating the product cycle theory.

67. E. Mansfield, A. Romeo and S. Wagner, 'Foreign Trade and U.S. Research and Development', *Review of Economics and Statistics* (Feb. 1979).

68. To some extent, this outcome had been anticipated. For instance, Wells had earlier written that 'with the establishment of efficient information networks among subsidiaries, the gap between introduction in the first market and a second market might be diminishing. If this is happening, the United States will have a shorter period of exports for new products'. Wells, *Product Life Cycle*.

69. J.H. Dunning and P.J. Buckley, 'International Production and Alternative Models of Trade', *Manchester School* (Dec. 1977).

70. R. Vernon, 'The Product Cycle Hypothesis in a New International Environment', *Oxford Bulletin of Economics and Statistics*, vol. 41, no. 4 (Nov. 1979).

71. Ibid., p. 257.

72. B. Balassa, ' "Revealed" Comparative Advantage Revisited: An Analysis of Relative Export Shares of the Industrial Countries, 1953–1971', *Manchester School* (Dec. 1977b), pp. 327–44.

73. The research intensive industries included: chemicals, drugs, office machinery, electrical machinery and power equipment, aircraft, scientific instruments and photographic supplies.

74. Ibid., p. 330.

75. Most have endorsed the hypothesis. For references to such tests, see: R. Arad and S. Hirsch, 'Determination of Trade Flows and Choice of Trade Partners: Reconciling the Hecksher-Ohlin and Burenstam Linder Models of International Trade', *Weltwirtschaftliches Archiv*, band 117, heft 2 (1981), p. 277.

76. J.N. Fortune, 'Some Determinants of Trade in Finished Manufactures', *Swedish Journal of Economics* (1971), pp. 311–17. J.W. Sailors, U.A. Qureshi and E.M. Cross, 'Empirical Verification of Linder's Trade Thesis', *Southern Economic Journal* (Oct. 1973), pp. 262–8.

77. M.I. Blejer, 'Income Per Capita and the Structure of Industrial Exports: An Empirical Study', *Review of Economics and Statistics* (Nov. 1978).

78. B. Balassa, 'A "Stages" Approach to Comparative Advantage', *World Bank Staff Working Paper*, no. 256 (May 1977a).

79. On p. 10, Balassa states that within his study emphasis is 'given to the estimates obtained by the use of the stock measure in evaluating the results'.

80. H.D. Tuong and A. Yeats, 'On Factor Proportions as a Guide to the Future Composition of Developing Country Exports', *Journal of Development Economics* (Dec. 1980).

81. Italics in the original.

82. G.K. Helleiner, 'Industry Characteristics and the Competitiveness of Manufactures from Less Developed Countries', *Weltwirtschaftliches Archiv*, band 112 (1976), pp. 507–24.

83. H. Lary, 'Imports of Manufactures from Less Developed Countries', *National Bureau of Economic Research* (New York, 1968).

84. Balassa, 'A "Stages" Approach to Comparative Advantage'.

85. Lary, 'Imports of Manufactures from Less Developed Countries', pp. xv, 40, 41.

86. Hirsch, 'Capital or Technology?', p. 541.

3 MULTINATIONAL CORPORATIONS IN WORLD TRADE

In the last decade or so, commentaries on various facets of the activities and ramifications of multinational corporations (MNCs) have proliferated. Practically every aspect of the MNCs' manifold involvements have been exhaustively examined, except those relating to their role as trade generators. While it is true that the MNCs' impact on a country's balance of payments is frequently assessed, stress is usually placed on profit remittances and/or investment flows. (In this regard, the MNCs' ability to effect illicit transfers through under or over invoicing has also attracted scrutiny.) When, however, one turns to literature dealing specifically with the relationship between MNCs and exports, the landscape is somewhat bleak. It is possible that this lacuna reflects the research interests of those of late who have been in the forefront of MNC studies. One significant group have mainly perceived MNC operations from an industrial economist's perspective, while another (the development specialists) have concentrated on the MNCs' contribution to less developed country (LDC) growth, especially in the sphere of appropriate technology, employment, capital accumulation and profits. Only since the advent of Posner's and Vernon's technological and product cycle models have trade theorists tentatively edged from perfectly competitive paradigms to those embracing imperfect markets; even though most must have long since realised that voluminous trade flows have been MNC induced. Perhaps serious data deficiencies have deterred many a would-be investigator, for the fact is that consistent and widespread MNC trade statistics are extremely difficult, if not impossible, to acquire. Except for the US, no other government regularly monitors MNC exports, and even in the US, information is not fully and freely available. Because international trade flows are invariably recorded in terms of countries and goods, but not in terms of companies, there are no general sources from which to draw. Instead, reliance has predominantly been placed on US Department of Commerce figures, as well as on snippets of information gleaned elsewhere. A few economists have conducted surveys of their own but considering the limited resources at their disposal, these can be no more than suggestive. Despite these obstacles, work in this field is beginning to see the light of day, and a small yet growing collection of publications is appearing. This chapter seeks to provide a partial review of some of these scholarly endeavours and to take stock of emerging issues.

MNC export participation can be viewed from various perspectives. One could try to determine the extent to which foreign investments substitute for or complement home country exports. Alternatively, current export flows actually emanating from MNCs could be estimated, accompanied by possible explanations as to why and in what circumstances MNCs are likely to stimulate trade. The growing phenomenon of intra-firm trade could also be highlighted, as could the MNCs' contribution to LDC trade and their increasing reliance on offshore processing. All these approaches will indeed be tackled, with special emphasis being given to trade in manufactures.

MNC Investments and Exports

The question of whether foreign MNC investments retard or stimulate home country exports has been a contentious one. At one end of the spectrum trade unionists in the US and elsewhere declaim that such disbursements reduce local employment prospects, while at the other end, MNCs retort that they bolster output. In the late 1960s this issue was more or less simultaneously pursued by Reddaway and others in the UK and by Hufbauer and Adler in the US.[1] To a large extent, their initial assumptions determined their conclusions. In one set, which Hufbauer and Adler designate as 'classical', foreign investment represents a net capital loss to the home country and a net gain to the foreign one. In another, the 'reverse classical assumption', foreign investments result in no net capital changes anywhere. Under both sets of assumptions, foreign subsidiary output is import substituting and therefore inimical to home country exports. However, this is thought to be partly countered by the subsidiary's initial importation of capital goods and ultimately by the influx of input components, as well as other final products. Sales of MNC products not actually manufactured by a foreign subsidiary could none the less be stimulated by it since the subsidiary could on its parent's behalf, capitalise on its goodwill and distributive facilities. Calculations based on a 'reverse classical' framework indicate that the *average* initial trade effect was of the order of 11 per cent of overseas direct manufacturing investment in the UK, and of 27 per cent for the US. For input components, the respective figures were 3.2 per cent and 4.2 per cent, while for finished goods, purchases for resale represented approximately 6 per cent and 4.5 per cent of respective foreign subsidiary sales.[2]

In the early 1970s the US Tariff Commission calculated that the linear correlation between US MNC foreign capital stocks and total US exports (for each industry) was .813 (significant at 1 per cent).[3] By contrast, from his correlation based study, Glejser concluded that between 1953 to 1971, direct foreign investments caused US exports to fall by $6.3 billion.[4] In reporting Glejser's results, Batchelor *et al.* cautioned that they might 'simply reflect the inability of certain American Industries to compete' and that such an inability may have stimulated foreign investments in the first place. It was certainly Batchelor's opinion that had US investors not acted, native ones 'would have established production facilities', and US foreign market stakes would have been relinquished.

As part of the quest either to endorse or refute claims that foreign investments rebound against exports, a medley of individual case studies were undertaken. Noting that these have pointed in either direction, depending on the industries chosen, Bergsten and others upbraided the case study approach and recommended sole reliance on statistical procedures based on aggregate data.[5] As a prelude to their own regression analysis, they ranked 75 US industries according to the 1965–71 average value of each industry's foreign investment proxy.[6] (A measure of each industry's export performance (the 1965–71 ratio of its exports to domestic shipments) was also recorded.) The industry investment ranking was subdivided into quartiles, and the average export performance for all industries and for those in each quartile were calculated. These are reproduced in Table 3.1, where in the top row it can be seen that the average industry exported 4.5 per cent of its domestic shipments. The next four statistics reveal that the average export performance was larger among goods grouped in higher foreign investment quartiles. In fact, the average for each group was directly and unambiguously connected to that group's quartile ranking, with a fairly sizeable discrepancy existing between the fourth quartile's average and the rest. Bergsten suspected that since US MNCs enjoyed technological advantages over their foreign competitors, they were on this account prone both to invest and export abroad more assiduously; in which case it became necessary to isolate the technology variable to forestall spurious conclusions. Accordingly, firms were divided into either a high or low technology classification on the basis of the proportion of scientists and engineers they employed. As Table 3.1 reveals, while high technology firms maintained a better export performance rating than low ones (8.1 per cent as against 2.3 per cent), within each

Table 3.1: 1965-71 – Export Performance of US Industries by Foreign
Investment Level and Other Characteristics

Industry Feature	All Industries	Foreign Investment Quartile			
		1st	2nd	3rd	4th
All kinds	4.5	6.0	5.7	4.4	1.4
High technology	8.1	7.6	9.7	7.8	2.3
Low technology	2.3	3.5	2.5	3.0	1.3

Source: Bergsten *et al., American Multinationals and American Interest*, Table
3.3, p. 81.

division, firms in the top three quartiles performed markedly better
than those in the bottom quartile.

This exercise was repeated for 13 other industry classifications (not
shown here).[7] Although some characteristics were export orientated
(such as the use of machinery) and others (such as unskilled labour) less
so, within every single subset, the export performance of firms in the
fourth investment quartile was uniformly and unmistakably the lowest.
These conclusions were reinforced by regressions (for the year 1967) of
export performance on foreign affiliate activity[8] and other variables,
including research and development, advertising, foreign market size,
market proximity and type of goods produced. An R^2 of .47 was
obtained and the foreign affiliate coefficient was both positive and
significant at the 1 per cent level.[9] On the basis of a similar procedure,
Swedenborg disclosed that in Sweden, firms with foreign affiliates
'actually succeed in exporting somewhat more than they would have
if they had not located abroad'.[10]

Moving beyond the precinct of viewing this issue solely in terms of
the foreign investment impact on the donor country, Lipsey and Weiss
explicitly took cognizance of effects on third parties.[11] As a first
measure, they alternatively regressed (using 1970 data) US exports, and
then the exports of 13 other major economies (in 14 industries to 44
countries) on variables representing destination characteristics (such as
market size, EEC membership and distance from the US and Germany)
and a measure of US owned affiliate activity (either net sales or net
local sales). In each case, separate regressions were run for developed
and less developed markets. Taking the set of equations in which US
exports were the dependent variables, all the affiliate activity coefficients that were statistically significant at the 5 per cent level, were
positive. These amounted to ten industries for developed country
destinations and nine for LDCs, where the coefficients were 'distinctly
higher'. With the 13 other countries' exports as the dependents, the

results were again comparatively more forthright with LDCs than with developed countries. Within the LDC regressions, all seven of the US affiliate coefficients that were significant, were negative. In this respect, Lipsey and Weiss' expectations that US owned subsidiaries (especially in LDCs) would displace foreign rival exports, were realised. What is more, since the absolute size of the negative affiliate coefficients in the 13 country case exceeded their positive counterparts in the US dependent regressions, it would seem that 'sales by U.S. owned manufacturing facilities cut exports by foreign countries by more than they added to U.S. exports'.[12] Turning specifically to the 13 country exports to developed countries, only four affiliate coefficients were significant at the 5 per cent level, of which one, relating to office machinery and computers, was actually positive. The latter outcome is not surprising once it is realised that the production of those two product types within the 13 countries is largely US controlled.

The final stage in Lipsey and Weiss' study involved regressions of US, and then the 13 other country exports, or similar variables, except that the activities of the 13's foreign affiliates were substituted for those of the US. As might be anticipated, all significant affiliate coefficients were negative for the US and positive for the others. In sum, 'just as U.S. manufacturing affiliates appear to promote U.S. exports and decrease exports by foreign countries, foreign-owned affiliates seem to increase foreign exports and reduce U.S. exports'.[13]

Virtually all of the above described works have disclosed some positive link between foreign investments and home country exports. While knowledge of such an association is enlightening, it is quite insufficient for a general appraisal of MNC participation in the world economy. For this, some inkling of the extent to which current trade flows originate from MNCs is needed. Considering the difficulties in gleaning such information, the compilation that follows is based on disparate sources.

MNCs and Current Exports

Partly because US corporations maintain a dominant profile among MNCs and partly on account of data accessibility, this section largely emphasises their trade participation. It has been estimated that in 1970, US MNCs cornered some 23 per cent of all world trade and 19 per cent of world manufactured exports.[14] Within the US itself, their MNCs were responsible for 69 per cent of all exports, while abroad, their

Table 3.2: 1970 — US MNCs' Share of OECD Manufactured Exports

Industry	% from all US MNCs	% from MNCs in the US	% from US MOFAS*
Grain mills	46	28	18
Soaps and cosmetics	39	16	23
Farm machinery	34	18	16
Office machinery	31	21	10
Computers	76	29	47
Transport equipment	42	23	19

Note: * Majority Owned Foreign Affiliates.
Source: US Tariff Commission, *Implications of Multinational Firms*.

affiliates held 42 per cent of Canada's trade, 36 per cent of Latin America's and 27 per cent of Asia and Africa's. Their 1970 share of OECD trade was particularly large. In overall terms they commanded 21 per cent of all OECD exports, but within specific groups their representation rose to as much as 76 per cent (see Table 3.2).

As Table 3.2 indicates, in most cases, the bulk of US MNC exports originated in the US, but a fairly large proportion was furnished by majority owned foreign affiliates (henceforth referred to as MOFAs) and this proportion has in fact been growing. Whereas in 1966 only 39 per cent of all US MNC exports were MOFA supplied, by 1970 44 per cent were. A summary of global MOFA trade for the years 1966 and 1976 is contained in Table 3.3. Throughout the world they have played an increasing role in their host countries' exports, for their contributions rose from 10 per cent to 13 per cent within developed countries (DCs) and from 24 per cent to 36 per cent in LDCs. In 1966, MOFAs directed most of their wares to local markets, but by 1977 there was a discernible shift towards the international economy, especially among Third World based companies.[15] In both blocs, the importance of the US as a destination for MOFA exports declined, and interestingly in both years, LDC based MOFAs relied absolutely and proportionally less on the US market.

Turning to trade in manufactures (see Table 3.4), there is a distinct difference in the pattern between DCs and LDCs. The overwhelming quantity of MOFA manufactures are exported from DCs, with there being no hint of any relative upsurge from Third World sources, in fact LDCs seem to have slipped behind, albeit marginally.[16] In both areas, ratios of exports to total affiliate sales are considerably less than those for the exports of all manner of goods. This is especially noticeable in the LDCs, where in 1976 only 9 per cent of total MOFA shipments

Table 3.3: US MOFA Exports (all goods) (in US $ million)

	1966	1976
From developed countries (DCs)	$14,044	$82,902
% going to USA	27	23
% of all DC exports	10	13
From LDCs	$ 9,481	$92,678
% going to USA	24	17
% of all LDC exports	24	36
Total MOFA exports	$23,525	$178,580
share from LDCs	40	52
Ratio to total MOFA sales		
in DCs	20	24
in LDCs	40	57

Source: Various issues of US Department of Commerce, *Survey of Current Business* (Washington, DC) and GATT, *International Trade* (Geneva).

Table 3.4: US MOFA Manufactured Exports (in US $ million)

	1966	1976
From DCs	$8,240	$48,036
% going to USA	30	27
% of all DC MOFA exports	59	58
% of all DC manufactured exports	8	10
From LDCs	$ 577	$ 3,096
% going to USA	37	37
% of all LDC MOFA exports	6	3
% of all LDC manufactured exports	8	7
Total exports	$8,817	$51,132
LDC share in total	7	6
Total as a share of all MOFA exports	37	29
Ratio to total sales		
In DCs	20	27
In LDCs	8	9
In Latin America	6	7
In Asia	23	21

Source: As Table 3.3.

(representing an amount equal to merely 7 per cent of all LDC foreign sales) were exported.[17] There is some variation among LDC areas, with MOFAs in Asia being much more trade disposed than their counterparts in Latin America. It may well be that even within DCs, MOFAs are more local market orientated than meets the eye, for many of them were primarily established in Europe to elude EEC trade barriers.

A comparative glance at the track record of foreign MNCs functioning in the US would be of relevance. While sources at hand only yield

Table 3.5: 1977 -- Foreign MNC Operations in the US (in US $ million)

	Exports	Imports
Total	$24,135	$42,541
From DC firms	$21,774	$40,558
From LDC firms	$ 2,361	$ 1,983
Ratio to sales		
All firms	13	
DC firms	13	
LDC firms	16	
Ratio to total US trade	21	28
Manufactured goods	$ 3,169	$ 5,055
Manufactures as % of all trade	13	12
Manufactured exports to sales	7	
Finished goods for resale	$19,415 (23,409)*	$30,586
As % total trade	80 (13)*	72
As % to/from affiliates	47	72

Note: * Bracketed figures relate to US MOFAs in 1976.
Source: N.G. Howenstine, 'Selected Data on The Operations of U.S. Affiliates to Foreign Companies, 1977' in US Department of Commerce, *Survey of Current Business* (Washington, DC, July 1980); and other issues.

1977 data (a summary of which is provided in Table 3.5),[18] this is close enough to the terminal data used in illustrating US MOFA trade. As might be expected, companies from DCs have a greater involvement in US trade than those from LDCs. They are also more inclined towards importing than exporting. On average, all foreign firms trade heavily in wholesale merchandise (finished goods for resale). Eighty per cent of their exports and 72 per cent of their imports are of this nature. (By contrast, only 13 per cent of 1976 US MOFA exports were in this category.) Many of these transactions, particularly in importing, are bridged with affiliates abroad, indicating that by and large, foreign MNCs base themselves in the US as procuring or distributing agents. Not shown in Table 3.5 is the fact that $11,064 million of wholesale exports (45 per cent of all MNC exports) were in the field of farm products, whereas in imports, motor vehicles totalled $11,093 million (26 per cent of all MNC imports). In overall terms, foreign MNCs appear to have had their hand in 21 per cent of all 1977 US exports and 28 per cent of all imports.

There is, to the author's knowledge, no systematic tally of the value of manufactured exports attributed to all MNCs (US and otherwise). One guess which is as good as any, has been ventured by Batchelor, who thought that in 1970, 'the share of multinationals, their

Table 3.6: MNC Shares of Selected LDCs' Manufactured Exports

Country		Percentage	Year
Singapore	(1)	nearly 70	1970
Singapore	(2)	over 50	1971
Singapore	(3)	30	1972
Brazil	(4)	44	1969
Colombia	(4)	35	1970
Argentina	(2)	30	1969
Mexico	(5)	30	1970
Philippines	(6)	20–25	approx. 1970
Taiwan	(1)	at least 20	1971
Taiwan	(3)	12–15	1972
S. Korea	(2)	15	1971
Hong Kong	(3)	10	1972
Pakistan	(1)	5–10	1972
India	(4)	approx. 5	1970

Sources: (1) Nayyar, 'Transnational Corporations', p. 62; (2) B.I. Cohen, *Multinational Firms and Asian Exports* (Yale University Press, New Haven, 1975), p. 10; (3) A. Hone, 'Multinational Corporations and Multinational Buying Groups: Their Impact on the Growth of Asia's Exports of Manufacturing — Myths and Realities', *World Development*, vol. 2, no. 2 (Feb. 1974), p. 148; (4) F. Long, 'Multinational Corporations and the Non-Primary Sector Trade of Developing Countries: A Survey of Available Data', *Economia Internazionale* (Nov. 1981), p. 396; (5) *Mexico's Manufactured Exports*, IBRD Report No. 79-ME (1973), p. 2; (6) Board of Investment Annual Report (1971), Makati.

subsidiaries and associates could approach two thirds of the (world) total'.[19] Although conventional wisdom has almost universally accorded the MNCs a dominant role in Third World trade, the figures in Table 3.4 attest that in manufacturing, exports by US MOFAs are anything but regnant. Their hold of LDC manufactured exports actually fell, particularly in Latin America, where between 1966 and 1974 their share receded from 37.8 to 19.2 per cent.[20] It is conceivable that a movement by US MNCs into minority owned ventures could have thrown the data out of kilter but on closer inspection this does not appear to have happened; for throughout all that period, over 80 per cent of US foreign investments were confined to MOFAs. Finally, in combining the participation of Japanese and West European MNCs with those of the US, Nayyar estimated that their aggregate 1974 share of LDC manufactured exports 'was probably not much greater than 15%'.[21] Among individual countries the importance of MNCs manifested considerable variance (see Table 3.6, where in some instances more than one country estimate is provided). Given any lack of statistical precision, the figures should be regarded as indicating minimum floor rather than ceiling levels.

MNCs and Trade: Some Conceptual Considerations

Up to this point, the MNCs' trade profile has been unravelled in terms of home country exports that ensue in the wake of foreign investments and in terms of overall export flows, especially those originating from foreign affiliates. With regard to investments, there are grounds for supposing that an overwhelming proportion of MNC affiliates are enticed abroad to pre-empt actual or potential trade obstacles. These might include tariff barriers, import quotas, high transport costs, discriminatory local government procuring, etc. Where MNCs respond defensively to protect their market standing, they could not justifiably be inculpated for all the home country export flows that are subsequently staunched. Bergsten reflected on the possibility that even though some early MNC ventures may be market penetrating, their very success may presage foreign production, for 'the more a firm can sell abroad, the larger the production volume over which start-up and overhead costs can be spread'.[22] However, it would be erroneous to attribute eventual foreign output solely to MNC machinations; for once corporations trade successfully, their activities may simply disclose market potentials which local enterprise could profitably exploit.

The general capacity of MNCs to engage successfully in trade is explicable in terms of their possessing resources not available to, or utilised by, others.[23] These include knowledge, entrepreneurial skills and access to markets, all of which may be ownership specific and which may be capable of being deployed in alternative areas in conjunction with location specific endowments. By and large, MNCs are able to scour the world in search of optimal geographic bases for the exportation of particular commodities. Once these places are identified, and unless it is superfluous for exporting firms to rely on anything but local endowments, MNCs are able to blend location and ownership-specific resources to their advantage. Location-specific endowments influence the point from which goods are exported, but the relative importance of ownership-specific factors determines the extent to which firms possessing them are able to capitalise on such ownership.

Three categories of firm specific advantages may be discerned. The first comprises attributes which yield monopoly power and which inhibit would-be competitors. These may consist of exclusive market or material access, the attainment of a foreboding corporate size or the possession of patents, trademarks or unique management skills. The second type deals with advantages that a newly formed branch plant would manifest over potential rivals whose entire organisations are inchoate. While the branch plant may have recourse to cheaper inputs (because of economies of bulk purchasing) as well as to 'knowledge of markets, centralised accounting procedures, administrative experience, R. & D., etc., at zero or low marginal cost, the de novo firm will have to bear their full cost'.[24] The third set of advantages arise specifically from the multinationality of a firm which being globally spread is better poised both to mobilise inputs from a variety of sources, and to consider alternative market outlets.

For an MNC to invest abroad either to capture markets in host countries or to export further afield, the possession of favourable firm specific endowments is a necessary rather than a sufficient condition. Apart from the attraction or need to locate in areas where in combination with the firm's ownership-specific factors, local inputs can profitably be harnessed, it must be in the firm's interest 'to internalize its advantages through an extension of its own activities rather than externalize them through licensing and similar contracts with independent firms'.[25] A firm would probably seek to internalise commodity trade to obviate uncertainty over the availability, price and quality of essential inputs, especially when they are highly firm-specific. In the firm's role as a supplier, internalisation may be compelling because of high property rights enforcement costs and because of a need to ensure minimum service standards to protect its products and its own general standing. Both as buyers and sellers, the internalisation of overseas transactions provides corporations with scope to manipulate transfer prices in order to maximise post-tax profits. Furthermore, the option of diverting activities to subsidiaries whose plants are momentarily underutilised constitutes another attractive internalisation by-product. Whether MNC internalisation promotes a more efficient global resource allocation by overcoming market distortions or whether these very market distortions are intensified, remains an open question. What is becoming increasingly apparent, is that intra-firm trade is a significant feature of all MNC international transshipments.

Intra-firm Trade

Intra-firm trade involves transmissions of merchandise from a company in one country, to its affiliates, parents or associated company in another country. As bad as is the data situation with regard to general MNC trade, information on intra-firm transactions is even more restricted and further hampered by diverse standards determining the minimum level of interlocking asset ownership necessary for parties to be deemed 'related'. As a proportion of both MNC and of overall exports, intra-firm trade appears to be quite extensive and growing. Lall's tabulated figures for US MNC exports to its MOFAs, indicate that as a share of US manufactured exports, they rose from 17.9 per cent in 1962 to 23.3 per cent by 1970.[26] A slight variation is contained in Batchelor's estimate which puts the 1966 US intra-firm trade with MOFAs at 19 per cent of all manufactured exports, and the 1970 share at 21 per cent.[27] (Just one percentage point larger than the 20 per cent figure subscribed to by Helleiner.[28]) Taken in the context of MNC trade alone, US 1970 manufactured intra-firm sales constituted 32 per cent and 27 per cent of exports and imports respectively.[29] Elsewhere, intra-firm trade has also been prominent. In the UK 24 per cent of 1970 manufactured exports were intra-firm[30] and in Sweden 29 per cent of 1975 exports were.[31] According to general consensus, intra-firm trade accounts for *at least* 20 per cent of all current OECD exports and it therefore warrants acknowledgement as a significant international trade phenomenon.

Most of the US intra-firm trade is conducted with developed countries, not just in absolute terms but also in terms of relative intensity. For instance, while 61.1 per cent of 1977 manufactured imports arriving from OECD countries were party related, only 37 per cent of LDC imports were.[32] Even with respect to non-oil primary products, the proportion of LDC intra-firm imports amounting to 13.6 per cent was considerably less than the 35.9 per cent figure for the OECD group. Needless to say, wide individual country differences in the incidence of LDC intra-firm imports were encountered, ranging from a 71 per cent share of Mexican manufactured imports to 10.1 per cent of India's.[33]

Finished goods for resale have been the mainstay of US intra-firm exports. Their 1965 share was in the region of 56 per cent[34] and judging from a sample of 100 leading corporations, the 1975 figure rose to 59 per cent. Similarly, in 1974, 74.9 per cent of inter-party imports entering under the auspices of non US owned firms were finished goods, while by contrast, only 4.5 per cent of intra-firm arrivals from US MOFAs were.[35] This reflects divergent objectives of US based importers. Foreign owned firms predominantly function to facilitate the consumer marketing of externally produced products, whereas locally owned firms are more predisposed to import components, as part of an international vertical integration production process.

Given that movements of finished products constitute a large, if not leading, segment of intra-firm trade, attempts have been expended in seeking to determine if any class of finished goods is particularly intra-firm trade prone. Such research may have been inspired by insights revealed by Torre who, in the early 1970s, grouped MNCs operating in Colombia into three categories according to the ease of market entry for the products they purvey.[36] He revealed that in 1966, firms in the easiest market entry classification distributed 31 per cent of their exports through affiliates, while those in the intermediate and hardest market entry group relied on affiliates for 57.9 per cent and 91.9 per cent of their respective exports.[37] Torre reasoned that 'the higher the marketing entry barrier, the more critical becomes the need for market information, marketing skills, and distribution channels that the exporting subsidiary's foreign affiliates are able to provide'.[38] On another tack, Buckley and Pearce discovered that among a sample of MNCs, those that were most research intensive realised intra-firm exports amounting to over half their total exports, whereas the intra-firm exports of the least research intensive were less than a fifth of their total.[39] A general systematic analysis was eventually undertaken by Lall,[40] who for the year 1970, regressed US intra-firm exports on research and development (R & D), value added per employee, a dummy variable for after sales service, advertising as a percentage of sales, a dummy for industries using tariff schedules 807 and 806.3,[41] and the ratio of foreign to domestic assets. The dependent variable was formulated either in terms of intra-firm exports as a percentage of total MNC industry exports or as intra-firm exports as a percentage of the sales of the affiliates receiving these exports. Generally speaking, better results were recorded in the case of the second specification, where R^2s of .49 were attained. Except for value added per employee, all of the independent variables registered at the 5 per cent (or better) significance level, the strongest being after service sales and the weakest in the sense of never attaining a 1 per cent significant level, being advertising. The sign of the latter variable was as expected: negative, postulated on the grounds that as highly advertised goods (which are usually mass produced) warrant scant after sales care, producers are less anxious to oversee and control distribution outlets.[42] In short, Lall demonstrated that in his model US intra-firm exports are affected by 'technological intensity, the extent of foreign investment, the "divisibility" of production processes and the need for after-sales service'.[43]

Apart from being confined to the US experience (where there was an element of Hobson's choice), Lall's analysis only took account of intra-firm exports. In this regard, Helleiner and Lavergne's work was a timely and propitious complement,[44] for in it they regressed the percentage of

US imports originating from related parties on: firm size (the proportion of an industry's workforce in firms employing 250 workers or more, as a proxy for entry barriers), a scale economy measure ('a source of quasi-rents'), a firm concentration index, the extent of advertising, the average wage rate ('a measure of skill intensity') and R & D. Separate tests were undertaken for the years 1975 and 1977, and in both periods runs were made on imports originating from all areas as well as those specifically from the OECD and LDCs. In general, variables relating to the average wage, firm size and R & D were significant intra-firm import determinants, but with respect to LDCs, R & D and advertising were the only two reliable explanators. In contrast to Lall, from Helleiner and Lavergne's point of view, they unexpectedly derived negative advertising signs since they assumed that large advertising outlays would reflect product differentiation; and hence market barriers. Two interpretations for what seemed to them a paradoxical outcome were tendered. One dwelt on the likelihood that this was associated with a comparatively successful MNC incursion, among newly industrialised LDCs, in standardised goods. On the fact of it, this is not very convincing; for the reason why such goods should be more conducive to intra-firm rather than arm's length trading is not apparent. In any case, it neither accords with Torre's research (cited above), or with their own disclosure of a high significance level for R & D. Their second explanation saw it as reflecting an unusually high proportion of intermediate product imports, where 'marketing' is not of much consequence. This is much more plausible considering that most LDC intra-firm imports into the US are indeed intermediate goods,[45] and considering that the 'divisibility of the production process' was significant in Lall's study.

Helleiner and Lavergne did not include among their dependent variables, any factor intensity measure other than the average wage rate. Considering that Lall's value added per employee variable was singularly insignificant, one might well be predisposed not to carp over this omission. However, in 'playing with the data', the author correlated (for 18 items) US related party imports as a percentage of total imports (as given in Helleiner and Lavergne's Appendix A), with capital per man ratios extracted from Hufbauer's seminal paper.[46] A significant correlation of .45 was attained. The smaller overall share of intra-firm LDC imports into the US as a proportion of total LDC imports (compared with the import pattern of goods from developed countries) has already been noted. Given that there is a significant positive correlation between capital intensity and intra-firm imports, and given that LDC exports are relatively labour intensive, this discrepancy is quite explicable. A casual perusal of data in Helleiner's book discloses that in 1977, those items that were particularly labour intensive maintained low proportions of intra-firm imports. For example, while the overall LDC manufactured intra-firm to total import ratio was 37 per cent; in leather, textiles, travel goods, clothing and footwear it was respectively 5, 7.8, 10.3, 11.5 and 4.4 per cent.[47] In each of these industries, the Third World maintained a share in excess of 40 per cent of all US imports. On correlating the incidence of Third World intra-firm imports on LDC import shares (in the US),[48] a negative and highly significant correlation of .519 emerged. Since the incidence of intra-firm trade is undoubtedly governed by the composition of the goods in question, the more LDC exports approximate developed country ones, the less will these two groups' intra-firm patterns diverge.

The mushrooming of intra-firm trade has a number of serious implications for both positive and normative trade theory. Where MNCs maintain an international network of large investment overheads and where subsidiaries are highly integrated both with one another and with a parent plant, market changes as manifested in price movements, are less likely to moderate trade flows than would have been the case had arm's length trade prevailed. In fact, Goldsbrough has actually shown, particularly in relation to US imports, 'that observed price elasticities are significantly lower for intra-firm than for conventional trade.'[49] On the normative side, intra-firm trade confers a daunting potential for the manipulation of transfer prices. This implies that a country's potential trade gains may be lessened by MNC intervention, especially when prices are rigged to deprive the host country of its due foreign exchange earnings. Losses could also be sustained by local governments, shareholders, workers and consumers as they respectively forego taxes, dividends, wages or cheaper prices. In countries like Australia, MNCs could conceivably underprice imported inputs to offset import tariff dues (where ad valorem duties are imposed) and thereby raise their level of effective protection (assuming duties are also imposed on the final products).[50] In such a case, not only would the host country be divested of tariff revenues, but local resources would probably be misallocated and the MNCs would generate unwarranted profits. A more sanguine view of MNC participation was upheld by Helleiner and Lavergne who believed that other things being equal, LDCs 'which welcome multinational corporations will expand their exports to developed countries faster than others'.[51] In their opinion, home based MNCs indulging in intra-firm imports, provide a shot in the arm for anti-protectionist forces. Apparently, US trade obstacles are smaller in industries where intra-firm trade is more pervasive. Helleiner and Lavergne attribute some of the expansion of US intra-firm imports from LDCs to a desire or need for MNCs to 'preside' and 'manage' integrated international production to avoid overall disruptions, and to control LDC export growth so as to minimise sudden incursions and 'surprises'. While this feature of intra-firm trade may bestow advantages to developed country enterprises, it is not patently clear that it also serves Third World interests in the sense of maximising their export effort.

MNCs and The Third World

If the information cited earlier can be relied upon, then it is clear that in general, MNCs maintain a fairly low profile as propagators of LDC manufactured exports. This is not unduly surprising, considering that labour intensive, standardised and technologically simple items constitute the bulk of Third World exports. Typically, items of these kinds neither loom large in intra-firm nor overall MNC trade. The range of goods in which MNCs as traders excel, has partially been identified by Torre, who (as it may be recalled), established an inverse relation between the degree of intra-firm trade and the ease of market entry. In addition, he proceeded to demonstrate that in Colombia, the more a product encountered market access difficulties, the more were foreign firms, *vis-a-vis* local ones, relatively successful exporters. From this he generalised that because foreign firms are well endowed with export promoting resources, 'they tend to export relatively more than domestic firms'.[52] By contrast, on the basis of a limited Asian sample, Cohen concluded that 'local firms have a slightly greater propensity to export than foreign firms'.[53]

The source of these conflicting statements merits further investigation. At this stage, relative export propensities of local and foreign firms have not been widely assessed. Furthermore, useful research could be directed to evaluate the widely held proposition that as development proceeds and LDC products become more sophisticated, MNC participation will become more imperative. Kirkpatrick and Yamin have recently shown that MNCs do indeed concentrate on LDC export subsidiary formation for goods in which R & D and after sales service are significant.[54] None the less, other tendencies should be heeded. In the first place, developed country retail chain stores, as well as import agencies, both of which have been an 'important motor of manu-factured export growth in Asia',[55] provide Third World manufacturers with a means of circumventing marketing problems. In fact, a symbiotic partnership of a kind is evolving, whereby LDCs ply developed country stores (such as Sears in the US) with competitively priced products while the stores activate their networks and reputations in disposing of them. There is some prospect, considering the enormous size of such retailers, that an element of monopsony power could be imposed to depress LDC terms of trade but once a country establishes a reputation for quality and reliability, this could be partially countervailed. Even if an escalation of MNC intrusion becomes necessary, there is no reason why Third World owned corporations cannot meet the challenge. Already, there are signs that newly industrialised LDCs are sprouting their own multinationals which could, over time, increasingly base themselves within developed countries to facilitate market penetra-tion. Finally, manufacturing firms within developed countries may subcontract with independent LDC producers, thereby sustaining inter-national vertical industrial integration in the context of arm's length trade. The extent to which contracts are settled with outsiders would depend on the relative profitability of either internalising or external-ising such transactions.

Offshore Processing

Although subject to various interpretations, offshore processing or international subcontracting can be regarded as an arrangement where-by a firm, in specific response to instructions from another located abroad, undertakes for foreign delivery, either some processing, com-ponent manufacturing or the production of an entire product. Freq-quently, the firm is likely to be a subsidiary of the organisation re-quisitioning the output but as mentioned, this need not necessarily be the case. 'For U.S. firms, slightly less than half of such activity has taken place through direct investment and intra-firm trade.'[56] Large retailers could initiate such trade, as could developed country manu-facturers who may wish to take advantage of existing independent LDC plant structures capable of meeting their requirements. At all events, final marketing is invariably handled by the commissioning party.

The scope for international subcontracting has been widening as a result of improved and cheaper communication and transport provi-sions, as well as by the increased ease of identifying and hiving off processing activities that could more appropriately be coped with else-where. In the US, tariff items 807.0 and 806.3, in certain circum-stances, exempt from customs duty the value of US inputs embodied in imports. Since these provisions foster offshore processing, it is widely believed that the growth of applicable imports is indicative of the growth of subcontracting in general.[57] Between 1966 and 1979, these imports rose from $953 million to $11,937.7 million, amounting in 1977 to 9.6 per cent of all US manufactured imports.[58] At first, the share originating from LDCs was no more than 6 per cent but by 1979 it rose to 44 per cent. Clearly, LDC imports will soon dominate in this sphere, but it is interesting to note that up to the close of the 1970s, they have taken second place and that in 1974, offshore processed goods constituted only 7.2 per cent of LDC manufactured exports to the US.[59] Likewise, products brought into the Netherlands and West Germany under similar offsetting tariff provisions, originated over-whelmingly from industrial countries, suggesting that international subcontracting 'is not always based on the exploitation of low-wage assembly sweatshops'.[60] With regard to the LDCs, the bulk of their trade in this field is in electronics and textiles, but food processing, services and repairs are also farmed out. Most of the work done on behalf of US enterprise is concentrated in Mexico, Hong Kong, Taiwan, South Korea and Singapore, which in 1970-4 collectively furnished 88 per cent of the LDC share of imports under tariff items 807.0 and 806.3.[61]

Whereas there are scattered instances of corporations putting out work within LDCs to utilise non-labour resources (such as in aluminium smelting in Ghana because of cheap electricity), by far and away the most significant enticement is the Third World's profusion of cheap unskilled labour. Not only is labour freely available at a fraction of the going US rate (for example, in 1969, hourly wage rates for Singaporean garment workers were $0.18 compared to a rate of $2.31 in the US)[62] but more often than not, it is 'possible to obtain labour productivity in the developing countries close to, or exceeding, U.S. levels'.[63] Output levels may flag in advanced countries where the tedium of repetitive tasks discourages industriousness and repels willing recruits. By contrast, within LDCs, workers steeled by the lack of more attractive alternatives could be hazed into applying themselves more diligently. Judging by case histories, it would seem that typically, US MNCs are forced to go 'offshore' as a last resort in their efforts to survive compe-titive pricing by foreign or sometimes even local rivals. Only after they actually take the plunge do they fully appreciate the benefits involved.

In Nayyar's view, 'there are two basic factors which influence the choice of transnational firms between low wage countries: political stability and labour docility'.[64] This, however, is much too simplistic, for even where these conditions are met, other equally valid considerations may come to mind. Ideally, MNCs would prefer to subcontract in a country devoid of bureaucratic interference and corruption, where goods could enter and exit free of duties and/or other restrictions, where the exchange rate is stable, where transport costs can be minimised and, if possible, where the country has preferential access into developed market economies. Such countries are more likely to be ones where previous MNC investments have successfully been attained and which have a reputation for good export performance. All told, they are unlikely to be among the LDC's poorest, and in fact, with the exception of Haiti (advantaged by US proximity), none of the UN's 31 designated 'hard core poverty' LDCs has made any appreciable subcontracting headway.

It is not to be denied that LDC offshore processing is primarily motivated by the cheapness and availability of Third World workers, especially non-unionised compliant ones. None the less, workers engaged in the system may have no current recourse to better job prospects or employment alternatives. In many ways it is far preferable to convey unskilled employment opportunities to LDC citizens in their own countries, than to lure them abroad as migrant 'guest workers' where they inappropriately perpetuate labour intensive industries, where the migrants encounter social disorientation and friction and where much of their earnings are spent externally. Even though offshore activities initially yield few economic linkages to the rest of the host country, over time 'local value added tends to rise in relation to gross value'.[65] On the basis of evidence gathered from companies maintaining international subcontracting plants, Moxon noted that 'they generally progressed from doing only the simplest manufacturing operations in the most standardized products offshore to getting involved in much more complex operations and products'.[66]

There are distinct dangers that in their eagerness to attract MNCs, LDCs may competitively fritter away potential gains as they provide corporations with tax free havens in industrial estates backed up by infrastructure deployed at subsidised rates. In extreme instances, foreign exchange earnings could even be negative. Apart from anything else, excessive offshore processing could expose a country to over-dependence on outside bodies and could deprive it of a fair measure of autonomous industrial development. The degree to which these negative features prevail in no small measure depends on the absence of any vigilance, integrity and determination on the part of LDC regimes.

At the other end, offshore processing has been assailed for shedding advanced countries of plant and equipment and for leading to 'de-industrialisation' and massive unemployment.[67] In part answer to these charges, research undertaken by Finger shows 'quite convincingly' that offshore processing does not 'displace domestic output nor produce a balance of trade deficit'.[68] Possibilities of an LDC and developed country both deriving foreign exchange gains arise when the LDC acquires an export activity and the developed country imports final products incorporating its own rather than a foreign rival's components.

Provided the negative features of offshore processing do not gain the upper hand, it could well serve to foster a rational restructuring of the international economy, augmenting total output and moderating prices for the general benefit of both producers and consumers.

Conclusion

In view of the relatively limited attention that MNCs, as traders, have attracted, only rather tentative conclusions emerge. It would probably be in keeping to state quite categorically that the MNCs play a major role in the world economy. Their foreign investments appreciably affect export flows and they dominate trade in high technology products. With respect to the LDCs, their involvement in manufacturing exports is currently rather low key, but over time their participation can be expected to increase. There certainly is evidence that they are moving into offshore processing at a rapid rate. Problems abound in relation to the MNCs' ability to rig transfer prices and in their excessive size and strength. It is possible that these challenges may be thwarted by countervailing MNC growth from within the Third World but the potential for this is not easy to gauge. What remains clear is that there are a number of questions that are yet unresolved; among which is the extent to which LDC manufacturers wishing to export, require or can forego MNC co-operation.

Notes

1. W.B. Reddaway, *Effects of U.K. Direct Invesment Overseas: Final Report* (Cambridge University Press, Cambridge, 1968); G.C. Hufbauer and F.M. Adler, *Overseas Manufacturing Investment and the Balance of Payments* (US Treasury Department, Washington, DC, 1968).

2. Considering that the 'reverse classical' assumption postulates that overseas investments would materialise through the medium of others if the home country's MNCs do not jump the gun, all exports induced by investments constitute net home country trade gains.

3. US Tariff Commission, *Implications of Multinational Firms for World Trade and Investment for U.S. Trade and Labor* (Washington, DC, 1978), p. 327.

4. As cited by R.A. Batchelor, R.L. Major and A.D. Morgan, *Industrialization and the Basis for Trade* (Cambridge University Press, Cambridge, 1980), p. 79.

5. C.F. Bergsten, T. Horst and T.H. Moran, *American Multinationals and American Interest* (Brookings Institution, Washington, DC, 1978).

6. This was a firm's foreign subsidiary dividends plus foreign tax credits deflated by the parent's total assets.

7. These hinged on the use of advertising, machinery, personnel experience, professionals, managers, clerks, salespeople, craft workers, operatives, unskilled workers, white workers, males, and the extent of worker education and experience.

8. Basically indicated by the sales of foreign affiliates less imports from US parents.

9. Interestingly, although the advertising variable was not significant, its sign was negative; more on this later.

10. B. Swedenborg, *The Multinational Operations of Swedish Firms* (Industrial Institute for Economic and Social Research, Stockholm, 1979), p. 223.

11. R.E. Lipsey and M.Y. Weiss, 'Foreign Production and Exports in Manufacturing Industries', *The Review of Economics and Statistics*, vol. LXIII, no. 4 (Nov. 1981).

12. Ibid., p. 490.

13. Ibid., p. 493.

14. US Tariff Commission, *Implications of Multinational Firms*, p. 493.

15. A good deal of the apparent upsurge in LDC exports can be attributed to oil price rises.

16. Their respective 1966 and 1976 MOFA shares were 7 per cent and 6 per cent. In 1976 only 3 per cent of all LDC MOFA exports were manufactures, compared with 6 per cent ten years earlier.

17. Similar manufactured exports to sales ratios were evident among Swedish overseas concerns. Over the period 1970-4, a ratio of 23 per cent applied to all affiliates but one of only 5 per cent to those situated in LDCs. See Swedenborg, *Multinational Operations of Swedish Firms*, pp. 271-2.

18. US based foreign affiliates were defined as US business enterprises 'in which a foreign person had a direct or indirect interest of 10 per cent or more'. By contrast, US MOFAs are enterprises in which at least 50 per cent of assets are held by US residents.

19. Batchelor *et al., Industrialization and the Basis for Trade*, p. 91.

20. D. Nayyar, 'Transnational Corporations and Manufactured Exports From Poor Countries', *Economic Journal* (March, 1978), Table 4, p. 65.

21. Ibid., p. 78.

22. Bergsten *et al., American Multinationals and American Interest*, p. 72.

23. See J.H. Dunning, 'Trade Location of Economic Activity and the MNE: A Search for an Eclectic Approach' in B. Ohlin, P. Hesselborn and P. Wiskam

(eds.), *The International Allocation of Economic Activity* (Macmillan, London, 1977).

24. Ibid., p. 401.

25. J.H. Dunning, 'Explaining Changing Patterns of International Production: In Defence of the Eclectic Theory', *Oxford Bulletin of Economics and Statistics* (Nov. 1979), p. 275.

26. S. Lall, 'Transfer Pricing by Multinational Manufacturing Firms', *Oxford Bulletin of Economics and Statistics* (Aug. 1973), Table 1, p. 183.

27. Batchelor *et al., Industrialization and the Basis for Trade*, Table E2, p. 295.

28. G.K. Helleiner, *Intra-Firm Trade and The Developing Countries* (Macmillan, London, 1981), p. 10.

29. Batchelor *et al., Industrialization and the Gains for Trade*, Table E2, p. 295.

30. Ibid., p. 296.

31. Helleiner, *Intra-Firm Trade and The Developing Countries*, p. 10.

32. Ibid., Table 2.2, p. 28.

33. G.K. Helleiner and R. Lavergne, 'Intra-Firm Trade and Industrial Exports to the United States', *Oxford Bulletin of Economics and Statistics* (Nov. 1979), Table 5, p. 307.

34. S. Lall, 'The Pattern of Intra-Firm Exports by U.S. Multinationals', *Oxford Bulletin of Economics and Statistics*, vol. 40, no. 3 (Aug. 1978), p. 211.

35. Helleiner, *Intra-Firm Trade and The Developing Countries*, p. 12. On the same page, Helleiner indicated that among a sample of German MNCs, 'fully two-thirds of the intra-group exports by parent companies were for resale by foreign affiliates'.

36. J.R. de la Torre, Jr, 'Exports of Manufactured Goods from Developing Countries: Marketing Factors and the Role of Foreign Enterprise', *Journal of International Business Studies* (Spring 1971); 'Foreign Investment and Export Dependency', *Economic Development and Cultural Change* (Oct. 1974).

37. Torre, 'Foreign Investment and Export Dependency', p. 145.

38. Ibid., p. 146.

39. As reported by D.J. Goldsbrough, 'International Trade of Multinational Corporations and its Responsiveness to Changes in Aggregate Demand and Relative Prices', *IMF Staff Papers* (1981).

40. Lall, 'The Pattern of Intra-Firm Exports by U.S. Multinationals'.

41. These tariffs facilitate offshore processing by virtue of the fact that designated imports may have duties waived on the value, if any, of US manufactured components.

42. At this point, the reader is reminded that advertising also manifested a negative sign in Bergsten's regressions. See note 9, p. 75 above.

43. Lall, 'Pattern of Intra-Firm Exports by U.S. Multinationals', p. 219.

44. Helleiner and Lavergne, 'Intra-Firm Trade and Industrial Exports to the United States'.

45. For example, in 1977 only 27.6 per cent of non US firm related party imports from LDCs consisted of finished goods compared to a figure of 80.1 per cent from developed countries. See Helleiner, *Intra-Firm Trade and The Developing Countries*, Table 2.4, p. 32.

46. G.C. Hufbauer, 'The Impact of National Characteristics and Technology on the Commodity Composition of Trade in Manufactured Goods' in R. Vernon (ed.), *The Technology Factor in International Trade* (National Bureau of Economic Research, New York, 1970), pp. 212–20.

47. Helleiner, *Intra-Firm Trade and The Developing Countries*, Table 2.3, p. 30.

48. All SITC groups 5 to 8 in Helleiner's table (ibid.), save group 57 (explosives).

49. Goldsbrough, 'International Trade of Multinational Corporations', p. 592.

50. No specific instances of this practice are at hand.

51. Helleiner and Lavergne, 'Intra-Firm Trade and Industrial Exports to the United States', p. 307.

52. Torre, 'Exports of Manufactured Goods', p. 28; 'Foreign Investment and Export Dependency', p. 137.

53. Cohen, *Multinational Firms and Asian Exports*, p. 116.

54. C. Kirkpatrick and M. Yamin, 'The Determinants of Export Subsidiary Formation by U.S. Transnationals in Developing Countries', *World Development*, vol. 9, no. 4 (April 1981), pp. 376–9.

55. Hone, 'Multinational Corporations and Multinational Buying Groups', p. 146.

56. Lall, 'Pattern of Intra-Firm Exports by U.S. Multinationals', p. 214.

57. As 'some international subcontracting is undertaken without benefit of "value added tariff" provisions, these statistics understate the extent of this type of trade'. Helleiner, *Intra-Firm Trade and the Developing Countries*, p. 37.

58. Ibid., p. 36.

59. Nayyar, 'Transnational Corporations', p. 67.

60. J.M. Finger, 'Offshore Assembly Provisions in the West German and Netherlands Tariffs: Trade and Domestic Effects', *Weltwirtschaftliches Archiv* (1977), p. 247.

61. Nayyar, 'Transnational Corporations', p. 62.

62. M. Sharpston, 'International Sub-Contracting', *Oxford Economic Papers* (March 1975), Table 4, p. 104.

63. Ibid., p. 98.

64. Nayyar, 'Transnational Corporations', p. 77.

65. Sharpston, 'International Sub-Contracting', p. 129.

66. R. Moxon, 'Offshore Production in the Less Developed Countries', *Bulletin of New York University, Graduate School of Business Administration* (July 1974), p. 54.

67. There is some logical incongruity in the radical proposition frequently articulated, that offshore processing simultaneously denudes developed countries of their industrial structures while failing to impact significantly on Third World manufacturing.

68. Finger, 'Offshore Assembly Provisions', p. 243.

4 PROTECTION

During the 1960s the world seemed to be on the threshold of a free trade era but unfortunately subsequent economic downturns resurrected the spectre of protectionism. This chapter addresses itself to issues in protection. At first, the positive theory of tariffs is adumbrated followed by a review of the policy implications of employing trade inhibiting devices. Thereafter, the general political economy of protectionism is outlined, the question of tariff preferences to LDCs is examined and, finally, the growth of the 'New Protectionism' is discussed.

The Theory of Protection

Until fairly recently, the tariff has been the dominant protectionist implement. An understanding of its economic import may best be attained by approaching the study of tariff theory through the use of partial equilibrium analysis. Accordingly, we shall assume that apart from the one industry under our consideration (in which production is virtually integrated) all other factors within the economy are basically kept constant. For this to occur, the industry in question must be relatively minute. In addition, it is also assumed to be perfectly competitive. As for the entire economy, the 'small country' assumption is initially employed, that is, the country is deemed to be incapable of influencing prices on the world market so that its international terms of trade are exogenously determined. The potential impact of a tariff within our hypothetical industry can be appreciated with the use of Figure 4.1. In that diagram, the commodity in question is shown to be obtainable on the world market at the price OA. The world supply curve (AE) is seemingly perfectly elastic (from our small country's perspective) analagous to the situation confronting an individual participant within a perfectly competitive market. Internal demand and supply schedules are represented by curves DD and SS. The good is essentially the same whether manufactured abroad or at home but because of national solidarity consumers are assumed to prefer the locally labelled product and resort to the imported equivalent only when internal supplies (at the prevailing price) are exhausted. Before

Figure 4.1

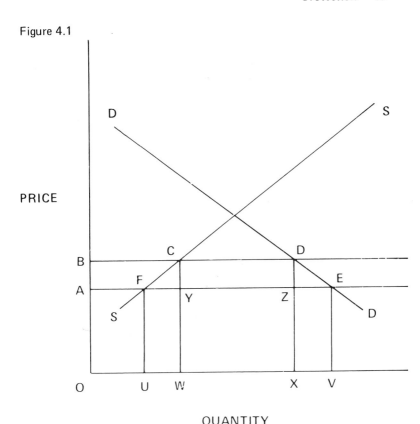

QUANTITY

tariffs are imposed and given the price OA, local suppliers produce OU
while consumers seek OV, UV the excess of local demand over supply
being the amount imported. Now assume that a tariff (which is of
course simply a tax on traded goods) is imposed, and that it is set at a
fixed absolute rate of AB per imported unit, or alternatively, at an ad
valorem rate of AB/OA. Whereas previously the imported good cost the
consumer OA, in the post-tariff situation the price rises to OB. In
essence, the tariff drives a wedge between internal and external prices,
equal to the amount of the tariff, and as the country cannot affect
external prices, the tariff is fully borne internally. From the local
producers' point of view, since local consumers no longer have recourse
to alternative sources of supply at less than OB per unit, they too can
and do charge OB, and in so doing, increase their output to OW. As for
consumers, now that they are confronted with a price hike, their
demand contracts to OX. Imports then fall to WX as a result of the

combined local supply and demand changes (UW plus XV).

Various welfare changes are set in train with the imposition of the above described tariff. Losses of consumer surplus equal to the area ABDE are sustained which are partly offset by an increase in producer surplus of ABCF and of government tax revenue equal to YCDZ.[1] Since total losses exceed total gains by the sum of the areas of triangles FCY and ZDE, the tariff results in a diminution of social welfare. Partly for this reason, economists look askance at tariff usage and argue that save in very exceptional circumstances, the objectives for which tariffs are employed can usually be secured by means of alternative policy instruments at lower welfare costs. For example, had the government merely wished to stimulate local production, it could instead have directly subsidised the industry in question. If a production subsidy of AB per unit had been allocated, the supply curve would have shifted downwards (by CY which equals AB) and local output would have risen by UW (as was the case with a tariff of AB). In this instance, the price to consumers would have remained at OA, and imports would only have contracted by UW instead of by UW plus XV. To finance the subsidy, ABCY of funds would need to be raised and allocated. Although the quantity of funds received by producers is equivalent to the quantity made available by taxpayers, the reader should not conclude that in this case, no social costs are entailed. Only ABCF of the ABCY subsidy can be regarded as a net producer gain, for the difference (FCY) is required to help coax the resources necessary to yield an extra UW of the good, from alternative placements. In fact, FCY reflects the net social cost of the subsidy, for had the economy simply wished to acquire an extra UW of the commodity as such, it could have, at prevailing world prices, mobilised resources worth UFYW to produce exports sufficient in value to enable it to import an extra UW units. In general, whenever imports are displaced by government intervention, the resulting curtailment of trade, with its concomitant reduction in specialisation and exchange, causes national income to fall.

When the 'small country' assumption is relaxed so that the economy is deemed capable of influencing world prices, at least in relation to specific goods, a tariff conceivably could improve that country's terms of trade, and thereby its wellbeing. Assume that a particular country imports cars, say from Japan, and that the Japanese charge $5,000 per delivered vehicle. Assume further, that production costs of locally produced equivalents are $6,000 per vehicle. In the absence of a tariff, only imported models would be purchased. Now assume that a per unit car tariff of \$1,500 is imposed. If the Japanese were to insist on obtaining their previous price, their cars would rise in price to \$6,500 within the tariff imposing economy and on that basis they would fail to compete with the locally made product. If this particular country's car market was a significantly large one, and if the Japanese producers were able to absorb a price fall, it may be in their interest to do so rather than forego their previous market share. They might for instance discount their product by \$500 so that their cars arrive at a landed price of \$4,500, to which a tariff is added, bringing the Japanese cars to price parity with the local ones. As before, the tariff creates a divergence between internal and external prices but in this example its burden is shared, \$500 by the foreign exporter and \$1,000 by the local consumer. From the consumer's perspective, the post-tariff price rise is once more a harbinger of welfare losses but from the national vantage, the fact that foreign prices have fallen means that less resources (embodied in exports) need be sacrificed for a given quantity of imports and, by that token, the country's welfare is enhanced. Whether social welfare improves in net terms, depends on the relative strength of the welfare promoting and welfare retarding forces. Common sense would suggest that there is obviously some point beyond which terms of trade improving endeavours are no longer worthwhile. If, for example, OPEC succeeded in driving up oil prices to say \$10,000 per barrel, the inevitable precipitous drop in total oil sales would deprive OPEC suppliers of adequate revenue. With this sort of problem in mind, scholars have developed the notion of an optimal tariff which *in theory* calibrates trade restrictions in order to maximise national welfare.

The mechanism by which a tariff can improve a country's terms of trade can be demonstrated with the use of a 'back to back' diagram as presented in Figure 4.2. The supply and demand curves for the importing country (1) are depicted on the right hand side and those of the exporting country (2) on the left. Both sides share a common price axis, and on this account, the supply curve on the left may appear to have the wrong slope but this is an illusion. In the pre-tariff case, at price A, country 1 imports JM (its excess demand at that price) while country 2 exports NQ (its excess supply). JM equals NQ and therefore, in world terms, overall supply and demand are balanced and A is an equilibrium price. In the context of Figure 4.2, if country 1 imposes an absolute per unit tariff of BC, its internal price would rise to C while the price of country 2's exports would fall to B. Country 1's imports would be reduced to KL, equal to country 2's now diminished exports of OP. As before, world demand and supply would be equated but

Figure 4.2

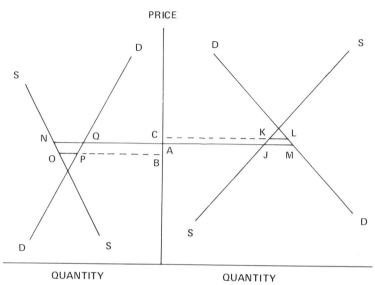

divergent prices would reign within the two countries, so that they would both bear some of the tariff burden. This would amount to a price fall of **AB** in country 2 and a price rise of **AC** in country 1. The overall difference between the set of the two post tariff prices would be equal to the value of the tariff.

Effective Protection

The theory so far outlined provides some understanding of the potential price impact of a tariff. In the small country case, an ad valorem tariff of a given percentage can be expected to raise the price of the protected item by that percentage, and as long as production is completely integrated, the extent of the price rise is indicative of the degree of protection that the tariff affords. In more general cases where firms purchase inputs from others, the degree to which a tariff protects a given industry is not immediately apparent. To determine this, our theoretical apparatus needs to be somewhat extended. Henceforth, we shall assume that the industry (or industries) in question acquires at least one input from another source, that both the input and final product can be imported, that there are fixed input-output production coefficients and that the 'small country' assumption is maintained.

The analysis that follows is derived in no small way from Professor Corden's seminal work.[2]

Imagine a table manufacturer who in the absence of tariffs requires $50 of imported wood to produce a table worth $100. Various primary factors of production in the form of labour, capital and land may be combined to transform the purchased material input — wood, into a final commodity whose overall value embodies the contribution of both the primary factors and the input. The value added by the primary factors (which in this case happens to be $50 per good) is simply the difference between the product's price and the material input acquisition costs per unit of output. Adopting Corden's usage, the per unit value added is termed the 'effective price', in contradistinction to the 'nominal' or selling price of the manufactured good as a whole. With the advent of a 10 per cent tariff on tables, the 'nominal price' rises to $110 and the 'effective' one (the difference between the selling price of a table and the cost of wood) to $60. Here the effective rate of protection (that is, the proportionate increase in value added made possible by the tariff structure) is 20 per cent. Clearly, we are now dealing with two tariff rate concepts; nominal and effective ones. With respect to nominal rates, their dimension has a direct impact on a final good's selling price, and thereby on consumer spending and welfare. Effective rates by contrast affect the degree to which tariffs succeed in stimulating extra production of the good in question. Whenever tariffs are levied on inputs, they diminish the effective price. Had a 10 per cent tariff been imposed on wood instead of on tables, tables would continue to be sold for $100 but as wood imports now rise to $55, value added per table or the effective price would now actually fall to $45, and effective protection rates would in this case be negative. Alternatively, had there been a 10 per cent tariff on both wood and tables, the effective price would have risen from $50 to $55 (post tariff table price of $110 minus post tariff wood price of $55) and in this case, nominal and effective rates would have been equalised. The reader could easily satisfy him or herself (by endless hypothetical examples) that whenever the tariff on the final product exceeds the one on the input, effective rates exceed nominal ones. As an illustration, let the nominal tariff on tables be 20 per cent and on wood 10 per cent. The nominal price of tables rises to $120 and the effective price to $65 ($120-$55) involving a 30 per cent value added increase.

One corollary of the above discussion is that when complete industry integration no longer holds, the amount of effective protection an industry receives is no longer exclusively dependent on the tariff rates bearing directly on that industry's own products, for as we have already noted, protection could even be negative in cases where no tariffs apply to the final good in question. Furthermore, effective rates are not only determined by the general tariff structure but also by the proportionate share of inputs in the value of the final product. When wood constitutes 50 per cent of the free trade price of tables, a 10 per cent table tariff generates a 20 per cent effective rate. If the share of wood is much larger, say 90 per cent, then the same 10 per cent table would yield an effective rate equal to 100 per cent. The implication of this is that even where various industries are subjected to the same nominal tariff structure, their effective rates are likely to diverge.

A formal algebraic presentation of the theory follows:[3]

Let:

P_v = value added per unit of j (j's free trade effective price).
P_v' = j's effective post tariff price (value added permitted by the tariff structure).
G_j = j's effective protective rate.
p_j = j's free trade nominal price.
a_{ij} = share of input i in cost of j at free trade prices.
t_j = nominal tariff rate on j.
t_i = nominal tariff rate on i.

then:

$$P_v = p_j(1 - a_{ij}) \tag{1}$$
$$P_v' = p_j\left[(1 + t_j) - a_{ij}(1 + t_i)\right] \tag{2}$$
$$G_j = \frac{P_v' - P_v}{P_v} \tag{3}$$

From (1), (2) and (3):

$$G_j = \frac{t_j - a_{ij}t_i}{1 - a_{ij}} \tag{4}$$

Some implications:

If $t_j = t_i$ then $G_j = t_j = t_i$
If $t_j > t_i$ then $G_j > t_j$
If $t_j < t_i$ then $G_j < t_j$

If tj > aijti then Gj < 0

If tj = 0   Gj = $\dfrac{-\text{aijti}}{1-\text{aij}}$

Equation (4) can be reformulated thus:

$$Gj = \frac{tj}{1-\text{aij}} - \frac{\text{aijti}}{1-\text{aij}} \tag{4.1}$$

The decomposition of equation (4.1) into two parts emphasises the two factors involved in determining the magnitude of the effective protective rate. The first section indicates the production subsidy potential of the nominal tariff on the final good, whereas the second component suggests how a tariff on the imported input penalises the value added activity. The ultimate extent of protection for the final product that the tariff system yields, and whether it is positive or negative, hinges on the strength of these conflicting tendencies. This matter can be further clarified with reference to Figure 4.3, where along the horizontal axis quantities of wood and tables are measured. A unit of wood is defined to be that quantity required for the production of one table. OA

Figure 4.3

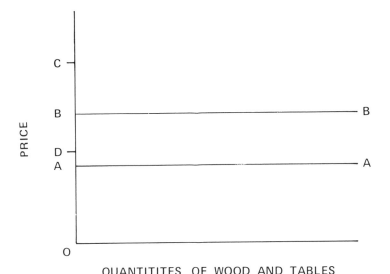

QUANTITITES OF WOOD AND TABLES

represents the free trade price of wood and OB of tables, so that the effective table price is BA. If a tariff on tables equal to BC is now introduced, the effective price will rise proportionately by BC/BA (equal to the first part of (4.1)). If instead, there is a tariff on wood equal to AD, the effective price would be CD which may exceed or fall short of the original price depending on whether BC minus AD is positive or negative. BC minus AD divided by BA yields the effective protective *rate*.

The analysis is easily extended to take account of situations where more than one imported input is involved; in which case effective protection (Gj) is defined as follows:

$$G_j = \frac{t_j - \Sigma a_{ij} t_i}{1 - \Sigma a_{ij}}$$

Two important connotations are worth mentioning. In various tariff bargaining forums, the apparent willingness of a given party to move towards a free trade position by reducing tariffs on say raw materials, might actually turn out to be a move towards strengthening effective protection, particularly if the raw materials are not in any case locally produced. For instance, if existing tariffs are abolished on wood and even marginally on tables, the effective table price would possibly still rise. To illustrate this (using equation (4)) let the first set of values equal: .1 for t_j and t_i and .5 for a_{ij}, so that G_j equals .1. Now let t_j equal .09, t_i 0 and a_{ij} remain .5. G_j now *rises* to .18!

The second consideration is that the study of effective protection helps to bring to light certain protected industries whose value added would be negative had they not been buttressed by tariffs. In our imaginary country, if the free trade prices of a unit of wood and a table were $105 and $100 respectively, then without protection it would be distinctly unprofitable to produce any tables whatsoever. However, if there was a 20 per cent table tariff, value added could potentially be $15, and if this is sufficient to meet primary factor costs, 'profitable' production could be sustained. Occurrences of this nature have been disclosed in a number of countries. Where they occur, countries coddling such import competing industries place themselves in the invidious position of sacrificing more in foreign exchange costs in importing inputs than in any savings they may incur in reducing final product imports. There are a number of reasons why free trade production costs are feasible profit-wise in some countries and not in others. For instance, certain countries may because of inherent inefficiencies employ a multiple of the input per unit of output than more skilful rivals elsewhere.

The effective protection concept certainly brings to the fore quantitatively opaque tariff measurements but its overall utility is often exaggerated. At the heart of the matter is the need to gauge how tariff structures affect resource allocation. Within the confines of a two good model, this poses no problem but as soon as we employ multi-commodity models, the mere ranking of industries by their effective tariff measurements is in itself of limited use. In many cases, particular resources are only transferable between a narrow band of industries. Not only would these need to be identified but we would also need knowledge of the relative elasticities of resource substitution in response to changes in relative protection levels. Furthermore, once the assumptions of fixed input output coefficients are relaxed and once certain inputs are no longer importables, accurate and reliable effective protection measurements become increasingly elusive.

Non-Tariff Barriers

Numerous means other than tariffs can be deployed to thwart imports. A government agency may conduct its procurement policy by favouring local suppliers over foreign ones even if foreign goods are cheaper or of better quality. Alternatively, unnecessarily stringent health, customs or technical regulations may be imposed on the entry of foreign merchandise. Of all non-tariff barriers, the one that has been the most commonly employed (at least up to the late 1970s) and which is fairly easily identified, is an important quota which places an absolute limit on the entry of designated goods regardless of terms of trade changes or the willingness of local consumers to purchase more imports at current prices. In some ways, import quotas are close substitutes for tariffs causing internal prices to rise and imports to fall. Glancing back to Figure 4.1, if in place of a tariff of AB, the government had simply imposed an import quota of no more than WX, prices would have risen from OA to OB giving rise to the same production and consumption effects that would have occurred with the tariff. In fact, in this case, the implicit tariff equivalent of the quota is AB/OA. The one major difference is that instead of the government collecting CYZD in tariff revenue, these funds are appropriated by those with access to the import licences. The state could avoid the loss of such proceeds by simply auctioning the quotas without restricting the participation of potential bidders. Where quotas are arbitrarily disposed, it is almost certain that their distribution would adversely affect resource allocation subsequent to the damage done by import restrictions in the first case.

Are Tariffs Economically Justifiable?

As indicated above, unless terms of trade alterations are feasible, tariffs (in a perfectly competitive framework) are likely to impair a country's social economic wellbeing. This proposition is believed to be tenable as long as pareto-optimality conditions apply. Where they do not, tariff usage may under certain circumstances be economically warranted, especially in the presence of private and social cost divergences. This can be shown with reference to Figure 4.4, where SS indicates an industry's supply curve based on private expenditure commitments and S'S' the supply curve based on social costs. The divergence between the two supply curves hypothetically may have resulted from a situation where in the face of massive unemployment, firms may be constrained to pay full employment salaries or, alternatively, the industry may induce external benefits through the propagation of skilled labour readily deployable elsewhere. Returning to Figure 4.4, HF represents the product's foreign supply curve and DD its local demand curve. In the absence of government intervention, the country will produce OZ of the product, consumers will demand OX and imports will amount to ZX. This is unsatisfactory in that local producers could expand their output from OZ to OW at less cost to the country as a whole than the corresponding imports that would be dislodged. An extra ZW of local output would require ZACW of the country's resources whereas ZW of imports could be obtained at no less than ZBCW. Triangle ABC represents the resource savings that would be enjoyed in the event of local output rising to OW. A tariff of JH per unit would induce the desired expansion and in so doing would be socially beneficial, provided the net loss of consumer surplus induced by the tariff (IEF) falls short of net production gains (ABC). Much, if not all of infant industry arguments hinge on this type of analysis, except that the private supply curve presumably originates above a point such as OH and that in general, dynamic considerations are involved so that ultimately the industry would be capable of producing socially optimal quantities without continuous government assistance. Other factors bearing on the infant industry case may arise as a result of imperfect

Figure 4.4

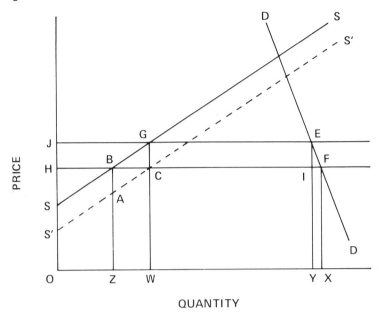

QUANTITY

capital markets or differences in the investment time horizons between private entrepreneurs and the government. A popular misconception is the assumption that potential scale economies or the expectation of medium term losses also constitute grounds for infant industry intervention. Why should a large industry anticipating negative cash flows consequent to the launching of a new venture be more worthy of public support than a newly established corner grocery store experiencing short term losses, as it accumulates experience and goodwill? Surely size in itelf cannot be a criterion in eliciting protection? In both small and large corporations, if satisfactory net profits cannot be realised in the long term their activities should cease, and if adequate returns are feasible, the early losses should be acknowledged to be part of investment costs. Where returns to such investments are privately appropriated there is no reason why they should be publicly funded.

Even though tariff usage may be meritorious in the event of market failure, tariffs are not necessarily the most appropriate option. With regard to the private and social cost divergence dealt with in Figure 4.4, a subsidy amounting to JHCG would have been far more preferable. Given that the subsidy would be financed by a non-distorting tax, it would have provided an apt production stimulus without inflicting consumers with adverse price movements so that social gains would equal ABC instead of the difference between ABC and IEF. The same sort of consideration applies to other fields where at first sight it would seem that a tariff is warranted.

If improvements in the balance of payments are needed, a tariff by restricting imports could be helpful but a devaluation would be a far more effective and efficient device. Although a tariff may seem to conserve foreign reserves, it would rebound against a country's exports if: it applied to crucial inputs, it caused resources to be drained from the export sector and it stimulated inflationary pressures rendering exports uncompetitive. A devaluation, by contrast, simultaneously boosts both the import competing and export sectors (at the expense of the non-traded sector) thereby improving the balance of payments without generating trade distorting side effects.

If increases in employment are sought, tariffs may (in the short term) create jobs but unfortunately in inappropriate areas. at a cost of long-term productivity improvements and of employment gains elsewhere. The marshalling of the workforce in industries where comparative advantage is weak, is a recipe for an abortive economic recovery and for ultimate stagnation. This proposition has been backed up empirically by Daly *et al.* who delved into the reasons why average manufacturing labour productivity in Canada has tended, by a sizeable margin, to trail behind that of the US.[4] They discovered that 'in general, the range of manufacturing products made in Canada does not appear to be much more limited that that produced in the United States' but this 'range is produced by a significantly smaller number of Canadian plants and firms, so that the range of items produced in a typical plant is usually substantially larger in Canada'.[5] Given that Canada's home market is comparatively small, product production runs are shorter than in the US, involving more time and hence costs, in retooling, resetting and gearing to the creation of an heterogeneous product mix. The ensuing 'limited specialization has turned out to be not only an important, but also a pervasive factor adversely affecting costs and productivity'.[6] Daly *et al.* were convinced that tariffs were responsible for Canada's intolerably high measure of product range diversification based on machines and plants not large enough to capture scale economies. Because of that country's protective structure, 'it has not been profitable to shift towards more specialized and longer production runs. In short, it is profitable for Canadian plants to be less productive than plants in the United States.'[7] The Canadian experience is pertinent to countries like Australia, which have also sheltered their manufacturing sectors behind protective tariffs and import quotas and which likewise have relatively limited internal markets. Apart from their malefic effects on labour productivity, tariffs are not always effective in ensuring net employment creation for (in large countries especially) a reduction in import spending deprives foreigners of the wherewithal to purchase the tariff ridden country's exports, so that while employment may expand in the import competing sector, this expansion could well be offset by job losses following a decline in export contracts. All in all, it would be far better for governments to redress the unemployment problem by appropriate macro-economic management.

Tariffs may also be utilised simply as a means of raising state revenue. This seems to be of considerable relevance in LDCs where tariffs not uncommonly account for no less than 25 per cent of LDC central government taxes. Here again, it could be argued that alternative revenue raising measures should, wherever possible, be adopted to avoid tariff induced distortions.

In practice, there may be occasions when tariff alternatives are not politically, practically or (given unusual circumstances) economically feasible. In some Third World countries the collection of direct taxes may be frustrated by difficulties in assessing a multitude of enterprises which refrain from collating and recording their transactions. Similarly, the cost of distributing subsidies may be daunting. Even where the subsidy is lodged, it may not be efficacious. This may be so in Third World countries where goods are 'shoddy' or qualitatively 'inferior' compared with importable substitutes. If the demand for local goods is low and inelastic, then subsidies that shift supply curves rightwards may not achieve perceptible market gains. If indeed the local products were not actually inferior but were only perceived to be so as a result of some irrational prejudice in favour of foreign products (partly stimulated by the prestige and promotional activities of well-known companies) then tariffs could function as transient devices causing enforced exposure to local alternatives. Even though credible arguments could be sustained for the use of tariffs in *certain* Third World countries, circumstances in developed countries are usually such that tariffs are likely to be more of an economic encumbrance than of assistance. If this is the case, one could well ask why tariffs persist and why protectionist pressures are a seemingly constant feature within the industrial world.

The Political Economy of Protectionism

Explanations accounting for the prevalence of tariffs typically draw attention to the fact that whereas individual producers usually obtain obvious and appreciable benefits from tariffs, the losses experienced by consumers, on an individual basis, are generally not as great nor as patent. Even though in the aggregate, consumer losses exceed producer gains, the costs that may be imposed on each individual consumer in terms of acquiring information and in canvassing tariff opposition tend to forestall effective action. By contrast, producers realise that time and money spent in propagating tariffs are likely to be financially well worth their efforts. In other words, there is an asymmetry of forces in contesting a tariff, with advantages heavily tilted towards those with vested interests in instituting protection. However, such an explanation is rather tentative in that in many instances, tariffs were widely installed as a prelude to local production, and in any case, it does not clarify why some industries receive more assistance than others.

In Australia, as a case in point, tariffs have long been regarded as an appropriate means for stimulating industrialisation. Tariffs contributed substantially to the historic influx of overseas capital and labour, and in so doing, *augmented the country's economic resources.* It is doubtful whether Australia's GDP would have reached its present level in a completely free trade environment, considering that many of its exports have confronted low income and price elastic demands. Above all, the Australian tariff has performed the socially accepted function of distributing the national product from its rural based enterprises towards industrial capital and wage earners. The tariff in fact has served as a proxy for a resource tax.

Workers have perceived the income redistributing function of the tariff with éclat, for historically, trade union strategy has been one of supporting manufacturers' bids for protection in order 'to apply to the Arbitration Court for higher wages'.[8] The possibility of attaining the same ends through other means, such as taxes and subsidies, while preferable on a theoretical plane, has not been deemed to be of practical significance.

Faced with a choice, producers would prefer tariffs to subsidies because they tend to be regarded as more durable and certain. Governments share this preference, for tariffs not only mask the implicit producer subsidy but are also revenue yielding. Furthermore, there may be something in the remarks of a leading Australian politician who declared that 'it would be absurd to channel all such aid through the

Budget because the spending rise would be so great that a prohibitive tax rise would be needed to finance it'.[9] This offhand declaration could readily be flaunted as an illustration of the necessity for subsidies to be made explicit, for if they are of the size suggested they should be subjected to open public scrutiny. However, what the speaker probably intended to convey was that either the likely distortions arising from the adoption of a tax-subsidy package were judged to be more onerous than those generated by tariffs or that such an approach was simply politically unacceptable.

Although tariffs may have in the past yielded clear cut dividends by virtue of their previous contributions to industrialisation (and this clearly seems to be the case for countries such as Germany, France, Australia, Canada, etc.) it does not of course follow that they are not currently an economic hindrance. On account of their historical importance, tariffs have obtained such widespread acceptance that few would have the temerity to advocate their total and immediate demise. Since the short run perpetuation of tariffs is commonly regarded as being part of the natural order of things, it is not difficult to comprehend the lack of public resistance to the issuing of 'temporary relief' to seemingly isolated industries incapable of withstanding foreign competition. This has been especially so in Australia where the former 'Tariff Board' adeptly devised idiosyncratic arguments in favour of specific sectors that clamoured for protection.

In terms of explaining inter-industry tariff variations, some economists have been captivated by models which posit tariff demand and supply functions. An example of both the specification and testing of such a model is provided by Anderson[10] who indicates that the effective demand for protection is determined by expected benefits in relation to lobbying costs. (The demand by people within an industry may partly be nullified by the lobbying strength of output users elsewhere.) Factors that bear positively on demand include: the extent to which an industry is in the process of decline, the extent to which imports have penetrated the home market, the extent to which an industry is labour intensive, the extent to which wage rates are below average and the extent to which there is industrial concentration (in order to avoid free-rider problems). On the supply side, it is suggested that governments would be more inclined to respond positively whenever their parties would stand to gain financially,[11] the more so if the industry is geographically concentrated, is a large employer and is sited in marginal electorates. In general, empirical tests do not yield significant results for the demand variables (save in the case of labour intensive industries) and the above approach has been taken to task for playing down the importance of voting strength and for overstressing the lobbying process.[12]

The influence of multinational corporations (MNCs) provides another dimension in tariff formation. As mentioned above, tariffs have been used in Australia to help attract foreign capital. Australia has not of course been unique in this regard for the Canadian government has likewise 'been perfectly aware of the relation between the branch plant movement (of MNCs) and tariffs' and that 'American investment in Canadian industry, far from being an unintended side effect of Canadian tariff policy, was its conscious and deliberative objective'.[13] The existence of a tariff-investment nexus has been confirmed separately by Hufbauer and by Aharoni[14] although Saunders' recent statistical investigation in Canada seems to suggest that as of late, 'effective tariff protection is negatively associated with foreign ownership').[15] Once MNCs migrate to overcome tariff hurdles, they are naturally reluctant to countenance any trade liberalising moves which could jeopardise their new investments, and hence they generally adopt a strong protectionist stance within host countries. In 1975, General Motors, for example, persuaded the Australian government to limit the importation of Japanese cars, a decision which in the words of one director, put the company 'in the best marketing position we've been in during the postwar years'.[16]

Within their own countries, some MNCs may have a predilection for reduced protection either to engage in intra-firm trade or out of fear that their own countries' import barriers could stimulate unwelcome incursions from foreign competitors or, alternatively, because they wish to forestall a movement towards offsetting barriers abroad.

Tariff Preferences

While the tariff controversy has continued to flare, a new twist has emerged, that is, the desirability or otherwise of providing LDCs with preferential import access into advanced country markets. Advocates of tariff preferences in favour of LDCs, have argued that they are necessary to offset an assumed inability of LDCs to compete on the same footing as developed countries, and to counter discriminatory trade barriers. Internally, LDC manufacturers are perceived as being handicapped on account of their limited local markets depriving them of possible scale economies, as well as by a general lack of satisfactory production factors, including the supply of adequate and reliable social capital. Externally, advanced country tariffs on goods of special interest to LDCs have been relatively high, and in many instances, formidable non-tariff barriers have been erected.

The provision of a generalised system of preferences (GSPs) to LDCs, has frequently been presented as an international extension of the infant industry assistance argument. However, the notion that GSPs can reliably nurture LDC infant industries may be open to question.[17] Normally, where the infant industry argument is employed, it is used to justify temporary protection to an industry, selected on the expectation that in the long run, it will be economically viable, and therefore local supply conditions are of relevance. On the other hand, when LDC industries are stimulated by external tariff changes, the stimulation accorded each specific industry is based not on internal comparative cost considerations but on the tariff structures of the developed countries. In such circumstances, it is conceivable that the GSP could inappropriately encourage capital intensive industries. The actual outcome would depend on the product coverage and tariff reductions of the GSP in operation. When the concept of GSPs was first mooted, it was generally expected that they would stimulate LDC exports at the expense of non-preferred sources causing trade diversion. Such a view was of course consistent with the belief that LDC manufacturers were inherently less competitive than their advanced country rivals. Iqbal[18] and Baldwin and Murray[19] reveal that under GSPs, 'trade diversion is considerably smaller than trade creation',[20] and that most items covered by GSPs are those for which LDCs are likely to have comparative advantages.

If so, the current operation of GSPs does not adversely affect resource allocation and aptly induces LDC industrial growth. What could well be challenged, is the assumption that LDCs actually need preferential treatment, without which they would make little headway. Before GSPs were generally introduced (in 1971), LDCs were exporting manufactured goods at above average rates and were increasing their share of the developed countries' imports. The patent ability of LDCs to compete successfully without beneficial discrimination is beginning to be widely acknowledged. For example, Chenery and Hughes have declared that some LDCs 'may have a comparative advantage so large that moderate tariff barriers — as hitherto in clothing and cotton textiles — are little impediment to them'.[21] Elsewhere, Finger has shown that the LDCs' relative penetration into the US import market, resulted from LDCs increasing their supply relative to their developed country competitors, 'rather than from a disproportionate increase in United States import demand for products in which the LDCs specialise'.[22] Finally, Murray in considering whether LDCs really need preferential access to world markets decided that 'the answer to this question is, in many respects, no. Obviously the developing countries enjoy an international comparative advantage for many manufactured products.'[23]

Even if LDCs do not actually need preferences to increase their trade, preferences conceivably could accelerate their export growth rates. In relation to existing schemes, since they have had as yet, a short lifespan, (with the US inaugurating its GSP in 1976) their overall impact has been difficult to gauge. Nevertheless, a UN study has suggested that in general, preferences can be an important factor in stimulating LDC exports,[24] while Iqbal has reported that within some schemes, there has been a faster movement of eligible as opposed to ineligible items.[25] Naturally, the ability of GSPs to provide meaningful export incentives depends on their scope.

With the onset of the US GSP in 1976, separate schemes were effectively provided by all developed countries or regions. Such an outcome fell short of LDC aspirations, for originally, a single comprehensive system with maximum product inclusions was sought. Instead, the various schemes differ with regard to the range of countries and commodities incorporated. While, at present, some 126 LDCs have preferential access into at least one developed country, 30 are excluded from either the European, Japanese or US market.[26] The US excludes all non GATT Communist states, members of OPEC or other cartels, countries granting reverse preferences (such as those providing concessions to the EEC, in return for associate status) and those nationalising US property without offering compensation. The EEC through the Lome Convention, maintains a special relationship with 46 LDCs, providing them with more favoured access than other Third World exporters, so that for all practical purposes, these 46 LDCs 'are not beneficiaries under the E.E.C. GSP scheme'.[27] Not only are the various GSPs not universally embracing but a small number of LDCs have appropriated an unduly large share of the gains. In 1975 two-thirds of GSP imports originated from ten countries,[28] and on the basis of 1970 trade flow data, five states, namely Taiwan, Mexico, Yugoslavia, South Korea and Hong Kong, were identified as exporting 55 per cent of the goods covered by major GSP benefactors.[29]

In terms of products eligible for preferences, it appears that after deducting goods exempt from duty in the first place, plus those excluded from GSPs, no more than 12 per cent of all LDC exports (and 12 per cent of LDC industrial exports) are covered.[30] This rather limited range results from the outright exclusions already mentioned, the setting of ceiling limitations and stringent rules of origin. Since preferences were unilaterally provided, donor countries took the view that they were entitled to limit such gestures in order to minimise any adverse employment and market consequences. The EEC for example, has offered textile preferences only to signatories of the multi-fibre arrangement, which in turn was instituted to restrict textile trade. Japan and the US excluded around three-quarters of their imports of dutiable industrial products, with the Americans barring textiles, shoes, certain electronics, glass and steel. Where European ceiling limitations apply, once the maximum quantities are imported, further imports are subject to normal most favoured nation (MFN) duties. In the US if an LDC supplies either more than 50 per cent of the imports of a specific item or an annual amount in excess of $25 million, then that LDC forfeits its beneficiary status with regard to that particular product. Such restrictions have reduced the effective product coverage of the combined US, EEC and Japanese schemes to 33 per cent of their nominal coverage or to only 4 per cent of LDC exports to these markets.[31] To these detractions must be added the burden of rules of origin, which by either requiring (as do the EEC and Japan) that outputs be classifiable under a different BTN (Brussels tariff nomenclature) heading than imported inputs, or (as is done in the US, Australia, Canada and New Zealand) that a given ratio of value added to total costs be maintained, certain goods are needlessly excluded. The case of electronic products being excluded from the EEC GSP because transistors (the imported inputs) fall under the same BTN classification as the industry's output, has frequently been cited.

From the above account, it is clear that GSPs, as they are currently structured, provide LDC exporters with limited benefits. The question arises whether improvements in GSPs should be canvassed or whether LDCs would be better served by further reductions in MFN duties, which could in fact be induced by the LDCs themselves participating as reciprocating negotiators. Obviously, GSP improvements would stimulate LDC exports but it could be argued that where LDCs already maintain comparative advantages, preferences, as opposed to non discriminatory tariff reductions, are not compelling, and where LDCs lack comparative advantages, preferences are inappropriate. In any event, the prospects for eliciting further significant GSP reforms are not too promising, considering that developed country governments are being pressurised by internal considerations to curb LDC imports. In view of the fact that policy makers within advanced economies perceive some costs in reducing tariffs on goods of interest to LDCs, their willingness to do so might be enhanced if LDCs, in turn, provided some reciprocal concessions. It is not enough to contend, as some have,[32] that reciprocation is implicit within GSPs because LDCs utilise their additional export earnings to import from industrial countries. Evident and explicit reciprocation is required to rally support of identifiable developed country exporters to counter the political clout of developed country protectionists. As it happens, a partial dismantling of tariffs within various LDCs, would assist these countries to shed themselves of inefficient industries and, in so doing, streamline their economies. Despite beliefs to the contrary, a number of areas have been disclosed where LDCs could with advantage lower their tariffs,[33] and although GATT has been widely berated for bypassing LDC needs, products of interest to Third World countries have been included in previous tariff reducing conferences. For example, the Kennedy Round yielded 'tariff reductions on products for which LDC exports in 1964 to the E.E.C., The United States, the United Kingdom and Japan came to well over $2 billion'.[34] Further MFN tariff cuts would clearly diminish the competitive advantages which GSPs provide and what may be at issue, is whether or not the net gain (to LDCs) of subsequent multilateral tariff reductions would be positive. With this in mind, two recent findings may be cited. The first by Baldwin and Murray,[35] reports that while (on the basis of 1971 trade figures) LDCs gained $479 million in increased exports from existing GSPs, a 50 per cent MFN tariff cut would instead have caused their exports to rise by $848 million. The second, by Cline and others,[36] based on an estimated $380 million GSP gain, derived by Iqbal[37] (also using 1971 values), calculated that by contrast, a 60 per cent MFN reduction (excluding textiles) would have yielded the LDCs a $1,110 million export gain. Although these sets of figures differ appreciably, they both suggest the likelihood that LDCs could realise higher returns by pursuing the MFN option. Presumably, MFN reductions would be permanent, they would not (unlike GSPs) be subject to ceiling limitations, they would apply to a broader range of products than GSPs, and no LDCs would be excluded. In this context, LDC interests may be better served if their spokesmen were to expend their energy in pressurising for general non discriminatory tariff reductions on goods of specific interest to them, rather than counting on unilateral GSP concessions.

The New Protectionism

As of late, opposition within developed countries to a general lowering of tariff and non-tariff barriers has been hardening in the wake of a renewed trend towards protectionism.[38] From the mid-1970s, trade restrictions were increasingly imposed, partly in response, to growing widespread economic difficulties and partly in response to structural problems associated with specific industries. This protectionist drift is considered to be 'new' in that it represents a reaction or setback towards the movement in establishing a liberal international trade era under the auspices of GATT. It is also new in the extent to which non-tariff barriers are being employed. With the completion of the Tokyo Tariff Round negotiations, average tariffs have been scheduled to fall to only 4.4 per cent for the US, 4.7 per cent for the EEC and 2.8 per cent for Japan. Given these commitments, protectionist pressures have surfaced in the form of non-tariff trade obstacles, partly legitimised by the EEC's insistence 'on the right to apply safeguard protection on a selective basis'.[39] Apart from resorting to outright import quotas, foreign suppliers are tending to be induced to restrain their exports 'voluntarily'. Surprisingly, this type of arm twisting has led to little acrimony, since established exporters have at least been provided with some minimum entry, mainly at the expense of newcomers. In effect, there seems to be an unofficial alliance between firms that have market allotments (conferring on them some monopoly status) and advanced country producers. Informal trade restrictions have grown quite rapidly and in Gard and Riedel's view they are particularly 'disquieting because they are so difficult to document'.[40] In the main, restraints have been imposed on individual goods but some observers believe that the range has increased prodigiously covering not only labour intensive sectors but also 'more complex, highly skilled and capital-intensive products such as man-made fibres and automobiles'.[41]

In the realm of textiles, a multi-fibre agreement (MFA) negotiated in 1973 and extended to the end of 1981, globally limited annual export growth rates to 6 per cent. The MFA also provided for bilateral quotas, and in terms of this provision, the EEC limited its 1978 textile imports from Taiwan, Hong Kong and South Korea to levels below those recorded in 1976. Likewise, the US restricted its 1978 purchases from these same three countries, to their 1977 values, while import ceilings were lowered in various amounts by Australia, Canada, Norway and Sweden.[42] By 1981 when the agreement was once more renewed, the US began restricting its textile imports from Hong Kong, South

Korea and Taiwan to an annual growth rate of 0.5 per cent on two-thirds of their items and no more than 2 per cent on the rest. Unfortunately, the squeeze on these three LDCs has not paved the way for better export growth rates from others who are in fact condemned to face the same obstacles they have hitherto encountered or even harsher ones. Ironically, between 1977 and 1980, 'E.E.C. textile imports from other developed countries jumped 44% dwarfing the 19% increase from developing countries and a rise in imports of less than 1% from Hong Kong, South Korea and Taiwan'.[43]

Other items such as cars, televisions, steel and ships began to be curbed with the onset of the 1975 recession, where sluggish markets co-existed with increased productive capacity. Each affected industry has sought protection on the basis of having experienced unique difficulties. In time, the number of 'special cases' has risen, with a growing danger of each temporary expedient becoming permanently institutionalised. Protection has been internationally transmitted, as frustrated exporters have focused on countries where access has been relatively easier, and in so doing have provoked those countries to restrain their newly enhanced imports. This is especially evident in steel where 'the E.C. has proposed that European steel imports be cut back by more than 10 percent in 1983 to make room domestically for steel displaced from the U.S. market, passing protectionist consequences along to Brazil and South Korea. Already the U.S. steel industry has announced a campaign to restrict imports from Japan on grounds that E.C. protection against Japan has diverted Japanese steel to the U.S. market.'[44]

Fortunately, although additional trade barriers have been imposed, they have not as yet, been too pervasive. In 1977, for example, only 3 to 5 per cent of world trade was 'being adversely affected by import restrictions introduced or seriously threatened, by the industrially advanced countries'.[45] Takacs' investigation led him to conclude that although in the US more protectionist pressure surfaces when the economy is depressed, 'the government does not necessarily respond to it',[46] and similarly, Gard and Riedel believe that apart from textiles and clothing, *official* changes in import barriers have not constituted a serious obstacle to combined LDC export growth.[47] What is of concern is that, throughout the Western world, there has been a change in public mood, in favour of further restrictions.

Within the US, protectionist sentiment has been rising in Congress, with the population no longer perceiving it as undesirable.[48] In Europe, fears of foreign competition, by LDCs especially, are widespread. Such phobia have been described graphically by Viansson-Ponte who, in relation to France, reports that many subscribe to the view that, that country's 'textile industry is dying. Manufacturers in Hong Kong and South Korea pay starvation wages, provide no benefits, copy our goods and even our labels and plunder our markets to the point of shamelessly invading France itself.'[49] Ironically, left-wing radicals have been amongst the forefront in clamouring for tighter import controls. For example, a Canadian Socialist journal in lamenting the fact that 'cheap imported clothing' has intruded into the Canadian market, concludes that 'the effects of these imports on employment in the Canadian clothing industry have been disastrous'.[50] At the other end of the globe, Australia's doyen of political economy has claimed that, during the last few years, his country has, because of trade, lost 200,000 jobs in manufacturing industry and that 'it is impossible for any country with free institutions to compete with the latest technology supplied by multi-nationals, and operated by repressed workers being paid $2 per day'.[51] What is particularly disturbing, from the viewpoint of LDCs, is that when it comes to preserving local protection, even self professed Third World supporters are among the ranks of those who perceive the growth of LDC manufactured exports as a threat to their country's economy. Such views are exemplified by Australia's National Education Officer of the Freedom from Hunger Campaign who, in a newspaper article, maintained that the rapid industrialisation taking place in SE Asia has contributed towards a global recession. This is supposed to have occurred because developed countries 'are losing out on income-generating investment' and because 'their trade balance is worsened as goods once produced locally are now imported'.[52]

In light of the sentiments described above, it would seem that 'the major trade issues facing developing countries are not how to gain preferential tariff treatment from industrialized countries, but rather how to prevent the further growth of non-tariff barriers against imports'.[53] Furthermore, it is worth re-emphasising that the LDCs' bargaining posture would be strengthened and protectionist pressures somewhat allayed, were the LDCs to enter GATT conferences as full negotiating partners. To some extent, moves in this direction have been made. During the Tokyo Tariff Round, 19 LDCs participated, some of which conceded tariff bindings and tariff reductions.[54] The Tokyo Round itself, which resulted in widespread agreements to lower tariffs (over an eight-year period starting in January 1980) and for the first time, to lower non-tariff barriers, was in part initiated to counter recent protectionist tendencies. Given that GATT member countries are committed to free trade, and given that large sections of their populations are fearful of its employment consequences, it is necessary to establish the extent to which such fears are warranted.

Notes

1. The per unit tariff AB which equals YC times the quantity imported WX equal to CD.

2. W.M. Corden, *The Theory of Protection* (Oxford University Press, London, 1971).

3. Derived from Corden, *The Theory of Protection*, pp. 35, 36.

4. D.J. Daly, B.A. Keys and E.J. Spence, *Scale and Specialization in Canadian Manufacturing* (Economic Council of Canada, Staff Study no. 21, March 1968).

5. Ibid., p. 20.

6. Ibid., p. 23.

7. Ibid., pp. 57, 58.

8. L. Glezer, *Tariff Politics: Australian Policy-Making 1960-1980* (Melbourne University Press, Melbourne, 1982), p. 10.

9. *Sydney Morning Herald* (23 Nov. 1981), quoting Doug Anthony, Australia's former deputy prime minister.

10. K. Anderson, 'The Political Market for Government Assistance to Australian Manufacturing Industries', *Economic Record* (June 1980).

11. 'The Prime Minister, Mr. Fraser, has been warned by major manufacturing interests who are vital Liberal Party donors that their funds will be withdrawn if the Federal Government cuts tariffs.' *Sydney Morning Herald* (27 Aug. 1981).

12. See for example, J.D. Quiggin and A.B. Stoeckel, 'Protection, Income Distribution and the Rural Sector', *Economic Papers*, vol. 1, no. 2 (Sept. 1982).

13. C.F. Bergsten, T. Horst and T.H. Morgan, *American Multinationals and American Interest* (Brookings Institution, Washington, DC, 1978), p. 49.

14. G.C. Hufbauer, 'The Multinational Enterprise and Direct Investment' in P.B. Kenen (ed.), *International Trade and Finance: Frontiers of Research* (Cambridge University Press, Cambridge, 1975); and Y. Aharoni, *The Foreign Investment Decision* (Harvard University Press, Cambridge, Mass., 1966).

15. R.S. Saunders, 'The Political Economy of Effective Tariff Protection in Canada's Manufacturing Sector', *Canadian Journal of Economics* (May 1980).

16. *Journal of Commerce* (31 March 1975).

17. In this regard, see H.G. Johnson, *Economic Policies Towards Less Developed Countries* (Allen & Unwin, London, 1965).

18. See Z. Iqbal, 'Trade Effects of the Generalized System of Preferences', *Pakistan Development Review*, vol. 15, no. 1 (Spring 1976); 'The Generalized System of Preferences and the Comparative Advantage of Less Developed Countries in Manufactures', *Pakistan Development Review*, vol. 13, no. 2 (Summer 1974).

19. R.E. Baldwin and T. Murray, 'MFN Tariff Reductions and Developing Country Trade Benefits under the GSP', *Economic Journal* (March 1977).

20. Ibid. Interestingly (or strangely), in another study by Zimmer and T. Murray, 'The Generalized System of Preferences' in K.P. Sauvant and H. Hasenpflug (eds.), *The New International Economic Order* (Wilton House, London, 1978), the authors claim (on p. 202), without reference to any facts, that trade diversion would largely result from GSPs.

21. H.B. Chenery and H. Hughes, *The International Division of Labour: The*

Case of Industry, World Bank Reprint No. 11 (1972).

22. J.M. Finger, 'Gatt Tariff Concessions and the Exports of Developing Countries – United States Concessions at the Dillon Round', *Economic Journal* (Sept. 1974), p. 572.

23. T. Murray, *Trade Preferences for Developing Countries* (Macmillan, London, 1977), p. 152.

24. UNCTAD, *Trade in Manufactures of Developing Countries, 1969 Review* (New York, 1970), p. 48.

25. Z. Iqbal, 'The Generalized System of Preferences Examined', *Finance & Development*, vol. 12, no. 3 (Sept. 1975).

26. See G. de Miramon and A. Kleitz, 'Tariff Preferences for the Developing World', *OECD Observer*, no. 90 (Jan. 1978), p. 31.

27. Murray, *Trade Preferences for Developing Countries*, p. 31.

28. Miramon and Kleitz, 'Tariff Preferences for the Developing World', p. 32.

29. Murray, *Trade Preferences for Developing Countries*, p. 60.

30. Ibid., p. 97.

31. See T. Murray in W.G. Tyler, 'Trade Preferences and Multinational Firm Exports from Developing Countries', *Issues and Prospects for the New International Economic Order* (Lexington, Toronto, 1977), p. 135.

32. See for example, Murray, *Trade Preferences for Developing Countries*, p. 9.

33. See G.M. Lage and F.F. Kiang, 'The Potential for Mutually Beneficial Trade Negotiations between the United States and Advanced LDCs', *Weltwirtschaftliches Archiv*, band 115, heft 7 (1979), p. 310.

34. J.M. Finger, 'Effects of the Kennedy Round Tariff Concessions on the Exports of Developing Countries', *Economic Journal* (March 1975b), p. 95.

35. Baldwin and Murray, 'MFN Tariff Reductions'.

36. W.R. Cline, N. Kawanabe, T.O.M. Kronsjo and T. Williams, *Trade Negotiations in the Tokyo Round* (Brookings Institution, Washington, DC, 1978).

37. Iqbal, 'Trade Effects of the Generalized System of Preferences'.

38. See e.g., B. Nowzad, *The Rise of Protectionism* (IMF, Washington, DC, 1978b); S.P. Cohen, 'Coping with the New Protectionism', *National Westminster Bank Quarterly Review* (Nov. 1978); B. Balassa, 'The "New Protectionism" and the International Economy', *Journal of World Trade Law*, vol. 12, no. 5 (Sept./Oct. 1978).

39. C.F. Bergsten and W.R. Cline, *Trade Policy in the 1980's* (Institute for International Economics, Washington, DC, Nov. 1982), p. 15.

40. L.M. Gard and J. Riedel, 'Safeguard Protection of Industry in Developed Countries: Assessment of the Implications for Developing Countries', *Weltwirtschaftliches Archiv*, band 116, heft 3 (1980).

41. G. Curzon, 'New Protectionism, the MFA and the European Community', *The World Economy*, vol. 4, no. 3 (Sept. 1981).

42. World Bank, *World Development Report* (Oxford University Press, New York, 1978), p. 15.

43. *The Economist* (10 April 1982), p. 73.

44. Bergsten and Cline, *Trade Policy in the 1980's*, p. 44.

45. Nowzard, *The Rise of Protectionism*, p. 78, reporting GATT estimates.

46. W.E. Takacs, 'Pressures for Protectionism: An Empirical Analysis', *Economic Inquiry* (Oct. 1981), p. 691.

47. Gard and Riedel, 'Safeguard Protection of Industry in Developing Countries', p. 47.

48. Balassa, 'The "New Protectionism" ', p. 417.

49. P. Viansson-Ponte, 'Undevelopment or Economic Miracle?', *Guardian*

(weekend ed., 20 May 1979).

50. *Canadian Dimension*, vol. 14, no. 1 (July/Aug. 1979), p. 20. The journal reports an absolute drop of 3,000 jobs between 1972 and 1975, equivalent to 2.5 per cent of the 1972 clothing workforce. It would seem that the term 'disastrous' is subject to various interpretations. In any case, no evidence was provided that import penetration alone was responsible for the fall in employment.

51. E.L. Wheelwright, 'The Australian Predicament'. Radio broadcast by Australian Broadcasting Corporation, Sydney (24 May 1979). Quoted from p. 4 of typescript supplied by the author.

52. S. Keen, 'Asia's Growth Seen as Threat to World', *Sydney Morning Herald* (12 March 1979).

53. World Bank, *World Development Report* (1978), p. 59.

54. IMF Survey (23 April 1979).

5 LDC IMPORTS AND JOB DISPLACEMENT

Recent Export Trends

During the last two decades, LDCs have been making increasing efforts to foster and stimulate their manufactured exports. Between 1960 and 1976, manufactured exports[1] from LDCs rose annually by 16.2 per cent outpacing the 14.1 per cent rate sustained by the industrialised countries and the 13.7 per cent rate for all world traded commodities[2] (see Table 5.1). Although having grown rapidly, LDC manufactured exports still constitute a small proportion of the world market (7.4 per cent in 1976). They are also characterised as contributing a small share of overall LDC exports (17.2 per cent in 1976), originating from a handful of countries and concentrated around a narrow range of items. For example, in 1968, ten states accounted for 69.9 per cent of all LDC manufactured exports. The countries in question (with their respective 1968 shares shown in brackets) being Hong Kong (23.2 per cent), India (10 per cent), Taiwan (7.9 per cent), Mexico (6.8 per cent), South Korea (4.9 per cent), Brazil (4.2 per cent), Argentina (4.1 per cent), Pakistan (3 per cent), Israel (2.6 per cent) and the Philippines (2.6 per cent).[3] Although only a few countries dominate LDC trade, their respective rankings have not been constant, for between 1963 and 1976, South Korea's, Brazil's and Singapore's shares rose from 1 per cent each to 16, 6 and 4 per cent respectively.[4] Furthermore, whereas in 1965 only 18 LDCs each exported over $100 million worth of manufactures (valued at 1975 prices) 40 countries exceeded that figure a decade later.[5] In terms of commodities, the LDCs have been heavily reliant on textiles, clothing and non-ferrous metals, which in 1963 represented 58 per cent of manufactured exports. If, as is sometimes the practice, non-ferrous metals are excluded, then textiles and clothing would have accounted for 40 per cent of the 1963 and 32 per cent of the 1975 totals. On the other hand, tremendous strides have been made in SITC category 7 (machinery and transport equipment) whose shares jumped from a low of 5 per cent in 1960 to 27 per cent in 1975. Over half the items in this group consist of electronic exports, many of which were initiated by multinational corporations in a limited number of mainly Asian states. Their recent upsurge has, however, altered the aggregate composition of Third World exports and disclosed areas in

Table 5.1: Trade in Manufactures (US $ billion)

	(1) World Trade	(2) World Man.	(3) All LDCs	(4) LDC Man.	(5) LDC Man. to DCs	(6) DC Man. Imp.	(7) % DC Man. from LDCs	(8) DC Man. Exp.	(9) % LDC Man. to DCs	(10) LDC Man. in World	(11) Man. as % LDC Exp.
1960	128	70	27	3.9	2.6	41	6.3	58	67	5.6	14.4
1961	133	74	28	4.0	2.6	44	5.9	61	65	5.4	14.2
1962	141	80	29	4.4	2.8	48	5.8	65	64	5.5	15.1
1963	153	87	32	4.9	3.2	54	5.9	71	65	5.6	15.3
1964	172	98	35	5.6	3.6	59	6.1	79	64	5.7	16.0
1965	186	109	37	6.4	4.0	67	5.9	84	63	5.9	17.2
1966	203	122	39	7.6	5.0	77	6.5	99	66	5.9	19.5
1967	215	131	40	8.1	5.4	83	6.5	107	67	6.2	20.2
1968	240	150	44	9.8	6.7	97	6.9	123	68	6.5	22.0
1969	273	176	50	11.7	8.1	116	7.0	144	69	6.6	23.4
1970	312	202	56	13.3	9.1	135	6.7	166	68	6.6	23.8
1971	348	226	62	14.8	9.6	151	6.4	187	65	6.5	23.9
1972	416	271	76	18.3	12.0	184	6.5	222	66	6.8	24.1
1973	576	365	112	28.3	19.3	247	7.8	296	68	7.8	25.3
1974	836	484	221	38.7	25.0	313	8.0	397	65	8.0	17.5
1975	878	519	213	36.5	22.5	313	7.2	426	62	7.0	17.0
1976	992	583	252	43.3	27.7	363	7.6	478	64	7.4	17.2
Growth rates per annum	13.7	14.1	15.0	16.2	15.8	14.6		14.1			

Notes: (1) Total world trade in all commodities; (2) Total world trade in manufactures; (3) Total LDC exports in all commodities; (4) Total LDC manufactured exports; (5) LDC manufactured exports to developed countries; (6) Total manufactured imports by developed countries; (7) % of developed countries' manufactured imports coming from LDCs; (8) Developed countries' manufactured exports; (9) % of total LDC manufactured exports bought by developed countries; (10) LDC manufactured exports as % of column (2); (11) Column 4 as % of column (3).

To provide a consistent series down to 1960, oil exporting and oil importing LDCs have been combined into one category. The decline in column (11) from 25.3 per cent in 1973 to 17.2 per cent in 1976, can be attributed more to burgeoning oil revenues rather than any loss of momentum on the part of LDC manufactured exports.
Source: UNCTAD, *Handbook of International Trade* (1969); GATT, *International Trade*, various issues.

Table 5.2: Industrial Countries' Imports of Manufactures (US $ billion)

	From World			From LDCs			% of Item Imported from LDCs	
	1963	1976	1963-76 Growth Rate	1963	1976	1963-76 Growth Rate	1963	1976
Non-ferrous metals	3.8	16.9	12.1	1.3	4.1	9.2	34.2	24.3
Iron and steel	4.3	24.4	14.2	.1	.8	17.3	2.3	3.2
Chemicals	5.7	46.9	17.6	.2	1.8	18.4	3.5	3.8
Wood and paper	2.1	10.9	13.5	.1	.8	17.3	4.8	7.3
Other semi-manufactures	2.8	20.9	16.7	.3	2.5	17.7	10.7	12.0
Engineering goods	23.2	183.6	17.2	.1	7.0	38.7	.4	3.8
Textiles	4.1	19.3	12.7	.5	2.8	14.1	12.1	14.5
Clothing	1.4	16.1	20.6	.2	6.8	31.2	14.3	42.2
Other consumer goods	3.6	28.4	17.2	.3	4.5	23.1	8.3	15.8
Total	51.0	367.1	16.3	3.1	31.8	19.6	6.1	8.7

Note: Due to rounding, the sum of column items may not equal the totals indicated.
Source: GATT, *Networks of World Trade* (Geneva, 1978).

which future gains could be made. Not only have LDCs diversified their output, they have also tended to manufacture proportionately more at higher production stages. Defining production stages in terms of successive processes in which goods are transformed into different products (say for instance, cotton into yarn (stage 1), cotton yarn into cotton fabrics (stage 2), cotton fabrics into clothing (stage 3), etc.), then, whereas, only 2.7 per cent of 1966 LDC manufactured exports to advanced economies had reached a fourth production stage, by 1974, 8.6 per cent had.[6] Finally, a noteworthy feature of recent trends is the growing competitiveness of LDC manufactures, whose share of advanced economy imports rose from 6.1 per cent in 1963 to 8.7 per cent in 1976. As can be seen from Table 5.2, relative inroads were accomplished across a wide sphere, with exceptional gains being achieved in clothing and engineering goods.

Employment and Trade

Research into the relation between import growth and employment can basically be divided into two components; one recording changes that have actually occurred, and the other; setting out to predict outcomes on the basis of hypothetical import movements or tariff rate reductions.

Commencing with the retrospective approach, the ILO, over the period 1961 to 1965, estimated the number of jobs lost as a result of LDC imports within certain industries of North America, the EEC and EFTA.[7] (The industries in question being processed food, textiles, clothing, footwear, wood products and furniture, leather goods, chemicals and some metal products.) All told, the estimates amounted to about 27,000 jobs in North America, 35,000 in the EEC and 20,000 in EFTA, numbers representing less than 0.2 per cent of each region's manufacturing workforce. The ILO study concentrated only on the negative job displacing effects of imports. During the course of time, countries also experience an expansion of exports, from which they derive employment benefits. To place import losses into proper perspective, corresponding export gains should be taken into account. With this in mind, Luttrell chose to survey, between 1965-6 and 1975-6, employment changes occurring in a selection of leading US import and export industries.[8] His calculations revealed that whereas 250,100 jobs were lost because of import growth (from all sources), 369,500 were gained by exports. (Incidentally, within this time interval, the absolute growth of exports surveyed fell short of the growth of imports by $3,647 million.[9])

The two studies thus far cited, assumed, in common with most others, that production varied inversely with imports and that within each industry or group, labour to output ratios remained constant. Both implied that employment changes attributed to trade, differed from those actually realised, indicating the influence on jobs of other factors such as movements in domestic demand or productivity improvements. The comparative impact of imports and other employment determinants have been explicitly assessed elsewhere. For example, during the years 1960 to 1965, Shelton reckoned that within the US manufacturing sector, the growth of imports displaced 234,400 jobs (equivalent to an annual loss of 0.3 per cent of that sector's entire workforce) compared to a decrease of 3,256,900 caused by improved productivity.[10] Similarly, Frank, in surveying trends between 1963 and 1971 within US industries, found that whereas the percentage contribution points of imports to the annual employment growth rate was −0.9 that of productivity changes was −2.9.[11]

Finally, utilising input-output tables, within a general equilibrium framework, Krause and Mathieson concluded that for the US, 'when the direct and indirect effects are taken together, a loss of 16,600 jobs between 1970 and 1971 (first quarters) can be attributed to changes in exports and imports',[12] constituting a minute fraction of the 1.7 million increase in unemployment that then occurred. Had the unemployment rate changed only because of trade disturbances, it would only have risen from 4.16 per cent to 4.18 per cent rather than to 5.93 per cent.

Turning to the second research category, where the emphasis is on assessing possible future employment outcomes, the approach generally taken has involved; forecasting import changes corresponding to specified tariff cuts, and then by assuming that imported goods replace local output on a one to one basis, an appropriate labour to output ratio is applied to calculate prospective job losses. Estimates of likely import increases are derived by computing post tariff price reductions (in percentage terms) and multiplying these by the relevant price elasticity of demand for imports. By assuming constant world prices, percentage changes in physical imports and import values are equalised. The procedure has various shortcomings and on some occasions, writers have used elasticity coefficients calculated at an earlier date or in relation to another country. The general consensus is that, if anything, the employment impacts are likely to be biased upwards. For example, since it is not feasible to identify the import increases that reflect consumers' responses to lower prices, all additional imports are erroneously assumed to replace local output. Alternatively, if world export supply elasticities are not infinite, then predicted imports would be unrealistically high.

While some writers have adopted the above procedure to investigate the impact of tariff cuts on employment within individual countries or industries,[13] attention has increasingly been concentrated on the possible consequences of multilateral tariff reductions. Among the first to break ground in this area was Baldwin who (using 1971 data), concluded that (if oil, certain textiles and agricultural products were excluded) a 50 per cent multilateral tariff cut would add only 15,200 to the US' unemployed.[14] A spate of similar studies has since been published,[15] of which the most recent and in fact most detailed, has been that of Cline and others[16] (referred hereto as Cline). Cline estimated (among other things) the potential employment effects within the US, Canada, Japan and the EEC, resulting from 12 alternative multilateral tariff cutting formulae. Table 5.3 indicates their results (using 1974 trade flows) in instances where the tariff formulae were: (a) a 60 per cent linear cut, (b) a 100 per cent linear cut and (c) a 60 per cent linear cut for tariff rates above 5 per cent and 100 per cent for those below. In all cases, the employment effects relative to the total workforce were very small; on the basis of formula (c) for instance, they amounted to 0.14 per cent for the US, 0.87 per cent for Canada, 0.47 per cent for Japan and 0.1 per cent for the EEC.[17] Canada and the EEC seem to experience negative employment outcomes, reflecting negative trade balances. These calculations were based on constant exchange rates and presumably, were they to be adjusted, their losses (already minor) would lessen. In all these estimates, textiles were excluded on the grounds that they were in any case subject to stringent quotas. Elsewhere, when textiles were taken into account (on the basis of 1971 data) they caused net direct employment effects to alter (in thousands) from 1.4 to −35.6 in the US, −17.9 to −23.6 in Canada, 48 to 88.7 in Japan and −90.7 to −107.8 in the EEC.[18] Though these changes are significant in absolute terms, as a proportion of each country or region's labour supply, they are still of little consequence. Even as a ratio of sectoral employment in the textile industry itself, the employment change is minimal, being of the order of −1.65, −2.93, 2.44 and −0.49 per cent for the US, Canada, Japan and the EEC respectively.[19] Considering that, in practice, multilateral tariff reductions are phased over a number of years, on an annual basis, any adverse

Table 5.3: Changes in Employment from Tariff Liberalisation ('000s of Jobs — excluding petroleum and textiles)

Area and Tariff Formula	Job Losses from Increasing Imports		Job Gains from Increased Exports		Net Job Balance	
	Direct	Total	Direct	Total	Direct	Total
USA						
(a)	65.2	140.7	84.0	169.6	18.8	28.9
(b)	108.7	224.4	139.0	280.6	30.3	46.2
(c)	74.4	161.7	88.7	179.0	14.3	17.3
Canada						
(a)	37.4	76.2	11.7	25.6	−25.7	−50.6
(b)	62.3	127.0	19.4	42.4	−42.9	−84.6
(c)	37.8	77.1	13.6	29.9	−24.2	−47.2
Japan						
(a)	98.4	239.9	101.0	263.8	2.7	23.9
(b)	163.9	339.9	167.5	437.7	3.6	37.8
(c)	101.1	246.1	108.3	287.9	7.2	41.8
EEC						
(a)	91.8	n.a.	−20.4	n.a.	−112.2	n.a.
(b)	153.1	n.a.	−27.8	n.a.	−180.8	n.a.
(c)	102.5	n.a.	−13.6	n.a.	−116.1	n.a.

Notes: n.a. — not available; for tariff formulae, see text; total effects include direct and indirect ones.
Source: Extracted from Cline *et al., Trade Negotiations in the Tokyo Round*, Table 3.14, p. 125.

trade disturbances would barely be perceived.

The Relative Job Impact of LDC Exports

Despite the evidence that trade extensions are not damaging, many continue to suspect that though this may be so in general, LDC imports are by contrast peculiarly disruptive. Such suspicions are held for a variety of reasons. For one, since LDC goods are predominantly labour intensive, it is natural to assume they are prone to depress employment. Statistical support for this view has been claimed by Marris, who contends that most studies suggest that 'a balanced increase in trade between OECD countries and the newly industrialized countries creates something like 5 to 25 percent fewer jobs than are displaced by imports'.[20] More specifically, Balassa (using 1976 trade data) has concluded that the OECD ratio of jobs gained to jobs lost, through balanced manufactured trade with LDCs, is of the order of .65.[21] In practice, net losses have not materialised, since developed country trade with LDCs has been imbalanced in favour of the former, both in terms of total exchanges and in terms of changes over time. For instance, in 1972 the advanced countries exported $30.7 billion of manufactures to non oil exporting LDCs and imported $11.7 billion from them, thereby obtaining a $19 billion trade surplus. By 1976, developed country exports rose to $67.4 billion, imports to $27 billion and their trade surplus to $40.4 billion.[22] Applying Balassa's findings, that for every million dollars' worth of exports to or imports from LDCs, 18.4 jobs are created or 28.5 lost,[23] then one may conclude that between 1972 and 1976 the growth in trade with non oil exporting LDCs, provided the developed economies with a net increase of 237,390 jobs!

Another source of concern regarding trade with LDCs, lies in a supposed tendency for inter- rather than intra-, industry trade to dominate. Within the confines of intra-industry trade, import competing firms may specialise and thereby forestall retrenchments. By contrast, inter-industry exchanges are considered more likely to cause entire sectors to contract as an industry's local demand is diverted to imports, without that industry being compensated with alternative markets abroad. Originally, Blackhurst *et al.* maintained that because intra-industry trade among developed economies had been growing relatively rapidly, 'the formation of the E.E.C. and E.F.T.A. resulted in surprisingly few adjustment problems'.[24] A year later, they adopted the view that the distinction between inter- and intra-industry trade was not meaningful, because of 'the ambiguity of the concept of an industry', and because there are few reasons for assuming adjustment costs to differ within rather than between industries.[25] If this is so, then whether trade with LDCs is of the inter- or intra-industry variety, is of no importance. Even if their earlier views were correct, the issue may have little long-term significance, if as Donges and Reidel predict, the expansion of LDC exports is likely to be accompanied by a widening of the product mix 'making trade with industrial countries more and more of an intra-industry, rather than an inter-industry type'.[26]

A third possible explanation of why LDC exports are sometimes viewed with misgivings, relates to the belief that their growth could readily accelerate causing a precipitous and unacceptable onrush of goods into advanced economies. Such a notion is not implausible, considering that technology and capital are readily transferable, and that once such transfers are effected LDCs could acquire, in instances where labour costs predominate, an immediate capability of radically penetrating and capturing developed country markets. However, when the extent of current LDC penetration is in fact noted, it is obvious that large additional increases could easily be accommodated. In 1970, manufactured LDC exports as a share of the industrialised countries' market was 0.7 per cent and although the growth of LDC exports continued to surge forward, their 1975 share rose to no more than 1.7 per cent.[27] Even in specific sectors, LDC shares have been small. For example, the 1971 proportion of LDC exports to US output of textiles, clothing and electrical goods was only 6.3 per cent, 6.5 per cent and 8.2 per cent respectively.[28]

Although LDCs have made market gains, they figure more prominently as customers than suppliers, even in terms of trade increments, for whereas between 1960 and 1973, they accounted for 9 per cent of the developed countries' increase in manufactured imports, they absorbed 29 per cent of the latter's export growth.[29] An expansion of imports from LDCs effectively paves the way for similar expansions from advanced countries and, given appropriate adjustment policies, the developed economies could derive substantial benefits from such exchanges.

Trade Benefits and Adjustments

The potential gains that may accrue to developed economies, as a result of the enhancement of their trade with LDCs, may be assessed in the light of the net losses that would be sustained were this option not to be pursued. From a static point of view, considerable consumer welfare improvements emanating from access to cheap imports, would be foregone. Assuming a 60 per cent linear multilateral tariff cut, Cline *et al.* calculated that the US, Canada, Japan and the EEC would each reap $49,110, $17,840, $28,990 and $45,300 million in terms of increased consumer surpluses.[30] By comparison, respective labour adjustment costs were thought to be $611.2, $286.8, $595.6 and $473.6 million.[31] While these figures apply to trade with all countries, it seems reasonable to suppose that dealings with the LDCs as such, would yield proportionately smaller, though still significantly large, impacts. This is partially confirmed by Szenberg *et al.*,[32] who reveal that in the US, as a result of a 10 per cent tariff reduction on imported footwear (in which Taiwan and Brazil rank among the principal suppliers) net social welfare would increase by about $78.69 million.

In dynamic terms, restrictions on LDC trade erode the developed economies' long-term growth prospects by effectively protecting labour intensive industries at the expense of high productivity sectors elsewhere, particularly in exports. Ample evidence exists suggesting that a movement of a developed country's workforce from its import to export sector would upgrade its labour skill composition.[33] The curtailment of LDC trade permits import competing industries to pay higher wage rates and attract more labour than is economically warranted, while at the same time exports are restrained, since LDCs are denied additional foreign exchange earnings. Consequently, resources are misallocated. Weak, stagnant and internationally uncompetitive industries are buttressed and even expanded, while innovative and progressive ones are stifled.

One can argue that the potential net trade welfare effects, alluded to above, are somewhat exaggerated. Within the confines of traditional economic analysis this may not be the case but what if the methodology is misplaced? Standard theory assumes that monetary gains accrued by consumers can be equated with equal monetary losses sustained by producers. Apart from ignoring possible unfavourable distributional effects, there may in practice be a welfare asymmetry with regard to equal monetary losses and gains, i.e. the psychic costs to workers of losing say $5, may exceed psychic gains to consumers of acquiring $5. If so, then reported gains, conventionally assessed, are subject to error. Furthermore, studies examining recent imports may have inadvertently understated their negative employment impacts and incorrectly implied that compared to productivity changes, they have been of minor significance. In the first place, technological changes are often accompanied by the growth of new industries, so that while labour requirements may be curtailed in some sectors, they may be expanded elsewhere. Secondly, assuming productivity changes to be detrimental to aggregate employment, the data analysed do not reveal whether or not import growth itself has stimulated labour saving innovations. A situation could be envisaged where at one stage, a tariff protected industry profitably operates with traditional production techniques. If the industry is internally competitive, firms may not innovate for fear of being emulated by rivals. If the industry is monopolistic, it may not innovate for fear of stimulating tariff reductions that may in turn negate returns to its innovation. However, if at a later stage, the industry begins to face increased foreign competition and further tariff hikes are not politically feasible, innovation may become imperative.

Although it is not difficult to flaw the procedures used to measure the likely effects of trade expansions, the evidence amassed overwhelmingly indicates potential benefits of so large a magnitude, that even allowing for some possible overstatement, there seems little doubt that it is to the advantage of developed countries to absorb more LDC exports and to adjust their economies accordingly.

Conclusion

LDCs have clear and obvious comparative advantages in most of their manufactured exports. They do not require preferences but rather the elimination of trade barriers as such. Unfortunately, developed countries have tended to protect their labour intensive industries to avoid 'market disruption' and to postpone structural adjustments, the burden of which may be concentrated on specific groups, which may be particularly disadvantaged due to skill deficiencies, an adverse age composition, lack of regional job alternatives, etc. In fact, the existence in both the US and West Germany of a positive relation between the degree of protection an industry is afforded and that industry's adjustment costs, has been observed.[34] In some instances, protection has been extended in response to increased LDC competition, indicating the unlikelihood of further preferences being conceded. These restrictions are in essence against the long-term interests of the developed countries themselves but they tend to be taken because of strong sectional pressures. They are even against the long-term interests of the protected workers ·because protection confines them and future entrants to relatively low paid occupations, since the expansion of more productive sectors is thwarted. LDCs could play a part in inducing developed countries to dismantle protection by offering where possible, mutual concessions. In so doing, they would mobilise potential developed country exporters to their cause and gain some political leverage.

Since the brunt of adjustments may be borne by a narrowly defined and easily identifiable section of the population, and since trade benefits are likely to be widely dispersed, developed country governments should accept social responsibility for alleviating and compensating those experiencing losses. As yet, industrialised countries have not initiated adjustment assistance schemes *specifically to promote LDC exports*.[35] On the contrary, instead of furthering the contraction of ailing industries, some have prompted their expansion. This is particularly manifest in the US textile industry where 'between 1961 and 1968 U.S. restrictions against textile imports not only protected vested interests, but also encouraged a 10.2% increase in the number of textile workers.'[36] By 1973, US textile mill production was 43 per cent higher than in 1967.[37] In Manitoba, Canada, the protected textile industry had actually sponsored the immigration of workers from the Philippines!

Notes

1. Defined as SITC items 5–6.
2. These rates are based on current prices. In terms of constant prices the growth rates between 1960–75 for LDCs and developed countries were 12.3 and 8.8 per cent respectively.
3. Calculated from UNCTAD, *Trade in Manufactures of Developing Countries, 1969 Review* (New York, 1970), Table 12, p. 19.
4. See R. Blackhurst, N. Marian and J. Tumlir, *Adjustment, Trade and Growth in Developed and Developing Countries* (GATT Studies in International Trade, no. 6. Geneva, Sept. 1978), p. 22.
5. World Bank, *World Development Report* (Washington, Aug. 1978), p. 10.
6. See A.J. Yeats, 'Recent Changes in Developing Country Exports', *Weltwirtschaftliches Arvchiv IV*, band 115, heft 1 (1979).
7. ILO, 'Some Labour Implications of Increased Participation of Developing Countries in Trade and Manufactures and Semi Manufactures' in *UN Proceedings of UNCTAD*, 2nd Session, vol. III, New York, 1968). See also C. Hsieh, 'Measuring the Effects of Trade Expansion on Employment', *International Labour Review* (Jan. 1973), for an excellent survey of this, and similar studies
8. C.B. Luttrell, 'Imports and Jobs – The Observed and the Unobserved', *Federal Reserve Bank of St Louis* (June 1978).
9. Computed from data in Tables I and III, ibid.
10. W.C. Shelton, Bureau of Labor Statistics, 'The Relationship Between Changes in Imports and Employment in the U.S. 1960-5', paper presented to American Statistical Association (Detroit, 1970).
11. C.R. Frank, Jr, *Foreign Trade and Domestic Aid* (Brookings Institution, Washington, DC, 1977).
12. L.B. Krause and J. Mathieson, 'How Much of Current Unemployment Did We Import?', *Brookings Papers on Economic Activity*, no. 2 (1971), p. 421.
13. See for example M. Szenberg, J.W. Lombardi and E.Y. Lee, *Welfare Effects of Trade Restrictions* (Academic Press, New York, 1977).
14. R.E. Baldwin, 'Trade and Employment Effects in the United States of Multilateral Tariff Reductions', *American Economic Review*, vol. 66, no. 2 (May 1976).
15. For a review of some of them, see M.E. Kreinin and L.H. Officer, 'Tariff Reductions under the Tokyo Round: A Review of their Effects on Trade Flows, Employment and Welfare', *Weltwirtschaftliches Archiv*, band 115, heft 3 (1979).
16. W.R. Cline, N. Kawanabe, T.O.M. Kronsjo and T. Williams, *Trade Negotiations in the Tokyo Round* (Brookings Institution, Washington, DC, 1978).
17. Ibid., p. 128. The percentage for the EEC relates to direct impacts only.
18. Ibid., pp. 132, 133.
19. Ibid., pp. 132, 133.
20. S. Marris, 'O.E.C.D. Trade with the Newly Industrializing Countries', *OECD Observer* (July 1979), p. 30.
21. B. Balassa, 'The Changing International Division of Labour in Manufactured Goods', *Banco Nazionale Del Lavoro* (Sept. 1979), p. 261.
22. Data extracted from GATT, *International Trade, 1976/7*, Table 7.

23. Balassa, 'Changing International Division of Labour in Manufactured Goods', p. 262.

24. R. Blackhurst, N. Marian and J. Tumlir, 'Trade Liberalization, Protectionism and Interdependence', (GATT Studies in International Trade, no. 5, Geneva, No. 1977), p. 11.

25. Blackhurst *et al.*, *Adjustment, Trade and Growth in Developed and Developing Countries*, p. 79.

26. J.B. Donges and J. Riedel, 'The Expansion of Manufactured Exports in Developing Countries', *Weltwirtschaftliches Archiv*, band 113, heft 1 (1977), p. 79.

27. World Bank, *World Development Report*, p. 28.

28. Frank, *Foreign Trade and Domestic Aid*, Table 3-8, p. 35.

29. World Bank, *World Development Report*, Table 12, p. 9.

30. Cline *et al.*, *Trade Negotiations in the Tokyo Round*, p. 130. Where tariffs were originally 5 per cent and below they were assumed to be abolished.

31. Ibid., p. 130. Adjustment costs are derived by multiplying the average earnings lost per displaced worker while seeking re-employment by the total number displaced.

32. Szenberg *et al.*, *Welfare Effects of Trade Restrictions*, pp. XV, XVI.

33. See for example Balassa, 'Changing International Division of Labour in Manufactured Goods', pp. 268-72.

34. For the US see J.H. Cheh, 'United States Concessions in the Kennedy Round and Short-Run Labor Adjustment Costs', *Journal of International Economics* (1974), pp. 323-40 and M.D. Bale, 'United States Concessions in the Kennedy Round and Short-Run Labor Adjustment Costs', *Journal of International Economics* (1977), pp. 145-8. For Germany see J. Riedel, 'Tariff Concessions in the Kennedy Round and the Structure of Protection in West Germany', *Journal of International Economics* (1977), pp. 133-43.

35. See B. Nowzard, *The Rise of Protectionism* (IMF, Washington, DC, 1978b), p. 51.

36. P. Isard, 'Employment Impacts of Textile Imports and Investment: A Vintage Capital Model', *American Economic Review*, vol. 63, no. 3 (June 1973), p. 402.

37. Nowzard, *The Rise of Protectionism*, p. 16.

6 TRADE ADJUSTMENT POLICIES

During the 1970s, a number of newly industrialised LDCs achieved rapid progress in their manufacturing sectors, while those of most advanced economies stagnated. These trends were reflected in an increasing penetration of LDC manufactured goods within developed economy markets, at a time when OECD states were experiencing record post-war unemployment levels. In contrast to the preceding two decades, when developed countries had undergone significant structural changes without undue trauma, the recession of the mid-1970s and thereafter heralded a growing concern with adjustment problems and a diffusion of protectionist sentiment. To counter the spread of import restricting measures and to grapple with the problem of factor immobility, attention has been focused on the feasibility of instituting appropriate trade adjustment assistance schemes. It has been argued that such schemes could contribute towards an improved allocation of resources while compensating those injured in the process. Such an argument, however, raises a number of issues. If structural changes displace labour and if the mobility of factors is impeded, should not the government adopt general measures to stimulate aggregate employment and remedy market imperfections, rather than create *ad hoc* agencies or programmes? Furthermore, why should workers in import competing sectors specifically be assisted, when a multitude of others, on account of technological progress, changes in market conditions or shifts in government policy, lose jobs?

While not questioning the desirability of maintaining broad policies to minimise any upheavals that might arise throughout the economy at large, advocates of trade adjustment schemes contend that, in the absence of effective measures, there are cogent reasons why import injured workers merit special attention. In comparing the plight of workers made redundant by changes in technology and by changes in tariffs, it might well be that those in the latter category are more regionally or industrially concentrated, and that their injuries (which follow a change of government policy) are imposed more abruptly. Technological changes, by contrast, are often more gradual and can in some circumstances be phased in (as a result of trade union negotiations) to lessen disruptions. They constitute an organic part of the growth process, they are not necessarily induced by governments and,

118

in any case, they usually provide alternative employment within new industries.[1] However, the essential difference between technological and general market changes on the one hand, and changes in imports on the other, is that in the main, changes of the first category are not amenable to pressure group manipulations.[2] If those adversely affected by technological improvements, lack the means to frustrate them, they need not be bribed to accept such changes. By contrast, since participants in import competing industries frequently possess sufficient political leverage to impede imports, it may be socially desirable to compensate them for any losses sustained, provided the net social benefits of increased imports are positive. Such expediency may accord not only with the dictates of practicality but also with equity and efficiency considerations. Industries most likely to be injured by foreign competitors, especially from LDCs, are frequently ones in which women and the elderly are disproportionately represented and which employ an abnormally high percentage of low paid, unskilled workers. They are often sited in areas offering limited job alternatives and, accordingly, they generally manifest chronically severe adjustment problems. These occur partly because married women workers generally cannot consider job offers entailing a change of residence, and similarly, because the elderly who are less prone (considering that seniority and pension rights may be at stake) and less able to seek new careers, experience difficulties in securing mortgages with reasonable instalments in alternative localities.[3] Generally, workers leaving depressed regions are likely to incur capital losses in disposing of their houses in a buyer's market, as well as possibly also experiencing capital losses resulting from a decreased demand for industry specific skills.

Taking the above points into account, it is believed that a prima facie case exists for trade adjustment schemes. Periodically, calls are made for the establishment of an international adjustment code,[4] and as of late, the ministerial members of the OECD council have emphasised their determination to 'pursue policies facilitating positive adjustment to structural changes in demand and production in the world economy to avoid protectionist measures'.[5]

This chapter attempts to evaluate whether, and in what circumstances, trade adjustment programmes are worth pursuing. To achieve this objective, as well as to provide readers with some scope in formulating judgements of their own, the experience of three OECD countries which have introduced such schemes is summarised. This is followed by a review of other measures generally undertaken in assisting industries or in facilitating resource mobility. Finally, an overall assessment of the issues is presented.

Trade Adjustment Assistance in the US

The United States' trade adjustment programme was initiated in 1962 under the Trade Expansion Act, which provided assistance to workers or firms injured by import competition, regardless of foreign source or industry. To qualify, the aggrieved had to establish that imports had been increasing, mainly as a result of previous tariff concessions, and that the increased imports were the major cause of injury. These conditions were quite stringent. If trade concessions originated in years past, it could be argued, as some officials have, that they should be treated as being 'part of the totality of market conditions'[6] and not be recognised as a significant import determinant. Although this view has some merit, it could rebound against claimants indeed harmed by concessions whose effects are felt over a lengthy period. Fortunately, in 1969, the majority of the Tariff Commission (the adjudicating body for the assistance scheme) ruled that it was enough simply to question whether except for concessions, imports could have reached, substantially, their current levels. Proving that imports were the major cause of injury was also no simple matter, especially since it had to be shown that imports exerted not only the largest influence but one greater than all other factors combined.

The procedure for obtaining redress was daunting. Appeals on behalf of an entire industry, for a finding of injury, were to be directed to the Tariff Commission and, if successful, the president could either increase import duties or authorise applications for adjustment assistance, or both. Alternatively, individuals could petition the Tariff Commission for aid and obtain a decision within 60 days. If it were positive, workers could request a certificate of eligibility from the Department of Labor, firms from the Department of Commcere. To be eligible, workers must have had employment for at least 78 weeks in the three years prior to the impact date, and must have served for at least 26 weeks in the preceding year in an adversely affected enterprise. Firms could claim assistance only after having submitted proposals for the adaptations they wished to make and after it had been established that no agency, other than the Department of Commerce, was prepared to provide the financial and technical assistance sought.

A variety of aid measures were available; for firms they consisted of technical advice in relation to production and marketing problems, financial support by way of direct government loans or 90 per cent loan guarantees and tax relief in permitting losses to be carried forward for five years, rather than three. Workers when out of work in a two year period after first becoming unemployed, were entitled to a trade adjustment allowance equal to either 65 per cent of their previous salaries or 65 per cent of the average manufacturing wage, whichever was less. This allowance could be drawn over no more than 52 (not necessarily consecutive) weeks or 65 weeks for those over 60 years of age.[7] If enrolled in an approved training scheme, an extra 26 weeks' allowance was provided. In addition, family heads who received firm job offers in other districts, could obtain relocation subsidies, while all had access to the testing, counselling, placement and training facilities generally available, there being no specific programmes for trade impacted workers.

At first, the number of petitioners achieving certification and assistance was extremely limited, partly because the Kennedy Round Tariff Reductions only began to be effected in 1968 and, as implied above, the trade commissioners initially interpreted the act's stipulations rather narrowly. Between October 1962 and November 1969 all 26 of the petitions submitted were denied; thereafter, between December 1969 and April 1975, approximately 54,000 workers were certified of whom close to 35,000 actually received benefits.[8] In 1974, the Trade Expansion Act was superseded by the less rigid and more accommodating Trade Act, which took effect in April 1975. Under the new law, workers are entitled to benefits if they become unemployed, and firms, if sales decline both on account of import increases (not necessarily due to tariff cuts) of like or directly competitive items contributing importantly to such injuries.[9] Displaced workers are now eligible for the lesser of 70 per cent of their previous salaries or 70 per cent of the average weekly manufacturing wage. A job search allowance of up to $500 has been introduced as well as adjustment assistance programmes for entire communities. To expedite claims, applications are no longer vetted by the Tariff Commission (renamed the International Trade Commission) but by the Secretaries of Labor (for workers) and Commerce (for firms).

The extent to which aid has been dispensed is in dispute. Williams indicated that within the first two year lifespan of the 1974 Act, a total of 209,075 workers were granted assistance[10] while Bale declared that 'from January 1975, when the act became law, until July 31, 1976, 435,000 workers have received trade adjustment allowances' and that 'clearly, under the new act workers beset by import-inspired displacement are receiving relief'.[11] This assertion is at odds with those of trade union spokesmen for 'Elizabeth Jager of the AFL-CIO reported that, after one and a half years of operation (of the 1974 Act), half a million workers had applied for relief but only 153,000 had received anything at all'.[12] Similarly, Finley who in dealing with beneficiaries under the initial act, complained that only an eighth of those seeking help received any and that the trade adjustment scheme was 'in fact a band-aid program, and a small one at that'.[13]

Studies analysing the adjustment experience of trade displaced workers and the impact of adjustment programmes on their ability to regain employment, have thrown light on the usefulness of the US programmes.[14] They indicate that in general, men have been able to adapt more easily than women by finding work more quickly and subsequently obtaining higher real wages than they had previously enjoyed. Women by contrast, when ultimately placed, encountered reductions in real wages. Case histories of those receiving assistance differed somewhat to those who hadn't. On the one hand, 'workers who received counselling, job testing, and training experienced longer durations of unemployment and found lower paying employment than those workers who did not receive benefits'.[15] Such a paradox is explained by the fact that 'the time lag between a worker being displaced and receiving assistance was so long (averaging 55 weeks) that the better qualified or more employable worker did not wait for these services' but sought and gained posts without them.[16] On the other hand, on the basis of a comparison of two particular shoe factories, where workers in one received assistance unusually promptly, the conclusion was reached that 'the expeditious delivery of adjustment benefits to trade displaced workers contributes to their rehabilitation'.[17] Ironically, workers so aided were unemployed for longer periods[18] but since they ultimately landed jobs offering higher wages than those obtained by otherwise equivalent trade displaced workers, it can be argued that timely (and of course substantive) benefits, permit recipients to undertake longer and more rewarding job searches. When workers were classified into sexual categories, empirical findings suggest that trade adjustment allowances had 'limited effect on the reemployment of females',[19] however, on further subdividing women on the basis of marital status, single women appeared to respond in much the same way as did men. Many married women 'did not search for a job while unemployed'[20] (their benefits serving merely as income compensation); for being constrained not to search further afield, because of family commitments, they may correctly have perceived a lack of local job opportunities.

The general effectiveness of trade adjustment assistance in the US has been marred by cumbersome bureaucratic processes. There has been widespread ignorance of the benefits available, with more than 60 per cent of potentially eligible claimants at one time being 'unaware of the training, placement and relocation aspects' of the programme.[21] Trade injured workers are not automatically notified of their entitlements and of the procedures to be taken to effect their claims, which is not altogether surprising, considering that many government service field officers have themselves not known how to handle petitions.[22] When first introduced, trade adjustment benefits exceeded normal unemployment allowances.[23] For this reason and to avoid 'entering into a limitless budgetary commitment',[24] the eligibility criteria were drafted to cover a narrowly defined range of potential applicants, which resulted in what was described by Frank as 'a classic case of legal requirements designed to prevent abuse reducing the effectiveness of the measures authorized by law'.[25] The primary purpose of both the 1962 and 1974 trade acts was to authorise US negotiations in the Kennedy and Tokyo GATT rounds. Considering that, assistance has not subsequently been widely disseminated, for example, by June 1978 only 62 firms (mostly in textiles, footwear and stainless steel flatware) had received loans or loan guarantees,[26] one might well conclude, that adjustment assistance provisions were inserted in both acts as a face saving formula to appease those opposing tariff concessions, rather than with any serious intent of significantly facilitating resource mobility or compensating trade impacted parties.

Trade Adjustment Assistance in Canada

Canadian adjustment assistance programmes embody both general and industry specific schemes. The special industry arrangements which apply to automobiles, and textiles and clothing, will be described later.

In December 1967, the General Adjustment Assistance Program (GAAP), was launched. It was designed to assist firms which, as a result of Kennedy Round tariff reductions, were either adversely affected by import competition or those which wished to capitalise on new export opportunities. The benefits consisted of a 90 per cent government guarantee on privately raised loans or the direct provision, in special circumstances, of public lending. Aid was confined to firms without access to alternative finance and was subject to the submission and approval of plans detailing viable adjustment projects.[27] Unfortunately, import competing firms were not required to shift from products in which Canada had a comparative disadvantage. On the contrary, much emphasis was 'placed on the reorganization and reequipment of companies to compete more effectively' within existing product lines.[28] In practice, since the tariff reductions realised were initially quite modest, and imposed little hardship on import competitors, the scheme's beneficiaries at first turned out to be exporters, who between 1968 and 1971 obtained all the loans the GAAP board authorised. From 1971, coverage was widened to include manufacturers who wished to restructure their plants to improve their international competitiveness, who perceived new opportunities to participate in international trade or who wished to adapt to disruptive import inflows, there no longer being any required link between prior trade concessions and injuries sustained.

The GAAP catered for workers, only in the sense that to be entitled to assistance, firms laying off 20 or more employees were required to serve them with three months' notice. Apart from that, trade displaced workers obtained the same services as the other unemployed which, in addition to maintenance allowances, included travel subsidies for job searches and grants to help meet relocation expenses. It should be realised that the GAAP is but one component of a general strategy to provide incentives and development stimuli to Canadian industry. For instance, the Department of Regional Economic Expansion provides financial assistance to firms proposing to establish or expand production in less developed regions, and conceivably appropriate enterprises adversely affected by trade could call upon it.

Recently, 'there has been a growing concern that the programs were not meeting their objectives',[29] and 'have not significantly satisfied demands for special protection'.[30] The GAAP's lack of adequate provision for workers, an absence of any abandonment compensation for firms and the government's readiness to assist inefficient enterprises to withstand foreign competition, have provoked a call for the establishment of an industrial adjustment and redeployment fund to help shift the country's 'industrial structure away from highly protected, labour-intensive, and standard-technology activities'.[31] It is suggested that the fund's proposed disbursements of $4 billion over 15 years, be accompanied by a progressive dismantling of import quotas and other trade constraints, whenever low levels of unemployment prevail. Since an overwhelming majority of workers who are particularly vulnerable to competitive pressures from newly industrialising LDCs, reside in Quebec,[32] an effective Canadian trade adjustment programme would obviously have to incorporate appropriate regional policies.

Trade Adjustment Assistance in Australia

Australian enterprise has long been inured to protection. In the mid-1960s, something like 60 to 70 per cent of manufacturing (measured by output values and employment) were dependent on tariffs,[33] with a similar situation continuing in the 1970s, when in 1974-5, nearly 50 per cent of the manufacturing workforce 'were employed directly or indirectly by highly protected industries'.[34] In view of a general resistance of manufacturers to tariff cuts and of administrators' supposed reluctance to concede them, it may be somewhat surprising to note that the Australian government in July 1973, announced a unilateral tariff reduction of 25 per cent across all goods. The reduction, made when the economy was particularly buoyant, was primarily motivated to combat inflation and to ease local resource shortages. Employment was expected to fall by no more than 33,000 as a result of a predicted import increase of $400 million[35] and only minor problems were anticipated. In fact, in the 12 months or so following the reduction, there was very little dislocation 'in view of the generally high level of demand in all sectors of the economy'.[36]

When the 25 per cent tariff cut was introduced, it was accompanied by an interim adjustment assistance programme, administered by a one man tribunal. In April 1974, a permanent Special Adjustment Assistance (SAA) programme was formulated 'to promote and ease the process of desirable change'.[37] Assistance was available to firms and workers directly hurt on account of government actions (not necessarily trade related ones), provided the actions in question were officially prescribed. Guidelines for prescription suggest that they should encompass the policy measures likely to stimulate beneficial structural change that are also prone to affect, adversely, components of the economy which cannot secure adequate compensation from generally available channels. The following government actions were prescribed: the 25 per cent tariff cut, tariff decisions in connection with consumer electronic equipment and components, domestic appliances and woven manmade fibre fabrics, the lifting of import quotas on woven shirts and knitted outwear, the reduction of subsidies to shipbuilders, actions involving dairy industry adjustments, the passenger and motor vehicle and components decision and the removal of sales tax exemption on aerated waters.

Workers, self employed or small scale employers falling under a prescribed category, could apply for income maintenance (usually within 12 months of the announced prescription) provided they became unemployed as a result of the policy change in question.[38] The income maintenance available was equal to the recipient's average non-overtime earnings over the preceding six months, subject to a ceiling of one and a half times the national average wage. Payments were made for up to six months, and if in that period lower paid employment was secured, wages were supplemented to help maintain previous standards. A firm was eligible for aid if a prescribed change rendered a significant part of its assets incapable of economic production or if lacking the financial wherewithal, it was incapable, without assistance, of expeditiously effecting desired modifications. Benefits consisted of a closure compensation equal to 85 per cent of the difference between the declared value of a firm's assets for taxation purposes and their realised sales value, 50 per cent of the costs of acquiring technical consultative services (up to a maximum of $10,000) and 90 per cent loan guarantees for undertaking adjustments consistent with government policy.

As an adjunct to the SAA, a supplementary scheme, the Special Assistance for Non-Metropolitan Areas (SANMA) was introduced to enable small town manufacturers affected by prescribed actions to sustain (or phase out gently) existing production and employment levels. To qualify, firms had to be significantly large local employers and had to undertake where possible, appropriate restructuring. From 1974-5 to 1975-6, $5.1 million, constituting SANMA's sum total of funds, were allotted for employment subsidies, while the benefits distributed under SAA consisted of $59.4 million for individual income maintenance and $1.2 million for firm closure compensation.[39] Thereafter, no further payments were made under SANMA. In 1976-7, SAA's budget declined to less than $0.5 million, finally winding down to a figure of $97,000 in 1977-8, for after 30 June, 1976, applications for assistance were no longer accepted. Because of ultimately large increases in aggregate unemployment which generated mounting dissatisfaction with the efficiency and equity aspects of the schemes, and because of the government's decision to reimpose import quotas to sustain output in 'sensitive' industries, both adjustment programmes were permanently suspended.

Criticism of the programme was widespread. Decisions to prescribe particular injurious government actions appeared quite arbitrary. Apart from covering various categories of import displaced workers, groups such as those in the dairy industry (following the abolition of free school milk) were included while others effectively unemployed in part because of government policies, were not. In some cases job losses could ultimately be attributed to the same cause but only those directly involved were assisted. Conceivably this could be justified on the grounds of a political need to 'bribe' those in the front line to accommodate socially desirable changes but no such rationalisations were proffered. Indeed, by 'compensating' people a year or two after actions were taken, the government ruled out the possibility of such reasoning being accepted. Invidious comparisons between the weekly $36 single normal unemployment benefit and the 100 per cent income maintenance allowance (averaging $97 per week)[40] accruing to prescribed workers, fostered resentment against what was perceived to be an unnecessarily privileged class of welfare beneficiaries. The scheme was also open to abuse, in that it was technically possible for a firm within a prescribed group, to release excess manpower caused by say internal rationalisation, under the guise of dismissing workers in response to adverse government measures.

The SAA programme was supposed to ease structural change but, unfortunately, it was implemented some 14 months after many of the policy decisions affecting resource allocations were taken, and at a time when the economic environment had deteriorated. In the new circumstances, 'Government policy had shifted to the provision of temporary assistance to maintain employment', and 'in this setting, the programs could not work as intended'.[41] They served merely as sources of compensation without providing incentives for resource transfers. Grants for company technical consultations were not made and no loans to stimulate restructuring were authorised. The SANMA programme was recognised as being helpful in sustaining country area employment but it did little to further adaptation to change.[42] Firms and workers lost confidence in the ability of both schemes to avert or mitigate massive disruptions and the Australian public have since shown little interest in reactivating them.

An Evaluation of the US, Canadian and Australian Schemes

None of the three schemes so far summarised has succeeded in placating opposition to free trade, for they have provided neither workers nor firms with sufficient cause to prefer adjustment assistance to protection.[43] From a firm's point of view, the 'bribe' component has generally been inconsequential. Closure compensation has not been available in the US and Canada and even though such payments were made in Australia, they naturally only partially compensated firms that went to the wall, and not those surviving, albeit at diminished profitability. What tends to be overlooked, is that firms capable of withstanding foreign competition and which would endure in a free trade situation would, as a result of tariff cuts, still experience losses in terms of curtailed rents. From an efficiency or even equity standpoint, there is no need for such losses to be socialised but by the same token, it would be in the firm's interests to resist measures causing them. Where firms are eligible to apply for assistance, be it in the form of guaranteed loans or consulting subsidies, etc., they are liable to become entangled with officialdom. Their operations are open to investigation and possibly regulation. Given most firms' hostility to government intervention (at least within their own enterprises), such involvements are viewed with misgiving. These reservations have been reinforced by tardy bureaucratic responses in terms of inordinate delays in processing claims, as well as by the actual uncertainty of ever receiving assistance (especially in Australia where specific government precription was a prerequisite). As for workers, the Canadian scheme accorded them no financial allocation, and in the US and Australia those indirectly affected by imports or prescribed actions were not covered.[44] While income maintenance payments exceeded unemployment benefits, only those able to obtain alternative jobs with no long-term salary cuts experienced minimal welfare losses. The more chronically unemployed by contrast, were not sufficiently compensated and more likely than not would have preferred the previous job security that protection appeared to afford them. Finally, considering that the governments of all three countries are anxious to prune public expenditures as vigorously as possible, it would seem that they too have a vested interest in preferring the continuation of protection to the establishment of adjustment assistance schemes, for the former usually contributes to fiscal revenue while the latter tends to detract from it.

Typically, European governments have shunned trade adjustment programmes, claiming that in establishing a battery of facilities to cope with unemployment, regional problems, labour retraining, assistance to small enterprises, etc. they have not only buttressed the market mechanism but have also prepared a safety net for workers and firms dislocated by structural changes originating from any cause.[45] Some of the measures adopted are mentioned below.

General Measures Assisting Adjustments

Within the broad confines of the EEC, a social fund established by the Treaty of Rome provides member states with finance to alleviate economic disruptions caused by the mutual integration of their economies. Assistance is available to enable workers to undergo retraining and/or to resettle in more job promising localities. Unemployed workers receiving retraining have been eligible for 80-100 per cent of their previous annual wages while those re-engaged (after retraining) at lower wage rates, could claim compensation for up to a two year period. Each country has been responsible for organising its own projects for which the fund has contributed 50 per cent of costs. Between 1960 and 1972, over 1½ million workers, mainly in Italy, Germany and France, were aided, 879,000 having been retrained and 712,000 resettled.[46] Although the 'fund has never had enough financial resources to meet all the demands put upon it',[47] it has, through its aid to displaced labour, 'had a favourable influence on the EEC member states' import policies by avoiding social troubles that otherwise could have arisen'.[48]

In terms of providing a useful package of complementary facilities to ease the shocks of economic change, Sweden is a front runner, offering under the direction of its national Labour Board, the following: travel allowances for job interviews and resettlement, a lump sum 'starting help' grant, separation allowances in the event of a family not immediately being able to accompany its main breadwinner to a new locality, government house purchases in depressed areas where an inabiltity to sell would hinder migration, the provision of dwellings where jobs are available but housing scarce and, finally, retraining allowances. Furthermore, large scale employers are required by law to provide their employees with at least three months' notice to quit.

Similarly, workers in the UK are also legally entitled to advanced dismissal notices ranging from one to eight weeks depending on the length of years served. Those with two or more years of service are entitled to severance allowances varying with age and duration of employment. The allowances are partly financed through a government controlled redundancy fund, to which employers are obliged to contribute. To aid labour mobility, the Employment Transfer Scheme provides a rehousing grant of £400 as well as travel costs and living away expenses incurred during job searches.

In addition to the above outlined measures, which are replicated in varying degrees in other OECD countries, schemes tailored to the exigencies of particular industries could on occasion be appropriate. For one, 'if programs are limited to specific industries it becomes less necessary to establish elaborate rules for determining the eligibility of individuals' and for another, 'it may be possible to provide assistance to all firms and workers who need it in certain industries, without entering a more or less unlimited financial commitment'.[49] Alternatively, as Frank has argued, it might be that 'separate programs result in duplication of efforts and a welter of different standards for assistance that in themselves are not equitable'.[50] An example of a positive and successful industry specific programme is provided by the Canadian-American Automobile Pact.[51]

Adjustment Under the Canadian–American Automobile Pact

In 1965, the United States and Canada signed an Automobile Products Trade Agreement under whose terms US automobile corporations were to expand the scale of their Canadian operations. The fulfilment of this requirement was made economically feasible, since the agreement provided for the free trade of new automobiles and components among producers, which resulted in lower Canadian production costs.[52] Since the application of the Pact explicitly entailed industry reorganisation, the co-operation of US automobile workers was elicited by the enabling legislation, the Automotive Products Trade Act, which provided for an Automotive Agreement Adjustment Assistance Scheme, administered by its own board. Benefits were equivalent to those under the 1962 Trade Expansion Act but eligibility criteria were much less demanding. Workers were entitled to aid if their firms were dislocated on account of the Automotive Pact, with dislocation being deemed to have occured if a firm's production declined whenever automotive imports increased from or exports decreased to Canada.[53] Casual ties between dislocation and changes in trade were not required to be established. Since the scheme was focused on a few firms in a one union industry, its adjustment board could utilise data accumulated from preceding hearings. This advantage, coupled with the fact that conditions for obtaining aid were relatively easy to satisfy, enabled claims to be promptly processed and from most applicants' perspective, positively resolved. By 1969, in contrast to the complete failure of trade impacted workers to obtain benefits under the general adjustment programme, 1,950 displaced automotive employees had been granted awards totalling approximately $4 million.[54]

In Canada, disruption was feared by automotive product manufacturers who were independent of US corporations. To mollify them, an Adjustment Assistance Board was established to authorise loans to firms, if as a result of the Automobile Pact they encountered adverse production shifts, or if in order to remain competitive, they deemed it necessary to expand and re-equip their plants. Loans were issued subject to a manufacturer having a 'reasonable prospect of a profitable operation',[55] and not having access to alternative financial sources. By 1971, close to \$94 million were lent. Employees were aided, regardless of whether they worked for Canadian or US controlled companies, if as a result of the trade agreement, 10 per cent of a firm's workforce or 50 workers were laid off, in excess of a four week period. Compensation varied in duration and extent, according to the number of a worker's dependents and time served in the automobile industry. If enrolled in an approved training programme, workers could claim assistance, which ranged from 62 to 75 per cent of previous wages, for up to one and a half years.

In both countries, the assistance provided was regarded as reasonable and adequate and tended to moderate opposition to the industry restructuring that was induced by the trade agreement. Unfortunately, a number of other industry specific schemes, ostensibly engineered to provide an appropriate response to the changing international environment, have in practice retarded movements towards free trade and can be regarded as yielding negative adjustment assistance in the sense of having inhibited resource outflows from uncompetitive sectors. This is best exemplified by the arrangements widely made in clothing and textile industries.

Negative Adjustments and the Clothing and Textile Industries

Within advanced countries the labour intensive textile and clothing industries generally threatened by LDC exports, tend to clamour for tighter import controls and for some kind of 'adjustment' programme explicitly designed to guarantee their viability. Typically, investments are undertaken to increase the capital intensity of their production processes[56] and, as in the UK, small and inefficient firms have, with government backing, been weeded out to place the industries on a footing, where they 'could compete with success in the markets of the world'.[57] Practically every industrial country has some policy for perpetuation of their clothing and textile industries in the face of adverse foreign competition. To highlight the differences in scope and operation of these policies, those of Canada and Australia are contrasted.

Adjustment Assistance to the Canadian Clothing and Textile Industries

In keeping with the Canadian government's intention of arresting a decline of the clothing and textile industry, as a result of rising imports, the 1971 Textile and Clothing Board Act was passed. The legislation provided for an independent Textile and Clothing Board to inquire whether injuries were being sustained or threatened in the industries in question, and to assess whether requests for import restrictions were warranted. All such requests had to be accompanied by plans indicating measures that firms would adopt to attain long-term viability. Apart from market intrusions by foreigners in determining the existence of an injury, the Board has tended to take account of factors such as adverse charges in: inventories, capacity utilisation, profits, domestic prices and market growth.[58] In gauging the likelihood of firms ultimately achieving international competitiveness, matters such as prospective wage changes and price levels in the exporting countries, the potential for scale economies, market segmentation and product specialisation, the degree of capital intensity and the prospect of technological change in Canada, have variously been considered.[59] However, realising that firms withdrawing from the industry are not compensated, the Board has been 'tempted to be overly generous when examining the long-term viability of their operations and the acceptability of their individual plans'.[60] Accordingly, negative employment growth rates were reversed, with the number of employed in textiles and knitting mills rising between 1971 and 1976, from 87,000 to 92,000, and those in clothing from 95,000 to 102,000.[61]

Although the scheme tended to entrench the textile and clothing industries, as was its main purpose, it was not bereft of positive aspects. Protection was to be terminated once adjustment plans were implemented or if the time schedules for modifications were not met. The Board's investigations were, in the main, publicly conducted, consumer interests were nominally considered, and the protective restraints 'have almost all been closely circumscribed as to product, class and country'.[62] Unfortunately, arrangements with regard to these industries in Australia exhibit even less redeeeming features, demonstrating the pitfalls of sustaining continued protection in the absence of even token efforts to effect industry adjustments.

Protection of the Australian Clothing, Footwear and Textile Industries

The Australian clothing, footwear and textile industries predominantly employ unskilled workers at low wage rates and at low levels of productivity. Nearly 70 per cent of all their employees are women. During 1973-4, these industries experienced setbacks as a result of the 25 per cent tariff cut, the Australian dollar revaluation, rapid wage escalation (especially for females)[63] and a general increase in unemployment. The government initially responded to the industries' plight, by imposing quotas on imported items that were most competitive with local products. Shortly thereafter import restrictions were generally extended, raising, between 1973-4 and 1976-7, the nominal rates of assistance (expressed as a percentage of output valued in unassisted prices) from 36 per cent to 62 per cent for clothing and footwear and from 19 per cent to 24 per cent for textiles.[64] In 1977, the Industries Assistance Commission (IAC) argued that since stated government policy was to encourage 'development in activities which have the best prospect for expansion without the need for excessive support from consumers and taxpayers',[65] and since the clothing, footwear and textile industries 'had little scope for improving their competitiveness against imports',[66] assistance to them should substantially be reduced. In response, the government retorted that recommendations of that kind generated undue uncertainty in the industries in question and that it was determined to preserve them 'as efficient industries with an essentially permanent character'.[67] Accordingly, the government then decided on a continuation of import quotas up to mid-1980, in order to maintain, as far as possible the mid-1977 levels of activity and employment. Although firms were in the interim expected 'to improve their structure and efficiency',[68] they were provided with no incentives to do so. On the contrary, firms entertained expectations that high levels of assistance would continue throughout the 1980s.[69] As a result, by 1979, 1977 employment levels had endured and production had increased by 9 per cent,[70] with the average Australian household bearing $235 towards the cost of protecting those industries.[71]

Interestingly, there appears to be a higher proportion of youth in the clothing and footwear industries than for manufacturing as a whole. Whereas in 1978 males and females between 15-19 years of age constituted 9.9 per cent and 11.2 per cent of the total manufacturing workforce, the corresponding percentages in clothing were 10.6 per cent and 14.6 per cent and in footwear 15.1 per cent and 16.0 per cent. This trend is particularly disheartening since young people are disproportionately drawn into those low productivity industries, which objectively should be declining.

In 1980, the IAC once again called for a relaxation of import controls. It pleaded for modest reductions over a 5-year period which would involve annual rates of output decreases of 3 per cent to 4 per cent. Such cutbacks were expected to displace (over the five years) 11,500 workers, *a number in keeping with anticipated losses due to normal attrition* following retirements and voluntary withdrawals. The Commission indicated that its recommended import quota increases were 'chosen to ensure that the associated annual rates of output and employment can be accommodated without undue disruption',[72] and that if the industries are seriously to begin adjusting to the changing international environment, 'they should be given a clear indication by the government that excessively high assistance will not be provided in the longer term'.[73] As before, the government reacted by declaring in remarkably similar language to that used in its 1977 statement, that it would not expose the industries 'to the uncertainty that would result from full implementation of the IAC's recommendations'.[74] To eliminate this 'uncertainty', protection, largely in its present form, is to be continued until December 1988. A cynic might well deduce that any 'uncertainty' that might then be felt by the end of the decade, would once again be allayed by extending import restrictions further into the time horizon.

The Australian experience represents the worst in negative adjustment, for in this instance, the industries have not been induced to rationalise, scrap obsolete plants or prepare in any meaningful way for an eventual liberalisation of trade restrictions. Economic grounds for continuing existing high protection levels appear to be tenuous. The industries are not excessively concentrated in chronically depressed localities or regions. In 1977–8, only 11 per cent of clothing and footwear workers were in non-metropolitan areas as were 26.3 per cent of textile workers, compared with 20 per cent for all manufacturing. In a handful of non-metropolitan regions, these industries are *relatively* large employers but that does not seem to warrant *national* protection, particularly when these cases constitute a small ratio of the three industries as a whole.

Labour turnover rates are higher in the textile, clothing and footwear industries than for all industries, the respective figures being 8 and

6.4 per 100.[75] In addition, the three industries employ a disproportionate number of migrants, for example, 54 per cent of clothing workers are migrants as opposed to 39 per cent for the manufacturing workforce as a whole.[76] These observations suggest that these industries have above average recruitment problems. Similar observations have been noted elsewhere. As far back as 1968, 14 per cent of the female labour force in the German textile industry were foreigners.[77] In Holland it had been found that 'even in regions with a high unemployment rate, the Dutch clothing industry has been forced to attract foreign workers',[78] and in Canada, where turnover rates are 'habitually well above average', half of the female employees in the Montreal garment industry were immigrants.[79] Given the difficulties that these industries face in acquiring and retaining manpower, it is quite possible that, in this area, labour pressures are not as decisive in fostering protection as is often assumed. In these and perhaps certain other industries, the political leverage of employers may be more significant, which may partly explain why adjustment schemes ignoring the grievances of capital are no match for outright protection.[80] Whatever the case, to be effective, trade adjustment programmes must be devised to take account of all circumstances relevant to a specific industry or to the import sector as a whole.

Issues in Easing the Adjustment Process

Ideally, an adjustment programme should be relatively efficient in maximising resource transfers per unit of expenditure, subject to its meeting basic equity objectives. Although on account of differences among countries in regard to industrial and trade union structures, regional imbalances, the extent of state intervention, the functioning of market mechanisms, etc., an appropriate universally applicable scheme is unlikely to be devised, certain common problems and issues prevail. One is the question of timing, in terms of both when and of what duration, adjustment assistance should be provided. A period of full employment is generally regarded as an appropriate occasion to effect adjustments, since it is commonly assumed that within buoyant economies, resources released by inefficient industries are readily redeployed in more resilient ones. However, even in circumstances of feverish economic activity, there may be factors which inhibit restructuring. For instance, excessively large demand increases for import competing products may temporarily lock into those industries, production factors required elsewhere.[81] On the other hand, recessions afford an economy the opportunity of permanently winding down uncompetitive industries and placing larger quantities of inputs at the disposal of more dynamic ones. If import restrictions are used to bolster aggregate employment, the burden of a recession is shifted to the more competitive sectors, putting an economy in danger of ultimately emerging from its recession with archaic structures, giving rise to physical bottlenecks, skill shortages, inflation and possibly an abortive recovery. 'Even under conditions of slow growth, new jobs are continually being created', and where those jobs are created will depend in part on where resources are available.[82] New England has frequently been cited as a case in point. During the 1960s the region divested itself[83] of a large proportion of its traditional clothing and textile industries, even though its unemployment rate exceeded the national one. Nowadays, with a lower unemployment rate than the US average, 'the region appears, in fact to be enjoying a small boom almost by itself. Why then is the region doing so well? A principal reason is that the long shakeout of defunct industries seems at last to be over, and New England is now a relatively clean state. Those industries which have survived or arrived are those best suited to do so.'[84] As for the duration of adjustments, a long period has the joint advantage of minimising capital losses, since premature depreciation is avoided, and of allowing older workers to phase out into normal retirement. Against this, a long period nourishes hope that future import penetrations can be thwarted by increasing an industry's capital intensity.

The complete demise of existing import competing industries is not necessarily warranted, for even in say textiles and clothing, scope exists for efficient intra-industry trade, in which the developed countries could maintain advantages in items where quality and local fashions dominate. Nevertheless, handouts should not serve as aid to enable firms to re-adjust in order to withstand imports, for the natural survivors should be capable of fending for themselves. However, a conflict might arise between satisfying re-allocation and compensation objectives, for as indicated above, if programmes are premised on the need to 'bribe' the potentially injured, then even efficient firms should be included. This dilemma may partly be resolved by retracting compensation from firms that proceed over a given interval, to increase investments in the industries in question. In connection with this problem, the definition of an injured party is of significance. Murray and Egmund have indicated that it is possible to consider for assistance purposes, three subsets of a firm; a component of one of its plants, an entire plant and the entire firm.[85] If the government's primary consideration is to facilitate resource allocation, then only an injury sustained by the entire firm need be redressed, for if smaller subsets are harmed and not the firm as a whole, then the firm would normally itself bear all adjustment costs. Where the intent of politicians 'includes the prevention of economic hardships of a region', then eligibility should operate at the plant level, and where the primary goal 'is to reduce or eliminate domestic resistance to freer trade, the narrow definition (i.e. section of plant) may be appropriate'. Problems also arise in dispensing benefits to workers. Excessively generous compensation may provide workers with a disincentive to seek alternative employment until the payments expire, while meagre grants may not muffle resistance to change. The provision of payments in one lump sum would eliminate job search disincentives but at the cost of some inequity in that it would discriminate in favour of more able workers who would regain employment relatively quickly.

A notion which has had some currency, is that a system of early warnings should be established to provide firms with advance notice of impending injuries. As a corollary, governments are exhorted to 'pick the winners'[86] and to groom chosen sectors for future growth. However, there is no basis for assuming that government bureaucrats possess more prescience than private entrepreneurs, and if favoured sectors do not live up to expectations, they may inadvertently continue to receive public assistance, at least for the medium term.

A proposal for reducing protection while satisfying the welfare proposition that gainers should compensate losers, has been advanced by Stewart.[87] Basically, she favours the substitution of temporary and specific sales taxes in place of trade restrictions, with the former being set at rates 'lower than the difference in price between the home-produced goods and the imported items, so that the consumers of the items still gain something'.[88] The sales taxes' proceeds should be forwarded to the trade impacted parties to enable them to vacate the injured industries with minimum hardship. Stewart feels that once the sales taxes and allied redistributions are operative, the industries involved should no longer receive special protection of any kind. Unfortunately, there may be some industries that, in the wake of a sudden and complete removal of import barriers, encounter immediate setbacks of so large a magnitude, that the sales tax revenues would not nearly suffice to compensate the losers.[89] In these cases some form of temporary although diminished protection may be warranted. A specific sales tax has of course the disadvantage of needlessly maintaining (although in this case admittedly for only a limited period) a price distortion, and where the good is in any event purchased by the general population, the use of direct taxes may be preferable. None the less, it may be politically expedient to raise the compensation funds through a system of sales taxes, on the grounds that consumers in the industries concerned, are accustomed to price surcharges and the sales taxes could be set to effect post protection price reductions.

Conclusions

Ideally, it might be best to eliminate the market imperfections causing resource immobility but in practice, trade adjustment schemes present themselves as useful second best instruments, even though there is the danger of their degenerating into social insurance programmes for the inefficient. In some countries, such as Canada and Australia, where movements towards freer trade could initially result in an increase in aggregate unemployment,[90] schemes to help redirect workers to possibly non-existent jobs, would be inadequate, unless appropriate general industrial restructuring is fostered either by direct government involvement or through the provision of suitable economic incentives and stimuli.

In their role of neutralising political opposition to freer trade, the trade adjustment schemes hitherto adopted have not met with unqualified success. An approach which might be worth considering is one which attempts to depoliticise the tariff making process. Independent judicial agencies could be established to adjudicate upon tariff matters, with submissions being presented by the industries and consumers involved, as well as by representatives of the government, in much the same way as wage decisions are determined in the Australian Industrial Court. The government would naturally determine the general guidelines to be followed but if adjudicators were then given free rein, the government would no longer bear any political odium for decisions adversely relating to particular industries or groups. In this regard, internationally negotiated guidelines could apply, enabling countries to maintain, within the framework of GATT, common tariff and trade agreements. To protect groups from excessive injury, temporary safeguards, i.e. temporary protection, should be accorded even though the tariff authority might have ruled for a widening of trade. However, the safeguard should be permitted to operate only when a trigger level of *relative* sectoral unemployment is reached and it should clearly be temporary, say for no longer than two to three years and steadily declining.[91] Needless to say, each government would still retain the option of initiating its own general or specific trade adjustment programme to supplement the above procedures, if there is a perceived need to do so.

Notes

1. This may not of course be so where technology is largely imported.

2. It is also a question of perception. If exporters lag abroad, they are simply regarded by the public at large as being inefficient, if import competitors can't cope, they are regarded as being injured by 'unfair' foreign competition.

3. There may also be greater psychic costs to the elderly in having to leave an area where they have had long-term residence, continuity and a sense of belonging.

4. See for example, G. and V. Curzon, 'Global Assault on Non-Tariff Trade Barriers', *Thames Essay No. 3* (Trade Research Policy Centre, London, 1972) and S. O'Clearealain, 'Adjustment Assistance to Import Competition' in F. McFadzean, *Towards an Open Economy* (Macmillan, London, 1972).

5. IMF, *Survey* (25 June 1980).

6. M. Szenberg, J.W. Lombardi and E.Y. Lee, *Welfare Effects of Trade Restrictions* (Academic Press, New York, 1977), p. 112.

7. In the early 1960s 'most state unemployment compensation payments averaged less than 50% of the weekly wage for a shorter period, usually 26 weeks'. (G. Neumann, 'The Direct Labor Market Effects of the Trade Adjustment Assistance Program', in US Department of Labor, *The Impact of International Trade and Investment on Employment* (Washington, DC, 1978), p. 108.)

8. C.R. Frank, Jr, *Foreign Trade and Domestic Aid* (Brookings Institution, Washington, DC, 1977), p. 53.

9. H.R. Williams in an article ('U.S. Trade Adjustment Assistance to Mitigate Injury from Import Competition', *American Journal of Economics and Sociology* Oct. 1977), complains that the 'severing of the tie between increased imports and prior trade concessions opens the door to extensive government subsidization of American firms and workers' (p. 390). 'It is one thing to provide assistance when the need for such arises from prior and directly related concessions. It is quite another when the increased imports may be due to any cause whatever' (p. 387). Williams and others fail to grasp the point, that it might be in the national interest to 'bribe' trade impacted workers and firms to accede to tariff reductions *or to refrain from seeking new impositions*.

10. H.R. Williams, 'U.S. Measures to Relieve Injury Caused by Import Competition: The Eligibility Test', *Journal of World Trade Law* (Jan./Feb. 1978), p. 31.

11. M.D. Bale, 'Worker Adjustment to Import Competition: The United States Experience', *International Journal of Social Economics*, vol. 5, no. 2 (1978) p. 73.

12. As mentioned by G. Edgren in 'Employment Adjustment to Trade Under Conditions of Stagnating Growth', *International Labor Review*, vol. 117, no. 3 (May/June 1978), p. 295. Bale's figures also differ from those given in his combined paper with Baldwin. In R.E. Baldwin and M.D. Bale, 'North American Responses to Imports from New Industrial Countries', paper delivered at

Conference on Old and New Industrial Countries, University of Sussex, (6–8 Jan. 1980), it is stated on p. 15, that 'as of January 1, 1978, about 270,000 workers had received weekly trade-readjustment allowances'.

13. M.H. Finley, 'Foreign Trade and U.S. Employment' in US Department of Labor, *Impact of International Trade and Investment on Employment*, p. 131.

14. See for example, J.E. McCarthy, 'Contrasting Experience with Trade Adjustment Assistance' in B. Balassa, *Changing Patterns in Foreign Trade and Payments* (Norton and Co., New York, 1978); Bale, 'Worker Adjustment to Import Competition'; and Neumann, 'The Direct Labor Market Effects of the Trade Adjustment Assistance Program' (1980).

15. Bale, ibid., p. 74.

16. Ibid., p. 74.

17. Ibid., p. 78.

18. On average 5.4 per cent higher, see Neumann, 'The Direct Labor Market Effects of the Trade Adjustment Assistance Program', p. 107.

19. Ibid., p. 107.

20. Ibid., p. 120.

21. McCarthy, 'Contrasting Experience with Trade Adjustment Assistance', p. 33.

22. See Finley, 'Foreign Trade and U.S. Employment', p. 131.

23. In time the differences narrowed and in some states, the rankings have been reversed.

24. C. Mills, 'Adjustment Assistance Policies: A Survey' in OECD, *Adjustment for Trade* (Paris, 1975a), p. 22.

25. Frank, *Foreign Trade and Domestic Aid*, p. 54.

26. Baldwin and Bale, 'North American Responses', p. 16.

27. The government defrayed 50 per cent of the costs of drafting and submitting proposals.

28. UN, *Adjustment Assistance Measures*, TD/121, Supplement 1 (New York, Jan. 1972), p. 25.

29. Crawford Report, *Study Group on Structural Adjustment* (Australian Government Printing Services, Canberra, March 1979), vol. II, p. 6.2.9.

30. Frank, *Foreign Trade and Domestic Aid*, p. 133.

31. Economic Council of Canada, *For a Common Future* (Canadian Government, Ottawa, 1978).

32. See for example, R.A. Matthews, *Canadian Industry and the Challenge of Low-Cost Imports* (Economic Council of Canada, Discussion Paper No. 172, Ottawa, July 1980).

33. See for example, D. James, 'The Assessment of Adjustment Problems in Australian Trade' in K. Kojima (ed.), *Structural Adjustments in Asian–Pacific Trade* (Japan Economic Research Center, Tokyo, July 1973), p. 312.

34. Crawford Report, *Study Group on Structural Adjustment*, vol. II, p. 4:1.6.

35. F. Gruen, 'The 25% Tariff Cut; Was it a mistake?', *The Australian Quarterly* vol. 47, no. 2 (June 1975), p. 10.

36. Crawford Report, *Study Group on Structural Adjustment*, vol. I, p. 10.14.

37. OECD, *The Industrial Policy of Australia* (OECD, Paris, 1975b), p. 64.

38. This had to be verified by a statutory declaration signed by the employer or business man.

39. Crawford Report, *Study Group on Structural Adjustment*, vol. II, p. 6.2.1.

40. Figures expressed in terms of 1975 rates.

41. Crawford Report, *Study Group on Structural Adjustment*, vol. I, p. 19.

42. See for example, D. Gastin, *The Pursuit of Structural Change in Manufacturing Industry* (Australian Government Publishing Service, Canberra, 1978), p. 14.

43. Or even to be indifferent between the two. Firms are likely to prefer protection; for it is not subject to budgetary review and therefore does not have to be periodically defended. Excessive protection may also provide above average capital returns.

44. Indirect exclusions of course applied to firms as well.

45. For example, a German government document states that 'in its framework of growth-oriented structural policies the Federal Government by promoting structural adjustments and retraining of labour for new jobs with better chances for the future is taking into account the justified interests of the developing countries' (as quoted in UN, *Adjustment Assistance Measures*, p. 31).

46. P. Coffey, *Economic Policies of the Common Market* (Macmillan, London, 1979), p. 63.

47. Ibid., p. 63.

48. F. Bruan, 'The European Approach to Adjustment' in H. Hughes (ed.), *Prospects for Partnership* (Johns Hopkins University Press, Baltimore, 1973), p. 204.

49. C. Mills, 'Adjustment Assistance Policies', p. 111.

50. Frank, *Foreign Trade and Domestic Aid*, p. 150.

51. This is not a unique case, other examples are to be found in the arrangements for the European coal and steel industries, the coal industry in Japan, and so on.

52. Import duties for consumers were maintained.

53. Dislocation 'was defined as increased idle capacity or inability of a firm to operate at a reasonable level of profit and unemployment or underdevelopment of 5 percent of the work force or 50 workers whichever was less'. (L.B. Krause, 'The U.S. Economy and International Trade' in Kojima (ed.), *Structural Adjustments in Asian-Pacific Trade*, p. 402.)

54. UN, *Adjustment Assistment Measures*, p. 46.

55. Ibid., p. 24.

56. For example in Belgium, see OECD, *Adjustment for Trade*, p. 99; in Germany, see G. Fels, 'The Choice of Industry Mix in the Division of Labour Between Developed and Developing Countries', *Weltwirtschaftliches Archiv* (1972), p. 186; in Sweden, see OECD, ibid., p. 23; and in Japan, see Hughes, *Prospects for Partnership*, p. 259.

57. C. Mills, 'Adjustment Assistance Policies', p. 111.

58. C. Pestieau, 'Market Access for Manufactured Exports from Developing Countries', paper presented at 1975 Halifax Conference, *Canada and the New International Economic Order*, Table 7.

59. See G.K. Helleiner, 'Manufactured Exports from Less Developed Countries and Industrial Adjustment in Canada' in OECD, *Adjustment for Trade*, p. 272.

60. Pestieau, 'Market Access for Manufactured Exports from Developing Countries', p. 30.

61. Matthews, 'Canadian Industry and the Challenge of Low-Cost Imports', Table 7.

62. Pestieau, 'Market Access for Manufactured Exports from Developing Countries', p. 30.

63. Between October 1973 and October 1975, the relative increase in female wages caused the wage bill for industry as a whole to rise by 2.8 per cent but in terms of clothing, footwear and textiles, it caused the wage bill to rise respectively by 14.2 per cent, 9.3 per cent and 6.2 per cent (IAC, *Structural Change in Australia* (Canberra, June 1977b, Table 3.1.1.).

64. Crawford Report, *Study Group on Structural Adjustment*, vol. I, Table 10.3.

65. As quoted in ibid., vol. II., p. 11.2.15.

66. Ibid.

67. IAC, *Report on Textiles, Clothing and Footwear* (Canberra, April 1980), p. 2.

68. Crawford Report, *Study Group on Structural Adjustment*, vol. II, p. 11.2.15.

69. Ibid.

70. See IAC, *Report*, p. 22.

71. Ibid., p. 66.

72. Ibid., p. 119.

73. Ibid., pp. 85, 86.

74. Minister of Business and Consumer Affairs, Media Release no. 80/114 (15 August 1980).

75. IAC, *Structural Change in Australia*, p. 52.

76. Crawford Report, *Study Group on Structural Adjustment*, vol. II, Table 2.2.B.

77. H. Giersch (ed.), *The International Division of Labour, Problems and Perspectives* (Mohr, Tubingen, 1974), p. 205.

78. D. Evers, 'Industrial Adjustment in the Netherlands, with Special Emphasis upon the Clothing Industry' in OECD, *Adjustment for Trade*.

79. Matthews, 'Canadian Industry and the Challenge of Low-Cost Imports', p. 70.

80. That governments frequently rationalise their decisions to protect the textile and clothing industries on the grounds that they largely employ disadvantaged groups; women, migrants, unskilled and uneducated workers, etc. does not of course prove that these groups can effectively pressurise the government to act on their behalf. Note by contrast the relatively poorer treatment of government pensioners, the physically and mentally handicapped, etc. that is obtained in most Western societies.

81. The duration of the locking in effect would depend in part on the elasticity of supply of foreign commodities.

82. OECD, *The Case for Positive Adjustment Policies* (Paris, June 1979a), p. 89.

83. Admittedly, involuntarily.

84. *The Economist* (23 August 1980), pp. 20, 21.

85. T. Murray and M.R. Egmund, 'Full Employment, Trade Expansion and Adjustment Assistance', *Southern Economic Journal* (April 1970).

86. See for example OECD *The Case for Positive Adjustment Policies*.

87. F. Stewart, 'Adjustment Assistance: A Proposal', *World Development*, vol. 1, no. 6 (June 1973).

88. Ibid., p. 46.

89. In the long run net social gains may be positive but in the short run before displaced workers are re-engaged, they may in fact be negative.

90. It has been estimated that between 1971 and 1976, trade growth has contributed towards unemployment in Canada and Australia. See, A.V. Deardorff and R.M. Stern, 'Changes in Trade and Employment in the Major Industrialized Countries, 1970-6', paper presented at the Sixth World Congress of Economists (Mexico, May 1980).

91. Here too, international codes could be agreed upon. Also, investment in a 'safeguard sector' should be taxed to equate prospective returns to those likely to be attained in a free trade situation.

APPENDIX: EMMANUEL'S UNEQUAL EXCHANGE THESIS: A CRITIQUE

> This Appendix contains an esoteric discussion on the merits of a prominent trade critic's onslaught on free trade. For those who lack the inclination or patience to follow arguments couched in terms of Marxist jargon and which are based on tabulated illustrations, this Appendix can safely be bypassed.

Radical economists are inveterate critics of current international economic relations, particularly with regard to dealings between developed countries (DCs) and LDCs. Their writings abound with diatribes against imperialism, the multinationals and the prevailing global institutional structures. Among their voluminous works, Emmanuel's *Unequal Exchange*[1] has come to be regarded as a classic, which sets out to provide a theoretical foundation for proving that LDCs are exploited through trade, and that specialisation on the basis of comparative costs is more likely than not to yield detrimental effects. Emmanuel's book is explicitly addressed to economists of all persuasions but since it first appeared in English in 1972, conventional economists have, with few exceptions,[2] failed to debate the issues raised and, to the best of my knowledge, have neither closely examined nor manipulated Emmanuel's models, checking for internal inconsistencies while provisionally allowing all basic assumptions to pass unchallenged. By contrast, Emmanuel's book has generated intense interest and controversy among his radical colleagues,[3] and although his notions have been subjected to modifications and refinements, few, if any, have questioned his basic conclusions. More recently, in *Essays in the Political Economy of Australian Capitalism*, an entire chapter was devoted (or should one say 'dedicated'?) to an exposition of Emmanuel's book, a book which supposedly 'constitutes a challenge to orthodox international trade theory'[4] and which 'serves as a clear reminder of the variety of tools in the Marxian tool-box; tools which offer constructive alternative guidance to that proffered by orthodox, neo-classical economists'.[5] This appendix seeks to take up Emmanuel's challenge and to engage him in debate by providing a response which could reasonably represent the conventional economic viewpoint. Accordingly, a summary and critical scrutiny of the highlights of Emmanuel's thesis follows.

The Meaning of Unequal Exchange

Emmanuel's concept of unequal exchange is based on the labour theory of value. As a point of departure, he describes a simple model in which labour is the only production factor in a society comprising independent workers, each with their own tools (being their inalienable property). Given labour mobility, a free exchange of products and the means to reduce diverse efforts to a common unit of abstract and homogeneous labour time, then: 'equilibrium will be maintained only if commodities are exchanged in proportion to the length of time needed to produce them'.[6] By equilibrium, is meant a situation in which there is no tendency for labour to move from one production branch to another. If by chance, prices did not reflect relative labour inputs, workers would redeploy their efforts until the resulting output changes caused a realignment of prices, which eliminated discrepancies between relative exchange values and labour time.

In introducing a second factor,[7] capital, the same equilibrium conditions hold as in the preceding case, provided that within every branch, claims by capital are proportionate to the amount of labour expended. Since capital is assumed to be both perfectly competitive and homogeneous, in the sense that it is expressed as a claim, 'It is independent of the concrete form it may assume',[8] the equilibrium rate of profit must be the same in all branches.

On releasing the restrictive constant factor proportionality assumption, it becomes impossible to set prices simultaneously to reflect the relative labour hours and capital units that goods embody. This can be illustrated in terms of Emmanuel's own example. Suppose that the production of 1 unit of good A requires 10 hours of labour, and 1 unit of good B, 20 hours. When constant factor proportionality is assumed, 2A will exchange for 1B, permitting an equality of wage and profit rates between both industries. However, if 10 units of capital combine with each hour of labour in A compared with 5 units per labour hour in B, and if 2A are exchanged for 1B, then while each industry would have expended 20 labour hours, in A, the product's proceeds would, in addition to labour, have to be apportioned to the owners of 200 capital units, whereas in B, factor rewards would have to be divided between the same number of units of labour (20) and the owners of only 100 capital units. 'It will then be necessary either for the hour of labor, the unit of capital, or both to be rewarded at a different rate in A and B.'[9] To circumvent this impasse, Emmanuel adopted an approach devised by Karl Marx, which enabled equilibrium prices to incorporate profits

Table A.1: Country A

Branches	(c) Constant Capital	(v) Variable Capital	(m) Surplus Value	(V) Value = c + v + m	(T) Rate of Profit = $\frac{\Sigma m}{\Sigma c + \Sigma v}$	(p) Profit T(c + v)	(L) Price of Production c + v + p
I	80	20	20	120		20	120
II	90	10	10	110	20%	20	120
III	70	30	30	130		20	120
	240	60	60	360		60	360

Notes:

Constant capital = fixed capital, assumed to be totally consumed within one production cycle.

Variable capital = wages.

Surplus value = value added minus wages (assumed to maintain a constant ratio to wages across the entire economy).

Value = total intrinsic output of all labour (living and past).

Price of production = equilibrium price, ensuring equal factor payments across all branches.

NB. These same symbols will be utilised in later tables.

Source: Emmanuel, *Unequal Exchange*, p. 21.

in proportion to total capital invested. This is explained in terms of the figures in Table A1. In this hypothetical economy overall production expenditures, comprising wages (v) and constant capital (c) costs amount to 300 (expressed in dollars or any other standard). As a group, the capitalists obtain a net return of 60 (m). Relating this to their total outlays (v + c), the rate of profit for the entire economy is 20 per cent, a rate which, because of capital mobility, must apply equally to each sector. Absolute profits for each branch are calculated by multiplying the average profit rate by the sum of constant and variable capital invested. Finally equilibrium rates (L) being the sum of profits, wages and charges against constant capital, are such that factors are able to be imbursed at equal rates throughout the economy as a whole.

Although the transformation of values (V) into equilibrium prices (L) allows factor payments to be standardised, inequalities in exchange between values (V) and prices (L) arise. In terms of Table A1, branch II realises a surplus in exchange (at price 120) over the value of its output (110), with the converse applying to branch III. This occurs because to permit an equalisation of profit rates, inter-sectoral transfers of surplus value are required, involving branches with low organic compositions of capital contributing to those with higher ones.[10] The resulting inequality of such exchange is implicitly dismissed by Emmanuel as being of little or no consequence, presumably because within a closed economy, surpluses appropriated from one part are relocated in another, and therefore the economy as a whole experiences no net losses. More explicitly, Emmanuel maintains that 'inside a given country redistributive mechanisms wipe out the inequality of exchange that is due to differences in organic composition. The branches or regions with a higher organic composition pour back into the other branches and regions the extra surplus value they have drawn out of the common pool, either through social legislation and state expenditure or else through inter-branch financing carried out via the banking network or the stock exchange.'[11] Logically, such a proposition is at odds with the whole purpose of transferring values into prices in the first place, for if subsequent redistributions would 'wipe out the inequality of exchange', they would similarly wipe out the attained equality of factor payments, which would once again conflict with the factor mobility assumption. Furthermore, there are no practical grounds for assuming the transfer mechanisms that Emmanuel describes, that is, there is no basis for believing that labour intensive industries pay disproportionately lower taxes or obtain relatively greater social benefits than capital intensive ones, or for that matter that they are more favourably placed in receiving investment funds or credit. Be that as it may, Emmanuel is really concerned with exchanges between countries and it is to this issue that we now turn.

Emmanuel eventually supposed that the original economy would come into contact with another, also consisting of three branches and whose prices, wages, profits, etc. are as set out in Table A2.[12] At first, we are informed that profit rates differ between the two countries, and that at prices of 120 per branch in A and 80 per branch in B,[13] the two countries would, if they traded, exchange on average one hour of living labour of one economy for one hour of living labour of the other. In other words, if they both traded their entire incomes, A would receive a payment of 360, which after deducting 240 for constant capital (past labour) leaves 120, equal to the value of its living labour (v + m). Similarly, B would receive 240 to be disbursed equally between its past and present labour.

Next, it is assumed that 'free circulation of capital is introduced between the two systems, and as a result, equalization of profits takes place'.[14] Emmanuel's resulting data configuration is reproduced in Table A3. Strangely, we are now presented with a situation in which profit rates are equalised without any capital movements having occurred. Perhaps one might explain this by suggesting the possibility

Table A2: Country B

Branches	(c)	(v)	(m)	(V)	(T)	(p)	(L)
I	40	20	20	80		20	80
II	50	10	10	70	$33^{1/3}$%	20	80
III	30	30	30	90		20	80
	120	60	60	240		60	240

Note: See Table A1 for explanation of symbols.

Table A3: A and B Together

Branches	(c)	(v)	(m)	(V)	(T) $\dfrac{(\Sigma m)}{\Sigma c + \Sigma v}$	(p)	(L)
IA	80	20	20	120		25	125
IIA	90	10	10	110		25	125
IIIA	70	30	30	130	25%	25	125
IB	40	20	20	80		15	75
IIB	50	10	10	70		15	75
IIIB	30	30	30	90		15	75
	360	120	120	600		120	600

Note: See Table A1 for explanation of symbols.
Source: Emmanuel, *Unequal Exchange*, p. 55.

that, confronted with the potential for inter-country capital flows, prices (L) instantly adjust to equate profit rates internationally? This still of course begs the question as to why country B, which was (and still is) capital poorer and which initially had higher profit rates, would be prepared to accept lower ones, without offsetting capital inflows. Leaving this problem aside for the moment, Table A3 indicates that although wage and profit rates are internationally equal, country B experiences a deterioration in its terms of trade (it now receives only 75 per branch while having to pay A 125 per branch). In addition, whereas before, 'one hour of B's living labor was exchanged on the average for one hour of A's living labor, it is now exchanged on the average for 21/27 hours of labor'.[15] In total, A's output sells for 375, B's for 225. On deducting 240 from A's total (to account for its constant capital (c)) 135 remain for its living labour, and likewise on deducting 120 from B's total, 105 remains. Therefore, through trade, B's living labour exchanges for 105/135 or 21/27 of A's.

Thus far, constant capital was taken to be fully consumed during a single production cycle. As a tentative step towards greater realism,

Table A4

Country	(C) Total Constant Capital	(c) Constant Capital Consumed	(v)	(m)	(V) c + v + m	(T) $\frac{\Sigma m}{\Sigma c + \Sigma v}$	(p)	(L) c + v + p
A	240	50	60	60	170	25%	75	185
B	120	50	60	60	170		45	155
	360	100	120	120	340		120	340

Source: Emmanuel, *Unequal Exchange*, p. 57.

Table A5

Country	(K)	(c)	(v)	(m)	(V)	(T) $\frac{\Sigma m}{\Sigma K}$	(p)	(L) c + v + p
A	240	50	60	60	170	$33^{1/3}\%$	80	190
B	120	50	60	60	170		40	150
	360	100	120	120	340		120	340

Emmanuel divided the constant capital component into two categories, the total stock of constant capital and the amount (now much less than the total and assumed to be equal in all branches) that is eroded in each cycle. This modification is depicted in Table A4, where, instead of itemising each branch, the aggregate figures for countries A and B are presented. Henceforth, Emmanuel focuses on comparing (V), the overall value of national labour (living and past) and the price obtained on the international market (L) for a country's output. In the context of the Table A4 data, unequal exchange would occur, if the two countries should trade with one another and exchange their total products, both of which incorporate the same value of labour (170), for A would obtain 185 (an excess of 15 over the value of its labour value) while B would receive only 155 (a deficiency of 15 from its labour value).

Recognising that there may also be an element of constancy in wage payments, in that within some enterprises, 'turnover rate of variable capital is very slow',[16] Emmanuel decided on a new column in his tables representing 'the whole of the capital invested (K), that is, the sum of constant capital, both fixed and circulating, and variable capital, weighted by their respective turnover rates'.[17] This is shown in Table A5. In this instance, while both A's and B's output embodies 170 of national labour respectively, in trade, A obtains 190 and B only 150, that is, 'a transfer of surplus value (of 20 units) take place from country B to country A'.[18]

Since labour, by contrast with capital, is assumed to be internationally immobile, differing internal wage rates can co-exist with a universal profit rate. The significance of this is illustrated with reference to the hypothetical data of Table A6, where in trade, B's output realises 110, and A's 230, despite the fact that their respective outputs have equivalent values (170 each). It is this very disparity, in the presence of equal profit yet differing wage rates, that Emmanuel finally designates (on pp. 61, 62) as unequal exchange. To show that inequality of wages as such, all other things being equal, is alone 'the cause of the inequality of exchange',[19] the total quantity of capital invested in both A and B was equalised, and as can be seen from Table A7 prices (L) yet continued to diverge from values (V).

To demonstrate the doubtful validity of Emmanuel's thesis that LDCs are pillaged through their trade with DCs, we shall utilise the hypothetical data of Table A6. In their present form they depict aggregate figures for each country.

Let us arbitrarily disaggregate them to yield two branches per economy (see Table A8). If all four goods were different we may well

Table A6

Country	(K)	(c)	(v)	(m)	(V)	(T)	(p)	(L)
A	240	50	100	20	170	$33^{1/3}$%	80	230
B	120	50	20	100	170		40	110
	360	100	120	120	340		120	340

Table A7

Country	(K)	(c)	(v)	(m)	(V)	(T)	(p)	(L)
A	240	50	100	20	170	25%	60	210
B	240	50	20	100	170		60	120
	480	100	120	120	340		120	330

Table A8

Branch	(K)	(c)	(v)	(m)	(V)	(T)	(p)	(L)
Country A								
I	100	10	90	18	118	$33^{1/3}\%$	33	133
II	140	40	10	2	52		47	97
	240	50	100	20	170		80	230
Country B								
I	20	10	18	90	118	$33^{1/3}\%$	7	35
II	100	40	2	10	52		33	75
	120	50	20	100	170		40	110

Table A9

Country	(K)	(c)	(v)	(m)	(V)	(T)	(p)	(L)
A	60	50	100	20	170	$33^{1/3}\%$	20	170
B	300	50	20	100	170		100	170
	360	100	120	120	340		120	340

encounter unequal exchange (as defined by Emmanuel) but if the set of two goods that each country produces is the same, it would not be possible to tabulate four such rows in Table A8, for in free trade there cannot simultaneously be two different prices per good.[20] We cannot even present pre-trade prices because Emmanuel has assumed equal profit rates, even though the ratio of total surplus value to total capital ($\Sigma M/\Sigma K$) differs between each country. Under such conditions, equal profit rates can only occur in the presence of trade because trade provides the mechanism for redistributing surpluses, in this case from country B to A. This means that complete specialisation has to be assumed to demonstrate unequal exchange, which probably accounts for Emmanuel's practice of referring to entire economies (as in Table A6, etc.). Even in the event of complete specialisation, unequal exchange is not necessarily inevitable. In Table A6, Emmanuel indicates that there is a common rate of profit of $33^{1/3}$ per cent to both A and B. Since within B, 100 of surplus value is generated against a total capital outlay of 120, it might well dawn upon B's capitalists, whether locally or foreign domiciled, that they could extract higher profit rates if the country were to withdraw from the world economy. Alternatively, the question as to what B's profit rate would have been in the pre-trade phase, given B's existing capital stock, could have been posed. It seems that B's rate would have been 100/120, that is, 83.3 per cent, while A's would have been 20/240, that is, 8.3 per cent. At these initial returns, if capital flows were then unencumbered, capital movements would have occurred from A to B until profit rates equalised at 33.3 per cent. The appropriate equilibrium capital quantities being 60 for A and 300 for B. If we assume that complete specialisation now occurs in both countries and that they now trade, and if we substitute the equilibrium capital values in Table A6 we would arrive at a situation (shown in Table A9) where there is complete equality of exchange even though wage rates differ.

Our example is extreme in that it assumed that the capital flows in question had no impact on wages. This is in keeping with Emmanuel's assertion that wages are essentially independent of other economic variables. If they were not, then presumably in the course of capital rushing into country B to take advantage of higher initial returns, wages would be bid up and conversely in A. This would lessen the actual capital transfers needed for equilibrium while diminishing the potential for unequal exchange. Finally, even if unequal exchange does in fact occur, say because goods produced in A and B are different, this in itself presents no case for autarky. An LDC may for example, export coffee whose price does not correspond to its value but could still benefit from the transaction, if it uses the proceeds to acquire goods from abroad at a cheaper rate than could be obtained internally. Clearly, this elementary proposition based on the laws of comparative advantage, threatens Emmanuel's entire analysis, and for this reason he strove to dispel it. Let us see how this was attempted.

Emmanuel on Comparative Costs

Essentially, Emmanuel wished to demonstrate that unless all production branches maintain equal capital to labour ratios, minor institutional changes in wages could reverse the ranking of goods in which a country had comparative advantages 'without any change in the objective conditions of production', thus making 'nonsense of optimization through specialization dictated by comparative costs'.[21] For this purpose, the hypothetical data of Table A10 were employed.

In comparing the price ratio of wine to cloth in each country, we note that $80/90 < 120/100$, and therefore Portugal has a comparative advantage in wine, England in cloth. Before trade, the countries together utilise 1,000K and 390 hours of living labour (that is, 170 + 220) to produce 2 units of wine and 2 of cloth. However, in trade, with both specialising completely, 1,000K and 300 labour hours ($2 \times 126 + 2 \times 24$) are expended to produce the pre-trade output, saving 90 labour hours. As Emmanuel states it, 'everything has thus turned out for the better'.[22] Now suppose that wages in Portugal rises by a third, and as a result the configuration of Table A11 emerges. Since $95^{1/3}/74^{1/3} > 120/100$, Portugal now specialises in cloth and England in wine, employing 1,000K and 480 labour hours ($2 \times 44 + 2 \times 196$), involving an excess of 90 labour hours over the pre-trade case, to yield the same output. From this illustration we are invited to conclude that 'only a certain disparity in wages (in some cases, as in our example, a very slight one) between the different countries is needed for an international division of labor based on comparative costs to lead, not to gain, but to a loss for the world as a whole'.[23]

Amazingly, Emmanuel sets up these hypothetical economies to engage in trade while individually maintaining their own profit rates. This implies an absence of capital mobility which is at variance with virtually the entire spirit of the rest of his book. To be consistent, this particular discussion should likewise assume capital mobility. Utilising Emmanuel's usual procedure of applying a common rate of profit to

Table A10

Country	Article	(K)	(v)	(m)	(V)	(T)	(p)	(L)
Portugal	Wine	100	63	63	126	17%	17	80
	Cloth	400	22	22	44		68	90
		500	85	85	170		85	170
England	Wine	100	98	98	196	22%	22	120
	Cloth	400	12	12	24		88	100
		500	110	110	220		110	220

Note: Emmanuel ignored constant capital (c) 'to simplify'.

(L) = per unit price, for one of each good is produced.

Source: These figures, and others relating to this discussion, are derived from Emmanuel, *Unequal Exchange*, pp. 246–8.

Table A11

Country	Article	(K)	(v)	(m)	(V)	(T)	(p)	(L)
Portugal	Wine	100	$84^{1/3}$	42	126	$11^{1/3}$%	$11^{1/3}$	$95^{1/3}$
	Cloth	400	$29^{1/3}$	$14^{2/3}$	44		$45^{1/3}$	$74^{1/3}$
England	Wine	100	98	98	196	22%	22	120
	Cloth	400	12	12	24		88	100

Table A12

Country	Article	(K)	(v)	(m)	(V)	(T)	(p)	(L)
Portugal	Wine	100	63	63	126	19.5%	19.5	82.5
	Cloth	400	22	22	44		78	100
England	Wine	100	98	98	196	19.5%	19.5	117.5
	Cloth	400	12	12	24		78	90

Table A13

Country	Article	(K)	(v)	(m)	(V)	(T)	(p)	(L)
Portugal	Wine	100	84	42	126	16.6%	16.6	100.6
	Cloth	400	$29^{1/3}$	$14^{2/3}$	44		66.4	95.7
England	Wine	100	98	98	196	16.6%	16.6	114.6
	Cloth	400	12	12	24		66.4	78.4

both economies, equal to $\Sigma M/\Sigma K$ (Σm and Σk being the combined sum of both economies), we first equate profit rates while maintaining each country's initial capital stock: the appropriate rate being 19.5 per cent, which at original wages yields the data of Table A12. From Table A12, we note that $82.5/100 < 117.5/90$, and therefore Portugal specialises in wine. Now let wages in Portugal rise by one-third. Since this affects (m), the overall profit rate falls to 16.6 per cent (see Table A13). From Table A13 it can be noted that $100.6/95.7 < 114.6/78.4$ and *once again Portugal specialises in wine*, for no reversal of comparative advantage followed the Portugese wage rise.

Alternatively, assume that profit rates are equalised through an actual flow of capital from Portugal (where rates were 17 per cent[24]) to England (where rates were 22 per cent[24]). This is shown in Table A14. From Table A14, $80/90 < 120/100$ and therefore Portugal specialises in wine. Now let wages in Portugal rise by one-third. At first returns to capital in Portugal would be less than in England (on account of the wage rise) and therefore capital would flow from Portugal to England until rates equalised at 16.6 per cent per country (see Table A15). Once again, the ratio of Portugal's wine to cloth prices, 95.3/74.6, is less than England's, 125.5/94.1, and Portugal continues to specialise in wine. While we do not outrightly deny that large wage rises could reverse trade flows, the above examples indicate that even at fairly significant wage changes (in this case $33^{1/3}$ per cent), *in terms of Emmanuel's own parameters*, it is not inevitable that countries would inappropriately specialise.

The sensitivity of this analysis hinges on the existence of wide differences in capital usage between the wine and cloth industries. If for instance, cloth used only twice as much capital as wine, significant wage changes could be accommodated without incurring offsetting comparative cost rankings, even in direct relation to Emmanuel's own example and way of reasoning (as summarised in Tables A10 and A11). Simply let wine capital equal 166 and cloth capital equal 333, then Portugal's price ratio would (in terms of Table A10 wages and profit rates) be 91/78 which is less than England's 134/85. If Table A11's wages and profit rates are then used, the price ratios would be 102/67 for Portugal which is *again* less than England's ratio of 134/85.

Having attempted to prove that wage rate changes would adversely affect the direction of trade, Emmanuel contended that if countries maintained different scales for reducing complex to simple labour, inappropriate specialisations would occur. Unravelling his specific example, we once again have the two countries of Portugal and England,

Table A14

Country	Article	(K)	(v)	(m)	(V)	(T)	(p)	(L)
Portugal	Wine	87	63	63	126	19.5%	17	80
	Cloth	349	22	22	44		68	90
England	Wine	113	98	98	196	19.5%	22	120
	Cloth	451	12	12	24		88	100

Note: The overall profit rate equals $\Sigma m / \Sigma K = 19.5$. For this to be the same in both countries before trade, $\Sigma m / \Sigma K$ within each country must equal 19.5 from which we derive each country's required capital stock and apportion it to each industry at the rate of 20 per cent to wine and 80 per cent to cloth.

Table A15

Country	Article	(K)	(v)	(m)	(V)	(T)	(p)	(L)
Portugal	Wine	68	$84^{1/3}$	42	126	16.6%	11.3	95.3
	Cloth	272	$29^{1/3}$	$14^{2/3}$	44		45.3	74.6
England	Wine	165	98	98	196	16.6%	27.5	125.5
	Cloth	495	12	12	24		82.1	94.1

Table A16

Country	Wine			Cloth		
	Concrete Labour	Wine Coefficient	Abstract Labour	Concrete Labour	Cloth Coefficient	Abstract Labour
Portugal						
Engineer	1	5	5	6	5	30
Labourer	70	1	70	30	1	30
			75			60
England						
Engineer	1½	10	15	$6^{2/3}$	10	$66^{2/3}$
Labourer	105	1	105	$33^{1/3}$	1	$33^{1/3}$
			120			100

producing wine and cloth. In Portugal, an hour of an engineer's labour is deemed equivalent to five of an unskilled worker, whereas in England the ratio is one to ten. The data for the two economies in question are contained in Table A16, from which it is clear that within Portugal one unit of wine requires 75 labour hours, cloth 60, while in England the respective figures are 120 and 100. Since $60/75 < 100/120$, Portugal specialises in cloth and England in wine. According to Emmanuel such an arrangement is an adverse one, for in the pre-trade situation, 355 hours of abstract labour are used to produce 2 units of wine and 2 of cloth, yet in the trade specialisation phase, the same quantity of output requires 360 labour hours $(2 \times 60 + 2 \times 120)$.

Superficially, Emmanuel's reasoning seems plausible but a closer examination of his figures suggests that contrary to his assertions, there is indeed scope for both Portugal and England to gain by the type of specialisation in question. Within Portugal, the real cost of 1 unit of cloth is .8 of wine, within England, it is .83 of wine. In the post-specialisation trade phase let 1 cloth exchange for .81 of wine. In Portugal, in producing 1 cloth, .8 of wine is foregone but the 1 unit of cloth can now be sold to England for .81 of wine, and therefore Portugal could incur a net gain of .01 wine. Similarly, in England to produce .83 of wine, 1 cloth is foregone. England could now retrieve 1 cloth by handing Portugal .81 of wine, capturing a net gain of .02 of wine. A problem with Emmanuel's analysis is that we are not informed as to the total labour endowments of each country. If England produces 2 units of wine when trading, it must command at least 240 labour hours, in which case *if* in the pre-trade case it only produced 1 unit each of cloth and wine, 20 labour hours would have been unemployed. Similarly, Portugal to produce originally 1 unit each of cloth and wine must have been endowed with at least 135 labour hours. Let us assume that full employment reigned in the pre-trade case, and that while Portugal expended 135 labour hours to produce 1 unit of each good, England produced 1.2 cloth with 120 labour hours and 1 wine, also with 120 labour hours. Accordingly, with a global effort involving 375 labour hours, the world produced 2.2 of cloth and 2 of wine. On specialising the Portugese labour supply of 135 hours can produce 2.25 of cloth, while England's 240 manhours can yield 2 of wine so that with a constant world supply of labour, an extra .05 of cloth is extracted.

The issue of wage changes and and the issue of different coefficients in reducing concrete to abstract labour, were those on which Emmanuel relied most to rebuff the notion that gains could emanate on the basis of comparative cost trading. Hopefully the above discussion has somewhat scotched Emmanuel's contention, a contention which evoked a warm response among Emmanuel's radical admirers.[25]

The Independent Wage Assumption

Emmanuel believes that a low wage structure is responsible for low prices, which in turn permit DCs to purchase LDC goods at rates below their values. Furthermore, he asserts that LDCs, by *virtue of being low wage countries* are forever doomed to be exploited through trade. In his own words, he states that there is 'a certain category of countries (the low wage ones) that whatever they undertake and whatever they produce, always exchange a larger amount of their national labor for a smaller amount of foreign labor'.[26] Elsewhere, he suggests that even 'if the Third World becomes industralized, we may well see one day the locomotives or machine tools of the Congo or Indonesia being exchanged for tulips of Holland, the lace of Bruges, or the gowns of Paris, at a rate that will enable Europe to pay its rate of wages and the Third World to pay its much lower rate'.[27] To support this, he compares the prices of Swedish timber and Middle East oil and concludes that timber commands high prices because of high Swedish wages, whereas oil prices are doomed to be low because of low Middle Eastern wages.[28] In the light of OPEC hindsight, one wonders whether Emmanuel would still stand by such statements.

An assertion that wages determine development and income levels is followed by a statement that 'there is not a single example where high wages have not led to economic development'[29] and in reference to the US, we are informed that historically, migrants were accustomed to a high standard of living and 'when they migrated (to the US) they naturally demanded even higher incomes',[30] which caused the US to become a high wage country, developed and capable of extracting surpluses from LDCs. Not only are such declarations difficult to uphold from a point of logic but the historical perspective is flawed. To maintain high real wages, and therefore high living standards, an economy must be highly productive, that is, it has to be developed in the first instance.[31] If an LDC attempted to raise its general wage structure in the absence of accompanying or prior output increases, it would still be an LDC, and still be incapable of providing its citizens with Western lifestyles. Apart from anything else, if wage rises were at the expense of capital, profit rates would fall and since capital is internationally mobile, a resulting capital flight would exacerbate the LDC's capital shortage. In addition, a premature high wage structure would worsen employment prospects, as firms would seek to economise on labour. In terms of developments in the US economy, Emmanuel fails to understand that where wages were higher than Europe, this was in no small measure the result of land abundance and opportunities for profitable self-employment. Furthermore, many migrants arriving from Europe were in no position to 'demand' higher incomes, the Irish literally fleeing from starvation, being a case in point. It is well documented that many newcomers were consigned to the sweat shops of New York and anti-labour union factories in the hinterland, not to mention the plight of Blacks in terms of their slavery and continued poverty. What is also baffling in terms of Emmanuel's thesis is why he perceives the need for tariffs to protect wages in advanced countries. Surely, if wages are not determined by prices, protection is irrelevant (from labour's point of view) and secondly, if DCs exploit LDCs by buying from them at unfair prices, one would expect to observe a willingness to intensify trade with LDCs rather than the converse.

The experience of Singapore is a salutary one in the light of the above discussion. That island state, in no small measure owes its relatively high living standard, *vis-à-vis* other Third World countries, to its ability to capitalise on its cheap workforce by rapidly expanding its exports of labour intensive items. Currently Singapore, which enjoys comparatively low unemployment rates, is embarking on a strategy to upgrade its labour productivity and economy in general, through a policy of universal real wage increases. The government hopes that entrepreneurs will respond to higher labour costs by adopting more capital intensive production techniques, or in Marxist jargon, increasing the organic composition of capital. The point, however, is that without a prior period of rapid economic development, based on full participation in the international economy, Singapore would not now be poised to take such measures.

Conclusion

The conclusion of this appendix is straightforward. Emmaneul's notions of unequal exchange are neither internally consistent nor based on reasonable assumptions. It is unrealistic to maintain that wages are an independent variable in determining a country's level of development. In the realm of the discourse on comparative costs, Emmanuel's shortcomings in logic are most in evidence, for by manipulating and extending his model, it is not clear that countries would incorrectly specialise for the reasons he states. The proposition that price distortions could cause a country to experience welfare losses through trade, is one which is not only well known but which has been extensively explored in the conventional literature. Emmanuel's contribution does not extend that discussion and in general terms, it provides little for LDCs to be concerned about when participating in trade with DCs. Ironically, Third World spokesmen currently lament the manifold restrictions being placed by DCs on just such trade.

Notes

1. A. Emmanuel, *Unequal Exchange: A Study of the Imperialism of Trade* (Monthly Review Press, New York, 1972).

2. See for example, L. Mainwaring, 'International Trade and the Transfer of Labour Value', *Journal of Development Studies*, (Oct. 1980); E.L. Bacha, 'An Interpretation of Unequal Exchange', *Journal of Development Economies* (1978), pp. 319-30; A.C. Ross, 'Emmanuel on Unequal Exchange', *Journal of Economic Studies* (May 1976).

3. See for example, S. Amin, 'Imperialism and Unequal Development', *Monthly Review* (New York, 1977); R. Sau, *Unequal Exchange, Imperialism and Underdevelopment* (Oxford University Press, Bombay, 1978); A. de Janvoy and F. Kramer, 'The Limits of Unequal Exchange', *Review of Radical Political Economics* (Winter 1974); B. Gibson, 'Unequal Exchange', *Review of Radical Political Economics* (Fall 1980).

4. D. Clark, 'Unequal Exchange and Australian Economic Development' in E. Wheelwright and K. Buckley, *Essays on the Political Economy of Australian Capitalism*, vol. 3 (Australia & New Zealand Book Co., Sydney, 1978), p. 14.

5. Ibid., p. 163.

6. Emmanuel, *Unequal Exchange*, p. 4. In calculating labour times, weightings relating to the relative negative features of particular tasks are incorporated.

7. Factors of production are defined as established claims to the economic product.

8. Emmanuel, *Unequal Exchange*, p. 32.

9. Ibid., p. 15.

10. On p. 34 (ibid.), Emmanuel defines the organic composition of capital as; $v/c + v$ i.e. the ratio of wages to total capital outlays.

However, since on p. 21 and elsewhere, he refers to capitalists who *increase* their organic compositions 'so as to economize in living labor', to be consistent, the definition should instead be: $c/c + v$.

11. Ibid., p. 163.

12. Ibid., p. 54.

13. Strictly speaking, (L) (price of production) is not a per unit price, it is rather total revenue. Per unit prices are obtained by dividing (L) by respective output quantities.

14. Ibid., p. 54.

15. Ibid., pp. 54, 55.

16. Ibid., p. 58.

17. Ibid., p. 58.

18. Ibid., p. 60.

19. Ibid., p. 61.

20. Even Emmanuel concedes this, see ibid., p. 175.

21. Ibid., p. 245.

22. Ibid., p. 247.

23. Ibid., p. 248.

24. From Table A10.

25. In an appendix to Emmanuel's book, Bettleheim states that 'Emmanuel's critique constitutes an extremely important contribution to the overturning of what might be called the dogma of the theory of comparative costs'. See, Emmanuel, *Unequal Exchange*, p. 274.

26. Ibid., p. XXXI.

27. Ibid., p. 103.

28. Ibid., p. 174.

29. Ibid., p. 124.

30. Ibid., p. 126.

31. Or, as in the Middle East, it must be well endowed with precious resources.

BIBLIOGRAPHY

Adam, G. 'New Trends in International Business: Worldwide Sourcing and Dedomiciling', *Acta Oeconomica*, vol. 7 (1971), pp. 349-67

Aharoni, Y. *The Foreign Investment Decision* (Harvard University Press, Cambridge, Mass., 1966)

Ahmad, J. 'Tokyo Rounds of Trade Negotiations and the Generalised System of Preferences', *The Economic Journal* (June 1978)

Amin, S. 'Imperialism and Unequal Development', *Monthly Review* (New York, 1977)

Anderson, K. 'On Why Rates of Assistance Differ Between Australia's Rural Industries', *Australian Journal of Agricultural Economics* (August 1978)

—— 'The Political Market for Government Assistance to Australian Manufacturing Industries', *Economic Record* (June 1980)

Aquino, A. 'Intra-Industry Trade and Inter-Industry Specialization as Concurrent Sources of International Trade in Manufactures', *Weltwirtschaftliches Archiv*, vol. 114 (1978), pp. 275-96

Arad, K. and Hirsch, S. 'Determination of Trade Flows and Choice of Trade Partners: Reconciling the Heckscher-Ohlin and Burenstam Linder Models of International Trade', *Weltwirtschaftliches Archiv*, band 117, heft 2 (1981)

Arnt, H.W. 'The Modus Operandi of Protection', *Economic Record* (June 1979)

Australian Treasury, 'Flexibility, Economic Change and Growth', *Treasury Economic Paper*, no. 3 (Canberra, 1978)

Bacha, E.L. 'An Interpretation of Unequal Exchange', *Journal of Development Economics* (1978), pp. 319-30

Balassa, B. 'A "Stages" Approach to Comparative Advantage', *World Bank Staff Working Paper*, no. 256 (May 1977a)

—— ' "Revealed" Comparative Advantage Revisited: An Analysis of Relative Export Shares of the Industrial Countries, 1953-1971', *Manchester School* (December 1977b)

—— 'Export Incentives and Export Performance in Developing Countries', *Weltwirtschaftliches Archiv*, band 114, heft 1 (1978a)

—— 'The "New Protectionism" and the International Economy', *Journal of World Trade Law*, vol. 12, no. 5 (September/October 1978b)

—— (ed.) *Changing Patterns in Foreign Trade and Payments* (Norton and Co., New York, 1978c)

—— 'The Changing International Division of Labour in Manufactured Goods', *Banco Nazionale Del Lavoro* (September 1979)

—— 'Trade in Manufactured Goods: Patterns of Change', *World Development* (March 1981)

Baldwin, R.E. *Non-Tariff Distortions in International Trade* (Brookings Institution, Washington, DC, 1970)

—— 'Determinants of the Commodity Structure of U.S. Trade', *American Economic Review* (March 1971)

—— 'Trade and Employment Effects in the United States of Multilateral Tariff Reductions', *American Economic Review*, vol. 66, no. 2 (May 1976)

—— 'Determinants of Trade and Foreign Investment: Further Evidence', *Review of Economics and Statistics* (February 1979)

Baldwin, R.E. and Bale, M.D. 'North American Responses to Imports from New Industrial Countries', paper delivered at Conference on Old and New Industrial Countries, University of Sussex (6-8 January 1980)

Baldwin, R.E. and Murray, T. 'MFN Tariff Reductions and Developing Country Trade Benefits under the GSP', *Economic Journal* (March 1977)

Bale, M.D. 'Estimates of Trade-Displacement Costs for U.S. Workers', *Journal of International Economics* (1976), pp. 245-50

—— 'United States Concessions in the Kennedy Round and Short-Run Labor Adjustment Costs', *Journal of International Economics* (1977), pp. 145-8

—— 'Worker Adjustment to Import Competition: The United States Experience', *International Journal of Social Economics*, vol. 5, no. 2 (1978)

Batchelor, R.A., Major, R.L. and Morgan, A.D. *Industrialization and the Basis for Trade* (Cambridge University Press, Cambridge, 1980)

Bergsten, C.F. *The Future of the International Economic Order: An Agenda for Research* (Heath, Lexington, 1973)

Bergsten, C.F. and Cline, W.R. *Trade Policy in the 1980's* (Institute for International Economics, Washington, DC, November 1982)

Bergsten, C.F., Horst, T. and Morgan, T.H. *American Multinationals and American Interest* (Brookings Institution, Washington, DC, 1978)

Bhagwati, J. *Trade, Tariffs and Growth* (Weidenfeld and Nicolson, London, 1969)

——— 'The Heckscher-Ohlin Theorem in the Multi-Commodity Case', *Journal of Political Economy* (October 1972)

Bhagwati, J. and Srinivasan, T. 'Trade Policy and Development' in Dornbusch, R. and Frenkel, J. *International Economic Policy* (Johns Hopkins University Press, Baltimore (1979)

Blackhurst, R., Marian, N. and Tumlir, J. *Trade Liberalization, Protectionism and Interdependence* (GATT Studies in International Trade, no. 5, Geneva, November 1977)

——— *Adjustment, Trade and Growth in Developed and Developing Countries* (GATT Studies in International Trade, no. 6, Geneva, September 1978)

Blejer, M.J. 'income Per Capita and the Structure of Industrial Exports: An Empirical Study', *Review of Economics and Statistics* (November 1978)

Brander, J.A. 'Intra-Industry Trade in Identical Commodities', *Journal of International Economics* (February 1981)

Branson, W.H. and Monoyios, N. 'Factor Inputs in U.S. Trade', *Journal of International Economics* (May 1977)

Brenan, J. 'One Businessman's View of the Protection Debate', *Economic Papers*, vol. 1, no. 2 (September 1982)

Brock, W.A. and Magee, S.P. 'Tariff Formation in a Democracy' in Black, J. and Hindley, B., *Current Issues in Commercial Policy and Diplomacy* (Macmillan, London, 1980)

Bronfenbrenner, M. 'Predatory Poverty on the Offensive', *Economic Development and Cultural Change* (July 1976)

Bruan, F. 'The European Approach to Adjustment' in H. Hughes (ed.) *Prospects for Partnership* (Johns Hopkins University Press, Baltimore, 1973)

Bureau of Industry Economics, *Industrialization in Asia – Some Implications for Australian Industry* (Canberra, 1978)

Cable, V. 'Britain, The "New Protectionism" and Trade with the Newly Industrialising Countries', *International Affairs*, vol. 55, no. 1 (January 1979)

Cable, V. and Rebelo, I. 'Britain's Pattern of Specialization in Manufactured Goods with Developing Countries and Trade Protection', *World Bank Staff Working Paper*, no. 425 (October 1980)

Caves, R.E. *Trade and Economic Structure* (Harvard University Press, Cambridge, Mass., 1967)

——— 'Intra-Industry Trade and Market Structure in the Industrial Countries', *Oxford Economic Papers*, vol. 33, no. 2 (July 1981)

Caves, R. and Jones, R. *World Trade and Payments* (Little Brown and

Co., Boston, 1973 and 1977)

Cheh, J.H. 'United States Concessions in the Kennedy Round and Short-Run Labor Adjustment Costs', *Journal of International Economics* (1974), pp. 323-40

Chenery, H.B. and Hughes, H. *The International Division of Labour: The Case of Industry* (World Bank Reprint no. 11, 1972)

Chenery, H.G. and Kessing, D.B. 'The Changing Composition of Developing Country Exports', *World Bank Staff Working Paper*, no. 314 (January 1979)

Choudri, E.U. 'The Pattern of Trade in Individual Products: A Test of Simple Theories', *Weltwirtschaftliches Archiv*, band 115, heft 1 (1979)

Clark, D.P. 'The Production of Unskilled Labor in the United States Manufacturing Industries: Further Evidence', *Journal of Political Economy* (December 1980)

Clark, D. 'Unequal Exchange and Australian Economic Development' in Wheelwright, E. and Buckley, K. *Essays on the Political Economy of Australian Capitalism*, vol. 3 (Australia & New Zealand Book Co., Sydney, 1978)

Cline, W.R., Kawanabe, N., Kronsjo, T.O.M. and Williams, T. *Trade Negotiations in the Tokyo Round* (Brookings Institution, Washington, DC, 1978)

Coffey, P. *Economic Policies of the Common Market* (Macmillan, London, 1979)

Cohen, B.I. *Multinational Firms and Asian Exports* (Yale University Press, New Haven, 1975)

Cohen, S.P. 'Coping with the New Protectionism', *National Westminster Bank Quarterly Review* (November 1978)

Corbet, H. and Jackson, R. (eds.) *In Search of a New World Economic Order* (Croom Helm, London, 1974)

Corbo, V. and Havrylyshyn, O. *Canada's Trade Relations with Developing Countries* (Economic Council of Canada, Ottawa, 1980)

Corden, M. 'Intra-Industry Trade and Factor Proportions Theory' in Giersch, H. *On the Economics of Intra-Industry Trade* (Mohr, Tubingen, 1978)

Corden, W.M. *The Theory of Protection* (Oxford University Press, London, 1971)

—— *Trade Policy and Economic Welfare* (Oxford University Press, London, 1974a)

—— 'The Theory of International Trade' in Dunning, J.H. (ed.), *Economic Analysis and the Multinational Enterprise* (Allen and

Unwin, 1974b)

Crawford Report *Study Group on Structural Adjustment*, vols. I and II (Australian Government Printing Services, Canberra, March 1979)

Curzon, G. 'Neo-Protectionism, the MFA and the European Community', *The World Economy*, vol. 4, no. 3 (September 1981)

Curzon, G. and Curzon, V. 'Global Assault on Non-Tariff Trade Barriers', *Thames Essay No. 3* (Trade Research Policy Centre, London, 1972)

Daly, D.J., Keys, B.A. and Spence, E.J. *Scale and Specialization in Canadian Manufacturing* (Economic Council of Canada, Staff Study No 21, March 1968)

Dam van, A. 'The World's Work: Who Needs it Most?', *Columbia Journal of World Business* (September/October 1977)

Deardorff, A.V. and Stern, R.M. 'Changes in Trade and Employment in the Major Industrialized Countries, 1970-6', paper presented at the Sixth World Congress of Economists (Mexico, May 1980)

Dixon, G.L.R. and McGown, V.J. 'The Behaviour of Australian Manufactured Exports', *49th ANZAAS Conference* (Auckland, January 1979)

Dixon, P.B. and Powell, A.A. *Structural Adaptation in an Ailing Macroeconomy* (Melbourne University Press, 1979)

Donges, J.B. and Riedel, J. 'The Expansion of Manufactured Exports in Developing Countries', *Weltwirtschaftliches Archiv*, band 113, heft 1 (1977)

Dunning, J.H. 'Multinational Enterprises and Trade Flows of Less Developed Countries', *World Development*, vol. 2, no. 2 (February 1974)

—— 'Trade Location of Economic Activity and the MNE: A Search for an Eclectic Approach' in Ohlin, B., Hesselborn, P. and Wiskam, P. (eds.), *The International Allocation of Economic Activity* (Macmillan, London, 1977)

—— 'Explaining Changing Patterns of International Production: In Defence of the Eclectic Theory', *Oxford Bulletin of Economics and Statistics* (November 1979)

Dunning, J.H. and Buckley, P.J. 'International Production and Alternative Models of Trade', *Manchester School* (December 1977)

Economic Council of Canada, *For a Common Future* (Canadian Government, Ottawa, 1978)

Edgren, G. 'Employment Adjustment to Trade Under Conditions of Stagnating Growth', *International Labour Review*, vol. 117, no. 3 (May/June 1978)

Emmanuel, A. *Unequal Exchange: A Study of the Imperialism of*

Trade (Monthly Review Press, New York, 1972)

Evers, D. 'Industrial Adjustment in the Netherlands, with Special Emphasis upon the Clothing Industry' in OECD *Adjustment for Trade* (Paris, 1975a)

Fels, G. 'The Choice of Industry Mix in the Division of Labour Between Developed and Developing Countries', *Weltwirtschaftliches Archiv* (1972), pp. 71-119

Fieleke, N.S. 'The Automobile Industry', *Annals AAPSS* (March 1982)

Finger, J.M. 'GATT Tariff Concessions and the Exports of Developing Countries – United States Concessions at the Dillon Round', *Economic Journal* (September 1974)

—— 'A New View of the Product Cycle Theory', *Weltwirtschaftliches Archiv*, band 111, (1975a), pp. 79-98

—— 'Effects of the Kennedy Round Tariff Concessions on the Exports of Developing Countries', *Economic Journal* (March 1975b)

—— 'Tariff Provisions for Offshore Assembly and the Exports of Developing Countries', *Economic Journal* (June 1975c)

—— 'Offshore Assembly Provisions in the West German and Netherlands Tariffs: Trade and Domestic Effects', *Weltwirtschaftliches Archiv*, (1977), pp. 237-49

Finley, M.H. 'Foreign Trade and U.S. Employment' in US Department of Labor *The Impact of International Trade and Investment on Employment* (Washington, DC, 1978)

Fortune, J.N. 'Some Determinants of Trade in Finished Manufactures', *Swedish Journal of Economics* (1971), pp. 311-17

Frank, C.R. Jr. *Foreign Trade and Domestic Aid* (Brookings Institution, Washington, DC, 1977)

Frankena, M. 'Restrictions on Exports by Foreign Investors: The Case of India', *Journal of World Trade Law*, vol. 6, no. 5 (1972)

Frobel, F., Heinrichs, J. and Kreye, O. *The New International Division of Labour* (Cambridge University Press, Cambridge, 1980)

Gard, L.M. and Riedel, J. 'Safeguard Protection of Industry in Developed Countries: Assessment of the Implications for Developing Countries', *Weltwirtschaftliches Archiv*, band 116, heft 3 (1980)

Garnaut, R. and Anderson, K. 'ASEAN Export Specialization and the Evolution of Comparative Advantage in the Western Pacific Region' in Garnaut, R. (ed.), *ASEAN in a Changing Pacific World Economy* (ANU Press, Canberra, 1980)

Gastin, D. *The Pursuit of Structural Change in Manufacturing Industry* (Australian Government Publishing Service, Canberra, 1978)

General Agreement on Tariffs and Trade (GATT), *Industrial Pollution*

Control and International Trade (Studies in International Trade, no, 1, July 1971)

—— *International Trade* (Geneva), various issues

—— *Networks of World Trade* (Geneva, 1978)

Gibson, B. 'Unequal Exchange', *Review of Radical Political Economics* (Fall 1980)

Giersch, H. (ed.) *The International Division of Labour;' Problems and Perspectives* (Mohr, Tubingen, 1974)

—— (ed.) *On the Economics of Intra-Industry Trade* (Mohr, Tubingen, 1979)

Ginman, P. and Murray, T. 'The Generalized System of Preferences' in Sauvant, K.P. and Hasenpflug, H. (eds.), *The New International Economic Order* (Wilton House, London, 1978)

Glezer, L. *Tariff Politics: Australian Policy-Making 1960-1980* (Melbourne University Press, Melbourne, 1982)

Glisman, H.H. and Weiss, F.D. 'On the Political Economy of Protection in Germany', *World Bank Staff Working Paper*, no. 427 (October 1980)

Goldsbrough, D.J. 'International Trade of Multinational Corporations and its Responsiveness to Changes in Aggregate Demand and Relative Prices', *IMF Staff Papers* (1981)

Goodman, B. and Ceyhun, F. 'U.S. Export Performance in Manufacturing Industries: An Empirical Investigation', *Weltwirtschaftliches Archiv* (1976), pp. 525-54

Gray, H.P. *A Generalized Theory of International Trade* (Macmillan, London, 1976)

—— 'The Theory of International Trade Among Industrial Nations', *Weltwirtschaftliches Archiv*, band 116 (1980)

Gregory, R.G. 'Structural Change Prices, Employment and Imports in Australian Manufacturing Industry', *7th Conference of Australian Economic Society* (Macquarie University, Sydney, August 1978)

Grilli, E. 'Italian Commercial Policies in the 1970s', *World Bank Staff Working Paper*, no. 428 (October 1980)

Grubel, H.G. 'The Case Against the New International Economic Order', *Weltwirtschaftliches Archiv*, vol. 13 (1977)

—— 'A Reply to Helleiner's Comments', *Weltwirtschaftliches Archiv*, band 114, heft 1 (1978)

Grubel, H.G. and Lloyd, P.J. *Intra-Industry Trade* (Macmillan, London, 1975)

Gruber, W.H. and Vernon, R. 'The Technology Factor in a World Trade Matrix' in Vernon, R. (ed.), *The Technology Factor in International*

Trade (National Bureau of Economic Research, New York, 1970)

Gruen, F.H. 'The 25% Tariff Cut: Was it a Mistake?', *The Australian Quarterly*, vol. 47, no. 2 (June 1975)

Hamilton, C. and Kreinen, M.E. 'The Structural Pattern of LDCs' Trade in Manufacturing with Individual and Groups of Developed Countries', *Weltwirtschaftliches Archiv*, band 116, heft 2 (1980)

Harkness, J. and Kyle, J.F. 'Factors Influencing United States' Comparative Advantage', *Journal of International Economics* (May 1975)

Healey, D.I. 'Structural Adjustments within the Economies of Australia, Japan, Sweden and the U.S. in Response to Imports from Developing Countries: Lessons for Australia', *50th ANZAAS Congress* (Adelaide, May 1980)

Helleiner, G.K. 'Manufactured Exports from Less Developed Countries and Multinational Firms', *Economic Journal* (March 1973)

—— 'Manufactured Exports from Less Developed Countries and Industrial Adjustment in Canada' in OECD *Adjustment for Trade* (Paris, 1975a)

—— 'Industry Characteristics and the Competitiveness of Manufactures from Less Developed Countries', *Weltwirtschaftliches Archiv*, band 112 (1976)

—— 'A Bad Case: Grubel on the New International Economic Order', *Weltwirtschaftliches Archiv*, band 114, heft 1 (1978)

—— *Intra-Firm Trade and the Developing Countries* (Macmillan, London, 1981)

Helleiner, G.K. and Lavergne, R. 'Intra-Firm Trade and Industrial Exports to the United States', *Oxford Bulletin of Economics and Statistics* (November 1979)

Hirsch, S. 'Technological Factors in the Composition and Direction of Israel's Industrial Exports' in Vernon, R. (ed.), *The Technological Factor in International Trade* (National Bureau of Economic Research, New York, 1970)

—— 'The United States Electronics Industry in International Trade' in Wells, L.T. Jr. (ed.), *The Product Life Cycle and International Trade* (Harvard University Press, Boston, 1972)

—— 'Capital or Technology? Confronting the Neo-Factor Proportions and Neo-Technology of International Trade', *Weltwirtschaftliches Archiv*, (1974a), pp. 534-63

—— 'Hypotheses Regarding Trade Between Developing and Industrial Countries' in Giersch, H. (ed.), *The International Division of Labour, Problems and Perspectives* (Mohr, Tubingen, 1974b)

—— 'The Product Cycle Model of International Trade – A Multi-

Country Cross-Section Analysis', *Oxford Bulletin of Economics and Statistics*, vol. 37, no. 4 (1975)

—— 'An International Trade and Investment Theory of the Firm', *Oxford Economic Papers* (July 1976)

Hogan, W.P. 'British Manufacturing Subsidiaries in Australia and Export Franchises', *Economic Papers* (July 1976)

—— 'Devising Structural Adjustment Policies', *Malayan Economic Review*, vol. 24, no. 1 (April 1979)

Hone, A. 'Multinational Corporations and Multinational Buying Groups: Their Impact on the Growth of Asia's Exports of Manufacturing — Myths and Realities', *World Development*, vol. 2, no. 2 (February 1974)

Howenstine, N.G. 'Selected Data on the Operations of U.S. Affiliates of Foreign Companies, 1977' in US Department of Commerce *Survey of Current Business* (Washington, DC), various issues

Hsieh, C. 'Measuring the Effects of Trade Expansion on Employment', *International Labour Review* (January 1973)

Hufbauer, G.C. *Synthetic Materials and the Theory of International Trade* (Harvard University Press, Cambridge, Mass., 1966)

—— 'The Impact of National Characteristics and Technology on the Commodity Composition of Trade in Manufactured Goods' in Vernon, R. (ed.), *The Technological Factor in International Trade* (National Bureau of Economic Research, New York, 1970)

Hufbauer, G.C. and Adler, F.M. *Overseas Manufacturing Investment and the Balance of Payments* (US Treasury Department, Washington, DC, 1968)

Hufbauer, G.C. 'The Multinational Enterprise and Direct Investment' in Kenen, P.B. (ed.), *International Trade and Finance: Frontiers of Research* (Cambridge University Press, Cambridge, 1975)

Hughes, H. (ed.), *Prospects for Partnership* (Johns Hopkins University Press, Baltimore, 1973)

—— 'The Prospects of ASEAN Countries in Industrialized Country Markets', *10th Pacific Trade and Development Conference* (Australian National University, Canberra, 19-23 March 1979)

Hughes, H. and Woelbroeck, J. 'Can Developing Country Exports Keep Growing in the 1980s?', *World Development* (June 1981)

IBRD *Mexico's Manufactured Exports*, Report no. 79-ME (1973)

ILO 'Some Labour Implications of Increased Participation of Developing Countries in Trade and Manufactures and Semi Manufactures' in *UN Proceedings of UNCTAD*, 2nd Session, vol. III (New York, 1968)

IMF *Survey* (25 June 1980)

Industries Assistance Commission (IAC) *Annual Reports* (1973 to 1978) (Canberra, 1977a)

—— *Structural Change in Australia* (Canberra, June 1977b)

—— *Structural Change and Economic Interdependence* (Canberra, July 1977c)

—— *Some Issues in Structural Adjustment* (Canberra, 1977d)

—— *Report on Textiles, Clothing and Footwear* (Canberra, April 1980)

Institute of Southeast Asian Studies, *Multinational Corporations and their Implications for Southeast Asia* (December 1972)

Iqbal, Z. 'The Generalized System of Preferences and the Comparative Advantage of Less Developed Countries in Manufactures', *Pakistan Development Review*, vol. 13, no. 2 (Summer 1974)

—— 'The Generalized System of Preferences Examined', *Finance and Development*, vol. 12, no. 3 (September 1975)

—— 'Trade Effects of the Generalized System of Preferences', *Pakistan Development Review*, vol. 15, no. 1 (Spring 1976)

Ironmonger, D. 'Protection for Whom? Economy-Wide Effects', *Economic Papers*, vol. 1, no. 2 (September 1982)

Isard, P. 'Employment Impacts of Textile Imports and Investment: A Vintage-Capital Model', *American Economic Review*, vol. 63, no. 3 (June 1973)

James, D. 'The Assessment of Adjustment Problems in Australian Trade' in Kojima, K. (ed.) *Structural Adjustments in Asian-Pacific Trade* (Japan Economic Research Center, Tokyo, July 1973)

Janvoy, A. de and Kramer, F. 'The Limits of Unequal Exchange', *Review of Radical Political Economics* (Winter 1974)

Jenkins, G.P. and Montmarquette, C. 'Estimating the Private and Social Opportunity Cost of Displaced Workers', *Review of Economics and Statistics*, vol. 31, no. 3 (August 1979)

Johnson, H.G. *Economic Policies Towards Less Developed Countries* (Allen & Unwin, London, 1965)

—— *Comparative Cost and Commercial Policy for a Developing World Economy* (Almqvist and Wiksell, Stockholm, 1968)

—— (ed.) *The New Mercantilism* (Basil Blackwell, Oxford, 1974)

Johnson, H.G. and Salt, J. 'Employment Transfer Policies in Great Britain', *The Three Banks Review* (June 1980)

Junz, H.B. 'Adjustment Policies and Trade Relations with Developing Countries', *Nebraska Journal of Economic Business*, vol. 18, no. 2 (Spring 1979)

Kasper, W. *Charity Begins at Home – On Development, Trade and Structural Adjustment* (Australian National University Development Studies Centre, Monograph no. 16, 1979)

Kasper, W. and Parry, T.G. *Growth, Trade and Structural Change in an Open Australian Economy* (NSW University Centre for Applied Economic Research, Sydney, 1978)

Keen, S. 'Asia's Growth Seen as Threat to World', *Sydney Morning Herald* (12 March 1979)

Keesing, D.B. 'Labor Skills and Comparative Advantage', *American Economic Review* (May 1966)

—— 'Different Countries' Labor Skill Coefficients and the Skill Intensity of International Trade Flows', *Journal of International Economics* (November 1971)

Kenen, P. 'Nature, Capital and Trade', *Journal of Political Economy* (October 1965)

—— (ed.) *International Trade and Finance: Frontiers of Research* (Cambridge University Press, Cambridge, 1975)

Kerdpibule, W. 'Trends in Manufactured Exports in Southeast Asian Countries', *World Bank Staff Working Paper*, no. 139 (January 1972)

Kirkpatrick, C. and Yamin, M. 'The Determinants of Export Subsidiary Formation by U.S. Transnationals in Developing Countries', *World Development*, vol. 9, no. 4 (April 1981)

Kleiman, E. 'Metropolitan Exports Lost Through Decolonization', *Oxford Bulletin*, vol. 40, no. 3 (August 1978)

Kojima, K. (ed) *Structural Adjustments in Asian-Pacific Trade* (Japan Economic Research Center, Tokyo, July 1973)

Krause, L.B. 'The U.S. Economy and International Trade' in Kojima, K. (ed.) *Structural Adjustments in Asian-Pacific Trade* (Japan Economic Research Center, Tokyo, July 1973)

Krause, L.B. and Mathieson, J. 'How Much of Current Unemployment Did We Import?', *Brookings Papers on Economic Activity*, no. 2 (1971)

Krauss, M.B. *The New Protectionism* (Basil Blackwell, Oxford, 1979)

Kravis, I.B. and Lipsey, R.E. 'The Location of Overseas Production and Production for Export by U.S. Multinational Firms', *Journal of International Economics* (1982), pp. 201-23

Kreinen, M.E. and Officer, L.H. 'Tariff Reductions Under the Tokyo Round: A Review of Their Effects on Trade Flows, Employment and Welfare', *Weltwirtschaftliches Archiv*, band 115, heft 3 (1979)

Krueger, A.O. *Growth, Distortions and Patterns of Trade Among Many*

Countries (Princeton Studies in International Finance, no. 40, 1977)

—— 'ASEAN in a Changing Pacific and World Economy', *10th Pacific Trade and Development Conference* (Australian National University, Canberra, 19-23 March 1979)

Lage, G.M. and Kiang, F.F. 'The Potential for Mutually Beneficial Trade Negotiations between the United States and Advanced LDCs', *Weltwirtschaftliches Archiv*, band 115, heft 7 (1979)

Lall, S. 'Transfer-Pricing by Multinational Manufacturing Firms', *Oxford Bulletin of Economics and Statistics* (August 1973)

—— 'The Pattern of Intra-Firm Exports by U.S. Multinationals', *Oxford Bulletin of Economics and Statistics*, vol. 40, no. 3 (August 1978)

—— 'Offshore Assembly in Developing Countries', *National Westminster Bank Quarterly Review* (August 1980)

Landsberg, M. 'Export-Led Industrialization in the Third World: Manufacturing Imperialism', *The Review of Radical Political Economics*, vol. 11, no. 4 (Winter 1979)

Lary, H.B. *Imports of Manufactures from Less Developed Countries* (National Bureau of Economic Research, New York, 1968)

—— 'Comment on Hypotheses and Tests of Trade Patterns' in Vernon, R. (ed.) *The Technology Factor in International Trade* (National Bureau of Economic Research, New York, 1970)

Leamer, E.E. 'The Leontief Paradox Reconsidered', *Journal of Political Economies* (June 1980)

Leontief, W. 'Domestic Production and Foreign Trade: The American Capital Position Re-Examined', *Economia Internazionale*, vol. 11, no. 1 (1954)

—— 'Factor Proportions and the Structure of American Trade: Further Theoretical and Empirical Analysis', *Review of Economics and Statistics* (November 1956)

Leveson, I. and Wheeler, J.W. (eds.) *Western Economies in Transition* (Croom Helm, London, 1980)

Linder. S.B. *An Essay on Trade and Transformation* (Almqvist and Wiksell, Uppsala, 1961)

Lipsey, R.E. and Weiss, M.Y. 'Foreign Production and Exports in Manufacturing Industries', *Review of Economics and Statistics*, vol. 33, no. 4 (November 1981)

Lloyd, P.J. 'Protection for Whom?', *Economic Papers*, vol. 1, no 2 (September 1982)

Loerscher, R. and Wolfer, F. 'Determinants of Intra-Industry Trade:

Among Nations and Across Industries', *Weltwirtschaftliches Archiv*, band 116 (1980)

Long, F. 'Multinational Corporations and the Non-Primary Sector Trade of Developing Countries: A Survey of Available Data', *Economia Internazionale* (November 1981)

Luttrell, C.B. 'Imports and Jobs – The Observed and the Unobserved', *Federal Reserve Bank of St Louis* (June 1978)

Lydall, H.F. 'Employment Effects of Trade Expansion', *International Labour Review* (1975), pp. 219-34

MacBean, A. *A Positive Approach to the International Economic Order* (British-North American Committee, London, 1978)

McCarthy, J.E. 'Contrasting Experience with Trade Adjustment Assistance' in Balassa, B. (ed.) *Changing Patterns in Foreign Trade and Payments* (Norton and Co., New York, 1978c)

MacDougall, G.D.A. 'British and American Exports: A Study Suggested by the Theory of Comparative Costs', *Economic Journal* (December 1951)

McDowall, S. and Draper, P. *Trade Adjustment and the British Jute Industry* (Overseas Development Institute, London, 1978)

McFadzean, F. *Towards an Open Economy* (Macmillan, London, 1972)

McKinnon, W.A. 'Protection for Whom? The IAC View', *Economic Papers*, vol. 1, no. 2 (September 1982)

McMahon, P. 'Australian-Asian Trade: An Examination of Aspects of Comparative Advantage', *7th Conference of Australian Economic Society* (Macquarie University, Sydney, August 1978)

MacPhee, C.R. 'Martin Bronfen Brenner on UNCTAD and the GSP', *Economic Development and Cultural Change* (January 1979)

Magee, S.P. 'The Welfare Effects of Restrictions on U.S. Trade', *Brookings Papers on Economic Activity*, no. 3 (1972)

Mainwaring, L. 'International Trade and the Transfer of Labour Value', *Journal of Development Studies* (October 1980)

Majumdar, B.A. 'Innovations and International Trade: An Industry Study of Dynamic Competitive Advantage', *Kyklos*, vol. 32, fasc. 3 (1979)

Mansfield, E., Romeo, A. and Wagner, S. 'Foreign Trade and U.S. Research and Development', *Review of Economics and Statistics* (February 1979)

Marris, S. 'O.E.C.D. Trade with the Newly Industrializing Countries', *OECD Observer* (July 1979)

Matthews, R.A. 'Canadian Industry and the Challenge of Low-Cost

Imports', *Economic Council of Canada*, Discussion Paper no. 172 (Ottawa, July 1980)

Meier, G.M. *Employment, Trade and Development* (Institute of International Studies, Geneva, 1977)

Melvin, J.R. 'Commodity Taxation as a Determinant of Trade', *Canadian Journal of Economics* (February 1970)

Messerlin, P.A. 'The Political Economy of Protectionism: The Bureaucratic Case', *Weltwirtschaftliches Archiv*, band 117, heft 3 (1981)

Mills, C. 'Adjustment Assistance Policies: A Survey' in OECD *Adjustment for Trade* (Paris, 1975a)

Milner, C. and Greenaway, D. 'Rethinking Trade Policy', *Westminster Bank Quarterly Review* (February 1981)

Minhas, B.S. *An International Comparison of Factor Costs and Factor Use* (North Holland, Amsterdam, 1963)

Miramon, G. de and Kleitz, A. 'Tariff Preferences for the Developing World', *OECD Observer*, no. 90 (January 1978)

Monson, T.D. 'An Extension of Bale's Labor Displacement Cost Estimates', *Journal of International Economics* (1978), pp. 131-3

Morawetz, D. 'Clothes for Export: Not Made in Columbia', *Finance and Development* (March 1981)

Morrall, J.F. *Human Capital, Technology and the Role of the United States in International Trade* (University of Florida Press, Gainsville, 1972)

Morrison, T.K. 'International Subcontracting: Improved Prospects in Manufactured Exports for Small and Very Poor LDCs', *World Development*, vol. 4, no. 4 (1976)

Moxon, R. 'Offshore Production in the Less Developed Countries', *Bulletin of New York University, Graduate School of Business Administration* (July 1974)

Mueller, H.G. 'The Steel Industry', *Annals, AAPSS* (March 1982)

Mullor-Sebastian, A. 'The Product-Cycle Theory: Empirical Evidence', presented at the 44th Annual Meeting of the American Economic Association, Washington, DC (28 December 1981)

Murray, T. *Trade Preferences for Developing Countries* (Macmillan, London, 1977)

—— 'Trade Preferences and Multinational Firm Exports from Developing Countries' in Tyler, W.G. (ed.) *Issues and Prospects for the New International Economic Order* (Lexington, Toronto, 1977)

Murray, T. and Egmund, M.R. 'Full Employment, Trade Expansion and Adjustment Assistance', *Southern Economic Journal* (April 1970)

Mutti, J.H. 'Welfare Effects of Multilateral Tariff Reductions', *Southern*

Economic Journal (January 1979)

Nayyar, D. 'Transnational Corporations and Manufactured Exports from Poor Countries', *Economic Journal* (March 1978)

Neumann, G. 'The Direct Labour Market Effects of the Trade Adjustment Assistance Program' in US Department of Labor *The Impact of International Trade and Investment on Employment* (Washington, DC, 1978)

Nowzad, B. 'Differential Trade Treatment for LDCs', *Finance and Development* (March 1978a)

────── *The Rise of Protectionism* (IMF, Washington, DC, 1978b)

O'Clearealain, S. 'Adjustment Assistance to Import Competition' in McFadzean, F. (ed.) *Towards an Open Economy* (Macmillan, London, 1972)

OECD *Adjustment for Trade* (Paris, 1975a)

────── *The Industrial Policy of Australia* (Paris, 1975b)

────── *The Case for Positive Adjustment Policies* (Paris, 1979a)

────── *The Impact of the Newly Industrialising Countries on Production and Trade in Manufacturing* (Paris, 1979b)

Ohlin, B. *Interregional and International Trade* (Harvard University Press, Cambridge, Mass., 1967)

────── 'The Business Cost Account Approach to International Trade Theory', *Swedish Journal of Economics* (February 1970)

Ohlin, B., Hesselborn, P. and Wiskam, P. (eds.) *The International Allocation of Economic Activity* (Macmillan, London, 1978)

Pearson, C. and Pryor, A. *Environment: North and South* (Wiley and Sons, New York, 1978)

Pelzman, J. 'The Textile Industry', *Annals, AAPSS* (March 1982)

PEP *Non-Tariff Distortions of Trade*, Broadsheet no. 514 (September 1969)

Pestieau, C. 'Market Access for Manufactured Exports from Developing Countries', paper presented at Halifax Conference, *Canada and the New International Economic Order* (1975)

Posner, M.V. 'International Trade and Technical Change', *Oxford Economic Papers* (October 1961)

Priorities Review Staff *Assistance for Structural Adjustment, Income Maintenance, Etc.* (Canberra, 1975)

Quiggin, J.D. and Stoeckel, A.B. 'Protection, Income Distribution and the Rural Sector', *Economic Papers*, vol. 1, no. 2 (September 1982)

Rahman, A.H.M.M. *Exports of Manufactures from Developing Countries* (Rotterdam University Press, Rotterdam, 1973)

Ray, E.J. 'The Determinants of Tariff and Nontariff Trade Restrictions in the United States', *Journal of Political Economy* (February 1981)

Reddaway, W.B. *Effects of U.K. Direct Investment Overseas: Final Report* (Cambridge University Press, Cambridge, 1968)

Renshaw, G. (ed.) *Employment, Trade and North-South Co-operation* (ILO, Geneva, 1981)

Riedel, J. 'Tariff Concessions in the Kennedy Round and the Structure of Protection in West Germany', *Journal of International Economics* (1977), pp. 133-43

Robertson, D. 'The Multinational Enterprise: Trade Flows and Trade Policy' in Dunning, J. (ed.) *International Investment* (Penguin, London, 1972)

Ross, A.C. 'Emmanuel on Unequal Exchange', *Journal of Economic Studies* (May 1976)

Round, D.K. 'The Determinants of Profitability and Tariffs in Australian Manufacturing', *The Malayan Economic Review* (October 1980)

Sailors, J.W., Quereshi, U.A. and Cross, E.M. 'Empirical Verification of Linder's Trade Thesis', *Southern Economic Journal* (October 1973), pp. 262-8

Sampson, G.P. 'Contemporary Protectionism and Exports of Developing Countries', *World Development*, vol. 8 (1980), pp. 113-27

Sau, R. *Unequal Exchange, Imperialism and Underdevelopment* (Oxford University Press, Bombay, 1978)

Saunders, R.S. 'The Political Economy of Effective Tariff Protection in Canada's Manufacturing Sector', *Canadian Journal of Economics* (May 1980)

Sauvant, K.P. and Hasenpflug, H. (eds.) *The New International Economic Order* (Wilton House, London, 1978)

Schmid, G. and Phillips, O. 'Textile Trade and the Pattern of Economic Growth', *Weltwirtschaftliches Archiv*, band 116 (1980), pp. 294-305

Sekiguchi, S. and Krause, L.B. 'Direct Foreign Investment in ASEAN by Japan and the United States' in Garnaut, R. (ed.), *ASEAN in a Changing Pacific World Economy* (ANU Press, Canberra, 1980)

Sharpston, M. 'International Sub-Contracting', *Oxford Economic Papers* (March 1975)

—— 'International Subcontracting', *World Development*, vol. 4, no. 4 (1976)

Shelton, W.C., Bureau of Labor Statistics 'The Relationship between Changes in Imports and Employment in the U.S. 1960-5', paper presented to American Statistical Association (Detroit, 1970)

Sherk, D.K. 'The New International Trade Models and their Relevance for Developing Asia', *Malayan Economic Review* (October 1969)

Stein, L. 'The Growth and Implications of LDC Manufactured Exports to Advanced Countries', *Kyklos*, vol. 34, fasc. 1 (1981)

—— 'Trade Adjustment Assistance to Achieve Improved Resource Allocation', *American Journal of Economics and Sociology* (July 1982)

—— 'General Measures to Assist Workers and Firms in Adjusting to Dislocation from Freer Trade', *American Journal of Economics and Sociology* (July 1983)

Stern, R.M. 'Testing Trade Theories' in Kenen, P. (ed.) *International Trade and Finance: Frontiers of Research* (Cambridge University Press, Cambridge, 1975)

Stern, R.M. and Maskus, K.E. 'Determinants of the Structure of U.S. Foreign Trade, 1958-76', *Journal of International Economics* (1981), pp. 207-24

Stewart, F. 'Adjustment Assistance: A Proposal', *World Development*, vol. 1, no. 6 (June 1973)

Study Group on Structural Adjustment, *Report*, vols. 1 and 2 (Canberra, 1979)

Swedenborg, B. *The Multinational Operations of Swedish Firms* (Industrial Institute for Economic and Social Research, Stockholm, 1979)

Szenberg, M., Lombardi, J.W. and Lee, E.Y. *Welfare Effects of Trade Restrictions* (Academic Press, New York, 1977)

Takacs, W.E. 'Prospects for Protectionism: An Empirical Analysis', *Economic Inquiry* (October 1981)

Tharakan, P.K.M. 'The Political Economy of Protectionism in Belgium', *World Bank Staff Working Paper*, no. 431 (October 1980)

Torre, J.R. de la, Jr. 'Exports of Manufactured Goods from Developing Countries: Marketing Factors and the Role of Foreign Enterprise', *Journal of International Business Studies* (Spring 1971)

—— 'Foreign Investment and Export Dependence', *Economic Development and Cultural Change* (October 1974)

Tuong, H.D. and Yeats, A.J. 'On Factor Proportions as a Guide to the Future Composition of Developing Country Exports', *Journal of Development Economics* (December 1980)

—— 'Market Disruption, the New Protectionism and Developing Countries', *Developing Economies* (June 1981)

Turner, L., Bradford, C.I., Franko, L.G., McMullen, N. and Woolcock, S. *Living with the Newly Industrialized Countries* (Royal Institute of International Affairs, London, 1980)

Tyler, W.G. (ed.) *Issues and Prospects for the New International*

Economic Order (Lexington, Toronto, 1977)

UN *Adjustment Assistance Measures*, TD/121 Supplement 1 (New York, January 1972)

UNCTAD *Handbook of International Trade* (New York, 1969)

—— *Trade in Manufactures of Developing Countries, 1969 Review* (New York, 1970)

UNIDO *Industrial Development Survey* (New York, 1974)

US Department of Commerce *Survey of Current Business* (Washington, DC), various issues

US Department of Labor *The Impact of International Trade and Investment on Employment* (Washington, DC, 1978)

US Tariff Commission *Implications of Multinational Firms for World Trade and Investment, and for U.S. Trade and Labor* (Washington, DC, 1978)

Vanek, J. 'The Factor Proportions Theory: The N-Factor Case', *Kyklos* (October 1968)

Vernon, R. 'International Investment and International Trade in the Product Cycle', *Quarterly Journal of Economics* (May 1966)

—— (ed.) *The Technology Factor in International Trade* (National Bureau of Economic Research, New York, 1970)

—— 'The Product Cycle Hypothesis in a New International Environment', *Oxford Bulletin of Economics and Statistics*, vol. 41, no. 4 (November 1979)

Verreydt, E. and Waelbroeck, J. 'European Community Protection Against Manufactured Imports from Developing Countries: A Case Study in the Political Economy of Protection', *World Bank Staff Working Paper*, no. 432 (October 1980)

—— 'Protection, Employment and Welfare in a Developing Economy: Policy Issues for the EEC', *6th World Congress of Economists* (Mexico City, August 1982)

Viansson-Ponte, P. 'Undevelopment or Economic Miracle?', *Guardian* (weekend edn, 20 May 1979)

Walter, I. 'The Pollution Content of American Trade', *Western Economic Journal* (March 1973)

—— *International Economics of Pollution* (Macmillan, London, 1975)

Watanabe, E. 'International Subcontracting, Employment and Skill Promotion', *International Labour Review* (May 1972)

Wells, L.T. Jr. 'Test of a Product Cycle Model of International Trade: U.S. Exports of Consumer Variables', *Quarterly Journal of Economics* (February 1969)

—— *The Product Life Cycle and International Trade* (Harvard University Press, Boston, 1972)

Wheelwright, E. and Buckley, K. *Essays on the Political Economy of Australian Capitalism*, vol. 3 (Australia & New Zealand Book Co., Sydney, 1978)

Williams, H.R. 'U.S. Trade Adjustment Assistance to Mitigate Injury from Import Competition', *American Journal of Economics and Sociology* (October 1977)

—— 'U.S. Measures to Relieve Injury Caused by Import Competition: The Eligibility Test', *Journal of World Trade Law* (January/February 1978)

World Bank, *World Development Report*, various issues (Oxford University Press, New York)

Yeats, A.J. 'Recent Changes in Developing Country Exports', *Weltwirtschaftliches Archiv*, band 115, heft 1 (1979)

Zimmer and Murray, T. 'The Generalized System of Preferences' in Sauvant, K.P.P. and Hasenpflug, H. (eds.) *The New International Economic Order* (Wilton House, London, 1978)

INDEX

Adjustments 118–39
Adler, F.M. 56, 75
Advertising 39, 48, 58, 67–8, 75
Agricultural Products 110
Aircraft 54
AFL-CIO 122
Africa 60
After Sales Service 67, 70
Aluminium 72
Amin, S. 161
Anderson, K. 93
Anthony, D. 102
Aquino, A. 22
Arad, R. 54
Arbitration Court 92
Argentina 63, 105
Asia 14, 60–1, 71, 101, 105
Australia 69–91, 93, 94, 97, 99, 101,
    125–8, 133–4, 138
Australian Government 125
Austria 11
Automobiles 99, 123, 130–1; *see
    also* cars

Bacha, E.L. 161
Balance of Payments 90
Balassa, B. 24, 30, 36, 52, 43–4,
    46–8, 50, 54, 130, 111–12,
    116–17
Baldwin, R. 8, 28–30, 32, 38, 40,
    51–3, 95, 98, 102, 110, 116, 139,
    140
Bale, M.D. 117, 121, 139–40
Batchelor, R.A. 57, 62, 66, 75–6
Beer 12
Belgium 11
Belgium–Luxembourg 29
Bergsten, C.F. 57–8, 75, 102–3
Bhagwati, J. 8, 21, 24–5, 51
Bicycles 13
Blackhurst, R. 112, 116–17
Blejer, M.I. 45, 46
Brander, J.A. 11, 22
Branson, W.H. 30, 32, 36, 40, 52–3
Bruan, R. 141
Brazil 63, 100, 105, 115
Buckley, P.J. 42, 54

Canada 11, 48, 60, 90, 93–4, 97, 99,
    101, 110–11, 113, 116, 123–5,
    127–8, 130–2, 135, 138
Canadian–American Automobile
    Pact 130–1
Capital 10, 29–30, 32, 36–7, 45,
    49, 50; and Foreign 14, 57, 94;
    Human 27, 29–30, 32, 38, 48–9,
    50, 52; Intensities 30, 36, 38–9,
    47–50, 132, 136; Social 95
Capital Stock 49
Cars 13, 43, 100
Caves, R. 8, 24–5, 30, 50–1
Ceyhun, F. 36, 39, 52–3
Cheh, J.H. 117
Chemicals 54, 107–8
Chenery, H.B. 95, 102
Chouori, E.U. 52
Clark, D. 161
Cline, W.R. 98, 103, 110–11, 113,
    116–17
Clothing 69, 95, 100–1, 105, 107–8,
    131–35
Coal 141
Coffey, P. 141
Cohen, B.I. 63, 70
Cohen, S.P. 103
Colombia 63, 67, 70
Computers 59–60
Congress (US) 100
Consumer Supplies 80
Corden, M. 22, 83, 102
Cork 41
China 11
Cournot Model 12
Curzon, Z. 103, 139

Daly, D.J. 90, 102
Deardorff, A.V. 142
Denmark, 7, 11
Devaluation 90
Distance Factor 13
Donges, J.D. 112, 117
Drugs 36, 39, 54
Dunning, J.M. 41–2, 54, 75–6

Edgren, G. 139

Education 27, 35–8, 75
Effective Price 83
Effective Protection 82–7, 94
Egmund, M.R. 136, 142
Elderly 119, 139
Electrical Goods 113
Electronics 72, 97, 103, 125
Emmanuel, A. 142–61
Employment 90, 91, 97, 101, 104, 108–16, 118–19, 125
Employment Transfer Scheme 129
Engineering Goods 107–8
Engineers 38–9, 43, 57
Europe 13, 18, 43, 61, 63, 93, 100, 128, 141
European Economic Community (EEC) 58, 61, 96–100, 108, 110–13, 129
European Free Trade Association (EFTA) 108, 112
Evers, D. 142
Exchange Rates 110

Factor Intensity Reversals 28, 34
Factor Price Equalization 15, 27
Factor Proportions 12–14
Farm Machinery 60
Farm Products 62
Finger, J.M. 19–20, 22, 74, 77, 95, 103
Finley, M.H. 122, 140
Firm Specific Advantages 64–5
Food 108
Food Processing 72
Footwear 69, 108, 113, 123, 133–35; *see also* shoes
Foreign Exchange 73–4
Foreign Investment 42, 56, 57, 63, 95
Foreign Subsidiaries 56–60, 66, 71, 75
Fortune, J.N. 44–5, 54
France 11, 29, 93, 101, 129
Frank, C.R. 109, 116–17, 123, 130, 139–41
Fraser, M. 102
Freedom From Hunger 101
Furniture 108

Gard, L.M. 99, 100, 103
Garment Workers 72
Gatt 61, 96, 98–9, 101, 123, 138
General Adjustment Assistance Program 123–4

General Motors 94
Gibson, B. 161
Giersch, H. 22, 142
Glass 97
Glezer, L. 102
Golsbrough, D.J. 69, 76, 77
Goodman, B. 36, 39, 52–3
Grain Mills 60
Grubel, H.G. 110–11
Gruber, W.H. 38–9, 53
Gruen, F. 123

Haiti 73
Harkness, J. 29–30, 32, 52
Heckscher–Ohlin Theorem 3–10, 49; and Produce Cycle Theory 19; Commodity Version 10; Critique of 12, 13; Empirical Testing of 25–33, 34–6, 46–7, 52; Factor Content Version 10; Multi-Commodities and Countries 8–10
Helleiner, G.K. 48, 66–7, 69–70, 54, 76–7, 141
Hirsch, S. 19, 22, 36–7, 41, 52–4
Holland 135
Hone, A. 63, 77
Hong Kong 38, 63, 72, 96, 99, 100–1, 105
Howenstine, N.G. 62
Hufbauer, G.C. 16–18, 28–9, 33–5, 49, 52, 56, 68, 75, 94, 102
Hughes, H. 95, 102

ILO 108
Imperialism 143
Import Quotas 64, 87–8, 91, 94, 99, 124, 126, 133–4
Imports and Jobs *see* Trade and Development
Income, Per Capita 13, 37, 42, 45
Income Elasticities of Demand 18, 20, 40, 45
Income Elasticities of Ownership 40
India 38, 63, 66, 105
Industries Assistance Commission 133–4
Industry, Definition of 11, 15
Industry Concentration 38–40
Infant Industries 88–9, 95
Inflation 125, 136
Intensity of Trade 12
Inter-Regional Trade 12
Intra-firm Trade 56, 62, 65–71, 94;

see also Offshore Processing
Intra-industry Trade 7, 10–12, 47, 112, 136
Intra-regional Trade 12
Iqbal, Z. 95, 98, 102–3
Iron 107
Isard, P. 117
Israel 105
Italy 11, 129

Jager, E. 122
James, D. 125
Janvoy, de A. 161
Japan 13, 20, 28, 38, 43, 63, 94, 96–100, 110–11, 113, 141
Johnson, H.G. 102
Jones, R. 8, 24–5, 30, 51

Keen, S. 104
Keesing, D. 37–8, 53
Kenen, P. 51
Kennedy Round 98, 121–23
Kiang, F.F. 103
Kirkpatrick, C. 70, 77
Kleitz, A. 103
Kramer, F. 161
Krause, L.B. 109, 116, 141
Kreinen, M.E. 116
Kyle, J.F. 29–30, 32, 52

Lage, G.M. 103
Lall, S. 66–7, 76–7
Lary, H. 48–50, 51–2, 54
Latin America 60–1, 63
Lavergne, R. 67, 69–70, 76
Leamer, E.E. 30, 32–3, 52
Leather 69, 108
Leontief, W. 10, 25–8, 32, 51; his Paradox 25–35, 39
Less Developed Countries (LDCs) 14, 19, 43, 47–8, 48–61, 66–7, 69–70, 73–6, 91, 94–108, 111–15, 118–19, 124, 131, 141, 143–161 *see also* Third World
LOC Exports 105–8; and Jobs 111–13
Liberal Party (Australian) 102
Linder, S.B. 12–14, 22
Linder's Hypothesis 7, 12–14, 47; Test of 44–6
Lipsey, R. 11, 22, 58–9, 75
Lloyd, P.J. 10–11
Lobbying 93–4
Logit Analysis 29

Lome Convention 96
Long, F. 63
Luttrell, C.B. 108, 116

McCarthy, J.E. 140
MacDougall, G.D. 23–5, 50
Machinery 105
Mainwaring, J. 161
Man-made Fibres 99, 125
Manitoba 116
Mansfield, E. 41, 53
Marris, S. 111, 116
Marx, K. 144
Maskus, K.E. 32, 35, 40, 52
Mathieson, J. 109, 116
Matthews, R.A. 124, 142
Metals 108
Mexico 38, 63, 66, 72, 96, 105
Migrants 73, 135
Mills, C. 130, 140–1
Minhas, B.S. 28, 51
Miramon, G. de 103
Monoyios, W. 30, 32, 40, 52
Montreal 135
Morrall, J. 22, 35–6, 44, 52–3
Motor Vehicles 62
Moson, R. 73, 77
Mullor-Sebastian, A. 41, 53
Multi-fibre Agreement 97, 99
Multilateral Tariff Reductions 110, 113
Multinational Corporations 14–42, 55–77, 94, 105, 143, and Third World 70–1, 101, Trade Theory 64–5; Current Exports 59–63; Investments and Exports 56–9; Offshore Processing 71–4
Murray, T. 95–6, 98, 102, 103, 136, 142

Natural Resources 27, 29, 37, 45
Nayyar, D. 63, 73, 75, 77
Netherlands 11, 72
Neumann, G. 139
New England 136
New Zealand 97
Non-ferrous Metals 105
Non Price Competition 19–20
North America 108
Norway 99
Nowzad, B. 103, 117

O'Clearealain 139
OECD 48, 60, 66–8, 111, 118–19,

129
Office Machinery 54, 59–60
Offshore Processing 46, 71–4, 76
Ohlin, B. 6–8, 75
Oil 75, 106, 110
Oligopolists 16
OPEC 96

Pakistan 63, 105
Paper 107
Pestieau, C. 141
Philippines 63, 105, 116
Photographic Supplies 54
Posner, M.V. 14–16, 22, 41, 55
Producer Surplus 80
Product Concentration 20
Product Cycle Theory 17–20, 34–5,
    40, 43, 53
Product Differentiation 7, 33–4
Productivity 109
Profit Analysis 30, 32
Protection 78, 102, 115, 119, 124,
    128, 132, 134–8; and New
    Protectionism 99–102; Political
    Economy of 92–4; Theory of
    78–82; *see also* Tariffs

Quebec 124
Quiggin, J.D. 94

Reddaway, W.B. 56, 75
Research and Development 27, 36,
    37–40, 42–4, 58, 65, 67–8
Resource Tax 92
'Revealed' Comparative Advantage
    36, 43–4, 46
Ricardian Theory 1–3; Test of 23–5
Ricardo, D. 1, 3
Riedel, T. 99, 100, 103, 112, 117

Sailors, J.W. 44–5, 54
Sales Taxes 137–8
Sau, R. 161
Saudi Arabia 12
Scale Economies 6, 11, 18, 37–48,
    68, 90, 94, 132
Scientific Instruments 54
Scientists 38–9, 43, 57
Sears 71
Sharpston, M. 72
Shelton, W.C. 109, 116
Shipbuilders 125
Ships 100
Shirts 125

Shoes 97
Siberia 7
Singapore 63, 72, 160
Skills 10, 26, 34, 35–8, 42, 119
Smith, A. 1
Soaps and Cosmetics 60
South East Asia 48
South Korea 63, 72, 96, 99–101, 105
Special Adjustment Assistance
    Program 125–6
Special Assistance for
    non-Metropolitan Areas 126–7
'Stages Approach' to Comparative
    Advantage 46–8
Stainless Steel 123
Steel Industry 6, 97, 100, 107, 141
Stern, R. 24, 32, 35–6, 40–1, 51–3,
    142
Stewart, F. 137, 142
Structural Adjustments 47
Subsidies 89
Sweden 11, 29, 58, 66, 75, 94, 129
Swedenborg, B. 57, 58
Switzerland 15, 29
Synthetic Materials 17
Szenberg, M. 17, 113, 116–17, 139

Taiwan 63, 72, 96, 99, 100, 105,
    113
Takacs, W.E. 100, 103
Tariff Preferences 94–8
Tariffs 18, 24, 27, 64, 67, 72, 76,
    78–102, 108–11, 118, 120–1,
    123–5, 128, 133, 138–9; and
    Resources 92; and Terms of
    Trade 80–2; Arguments for 88–
    91; Effective Tariffs 82–7; *see
    also* Protection
Taxes 91–3
Technology 7, 118–19, 132, 139
Technology Based Theories 14–20,
    49, 55; Technological Group
    Trade 16, 34
Television 100
Textiles 69, 72, 95, 97–101, 105,
    107, 110, 113, 115–16, 123,
    131–3
Third World 18, 19, 63, 69, 70–3,
    91, 101, 105; *see also* LDCs
Tokyo Round 99, 101, 123
Torre, J.R. 67–8, 70, 76
Trade Act (US) 121
Trade Adjustments 113–15, 117–19;
    and in Australia 125–7, 127–8;

in Canada 123–5, 127–8; in
  Clothing and Textiles 131–5;
  in the US 120–3, 127–8
Trade and Unemployment 105–16
Trade Barriers 11, 70, 87–8, 95, 99
Trade Creation 95
Trade Diversion 95, 102
Trade Expansion Act (US) 120–1
Trade Unions 56, 92, 118, 122,
  135
Transfer Prices 65, 69, 74
Transistors 97
Transport 6–7, 11, 64, 73
Transport Equipment 60, 105, 107
Travel Goods 69
Treaty of Rome 129
Tuong, H.D. 48, 54

Unemployment 74, 108–11, 118,
  121–2, 124, 126–9, 133, 135–6,
  138, 141
Unequal Exchange Thesis 143–61
United Kingdom 7, 11, 23–5, 29,
  42, 56, 66, 98, 129
United States 11, 18–20, 22–30,
  32, 34–44, 47–8, 50, 53, 55–63,
  65, 67–9, 71–3, 75–6, 90,
  94–100, 108–11, 120–3, 127–8,
  130–1, 136, 157, 160
Unskilled Workers 75, 119, 133

US Department of Commerce 55, 60,
  62, 120
US Department of Labor 120
US Tariff Commission 57, 60, 75,
  120, 121

Value Added 20, 35–6, 41, 48–9, 67,
  73, 83, 97
Vernon, R. 18–19, 22, 38–9, 41–3,
  52–5
Viansson-Ponte, P. 101, 103

Wages 33, 35–6, 39, 48, 68, 72–3,
  93, 101, 114, 122, 129, 132–5,
  138
Weiss, M.Y. 58, 59, 75
Wells, L.T. 40–1, 53
West Germany 11, 29, 58, 66, 72,
  93, 115, 129, 135, 141
Wheelwright, E.L. 104
Williams, H.R. 121, 139
Women (in employment) 119, 122,
  133, 135
Wood 41, 107–8
World Production 41
World War II 17

Yamin, M. 70, 77
Yeats, A.J. 48, 54, 116
Yugoslavia 96